AMERICAN
POWER

In Memory of
Edward Kowalski
21
6-23-73

AMERICAN POWER

The Rise and Decline
of U.S. Globalism
1918–1988

JOHN TAFT

1817

HARPER & ROW, PUBLISHERS, New York
Grand Rapids, Philadelphia, St. Louis, San Francisco
London, Singapore, Sydney, Tokyo, Toronto

FIRST EDITION

Designed by Cassandra J. Pappas

Maps drawn by Paul Pugliese

Library of Congress Cataloging-in-Publication Data

Taft, John, 1950–
   American power:the rise and decline of U.S. globalism, 1918–1988/John Taft.
     p. cm.
   Bibliography: p.
   Includes index.
   ISBN 0-06-016133-7
   1. United States—Foreign relations—20th century. 2. Diplomats—United States—
Biography. 3. Statesmen—United States—Biography.
I. American power (Motion picture) II. Title.
E744.T126 1989
327.2'092—dc20
[B]   89-45068

89 90 91 92 93 CC/HC 10 9 8 7 6 5 4 3 2 1

Contents

Illustrations appear after pages 82, 146, and 210.

Maps appear after pages 55, 136, and 243.

Preface

The purpose of this book is to tell, partly by anecdote and partly by distillation, the story of America as a global power through the lives of its leading protagonists. It sometimes is said that America does not have the Big Story of this century—that supposedly happened in Eurasia during and after the two world wars. But if the Big Story was played out in Europe and Asia, American industrial capitalism has taken the most significant role in it.

The story of American power has been told in any number of versions, and evidence has been found for at least as many theories of what lay behind it. No doubt, U.S. diplomacy reflected America's great size and strength, a natural desire to preserve and to expand it, and a related fear of Soviet communism. There is much to be said for that standard presentation. But surely it is just as important to grasp the positive world view that guided the American colossus at the zenith of its power. This was a world view often forgotten in practice but nevertheless shared by many American policymakers from Woodrow Wilson onward.

This world view can best be summarized as "internationalist liberalism." First advanced in limited form by Woodrow Wilson, it had roots as far back as the eighteenth century and some closer forebears among the mugwumps of 1900. It meant a fairly consistent adherence to free trade and investment, anti-imperialism, the advancement of democracy, foreign aid, arms control, and multilateral institutions such as the United Nations and its agencies. Of course, different internationalist liberals put a varying degree of emphasis on each of their principles, and they could be quite hypocritical about them. All saw them as desirable goals—but in their zeal to promote their program against Communist challenges, they may have ended up running a U.S. empire of a different kind.

Internationalist liberalism grew out of the later stages of the Progressive movement and Wilson's intervention in World War I. Until 1916, progressivism was primarily a domestic affair; early U.S. incursions into the Caribbean basin had not entailed serious global ambitions. But during World War I, President Wilson was ready to enter into the quarrels of Great Powers, to join a de facto military alliance, and to recast the imperial metropoles of Europe. He pushed an American program that presumed to cure the world's most salient political and economic ills. No longer was it just a matter of expanding into foreign empires, of acting as a neutral mediator, or of issuing denunciations not backed up by deeds.

In analyzing what lay behind American foreign policy, I have had recourse to another term, "ultraliberal," which some ultraliberals may not like. Liberalism, one might argue, is a complex condition whose intensity cannot be measured across a spectrum. This argument neglects the fact that at its various post-Enlightenment stages liberalism usually had a fairly specific set of goals—even if those goals might seem contradictory or change later on. An ultraliberal is fundamentally a zealous advocate of current liberal goals. Perhaps this difference bears some relation to a distinction drawn by Ernst Nolte between "enthusiastic liberalism" and "critical liberalism." Enthusiastic liberals hold a conviction that to be "free" one must live according to a specific doctrine. Critical liberals believe that liberty requires adherence to a cluster of doctrines and values—including, perhaps, religious faith and patriotism—and that liberty's realization is a complex matter requiring endless adjustment.

Ultraliberals, by my reckoning, are purists or enthusiasts. In international affairs, they are liberals who believe with particular zeal in free trade and investment, anti-imperialism, the advancement of democracy, foreign aid, arms control, and multilateral institutions. Such liberals usually have opposed unilateral intervention by the United States, its support for right-wing dictators, or its reluctance to give aid to needy-but-neutralist countries. Of course they could be as hypocritical as most people when they tasted power, and at times they could soft-pedal parts of their program. But some were so zealous that they preferred the United States to retreat into a noisy geographic isolation, rather than compromise any important point of their agenda.

During most of the years after World War II, internationalist liberals believed that their chief enemy, other than communism, was American isolationism. In its more extreme forms, isolationism was indeed a serious inconvenience to them. But under a broader definition, isolationism is a world view which they often shared with other Americans. The term implies simply a reluctance to have any but commercial relations (and maybe not even those) with countries not under some ascendancy of the United States—countries that do not at least pay lip service to American values, and with which there is an ongoing need to compromise on principle. After World War II, America was so powerful that it could treat most of the industrial world as almost an extension of itself—usually with the acquiescence of countries that felt threatened by communism. In that subtle sense, most internationalist liberals never ceased to be isolationist at heart.

My version of their story begins with William Bullitt and a group of young men who came of age politically during the Wilson presidency. It has been said often, and quite correctly, that a prep school/Ivy League group dominated U.S. diplomacy for most of this century. These diplomats were an elite core even forty years ago; forty years hence they may seem an alien cadre to most Americans. It is no coincidence that some of its members were rich, and certainly they shared a very peculiar enthusiasm. As William Bullitt remarked to a group of Yale undergraduates in 1950, "The few Americans who have devoted their lives to foreign affairs since 1914 are so exceptional as to be almost oddities. As a nation, we are amateurs in the foreign field."

What usually is omitted is a description of their political case history. Their intellectual core, so to speak, was the New Liberalism associated with the *New Republic* magazine during World War I, a liberalism that in domestic politics advocated greater freedom for individuals through government intervention, expanded voting and criminal rights, income transfers, workingmen's protection, and the encouragement of large-scale industries. Like classical liberals, New Liberals shared a meliorist faith that people could be made freer by means of new insights and political and economic structures; they broke new ground for American liberalism by pushing for extensive federal intervention. The mission of bringing more freedom to Americans through central government action was extended to bringing more freedom to foreign countries through similar initiatives. America's enormous power after World War II, as well as its fear of Communist expansion, would be their means of bringing that agenda to the world.

It is well known that most of these people went to Washington because of World War II and made effective use of the crony system. Many of them could draw on substantial support from outside the State Department. Their movement, as one might call it, had a number of important fellow travelers—these included several presidents, but most of them were just very capable functionaries like John McCloy, Robert Lovett, and Robert Murphy. Some members like Henry Cabot Lodge joined up late, while others like George Kennan were involved only briefly. But it was the overall movement that made them effective.

Perhaps one of the nicest times and places to have lived was in America's upper middle class between 1900 and 1965—especially to have been among those born shortly before the turn of the century. These people enjoyed most the benefits, and few of the drawbacks, of modern industry. There was a Gatsbyesque sleaze beneath their power and prosperity, as there always has been in American expansion. From the very start, U.S. foreign policy has been a mixture of idealism and commercial self-interest. While an element of sleaze does not make the whole thing rotten, it is well not to exaggerate their vision or intelligence. I began this book with some enthusiasm for what these people accomplished, or set out to accomplish, in the world arena. A closer examination of the record has left me far more skeptical.

Theirs was an unusually self-conscious generation that thought very highly of itself. As F. Scott Fitzgerald wrote just before his death in 1940, "I have never loved any men as well as those who felt the first springs when I did, and saw death ahead, and were reprieved—and who now walk the long stormy summer step in step with me. If my generation was ever lost it certainly found itself. It stands by nature, sophisticated by fact— and rather deeply wise. And in this tragic year, so like another year, I keep thinking of a line of Willa Cather's, 'we possessed together the precious, the incommunicable past.' " The picture is overdrawn. Fitzgerald's generation was no wiser than most. But on the central importance of their precious past he got it right, and that is what this book tries to show.

On a personal note, a number of my relatives have been diplomats, starting with a great-great-grandfather who was a minister plenipotentiary in Europe. This perhaps is the past that started me on the road to writing this book. But I want here to express my appreciation to many people outside my family who have helped me along the way. First, I am grateful to Aleksandar Pavcović, who gave me the idea of writing on this subject; also helpful at the early stages was Michael Kinsley, who as editor of the *New Republic* commissioned me to do a series of articles on U.S. diplomats. Tom Wallace and Marc Granetz played a crucial role in contracting this book with an unknown author.

None of these people foresaw that my authorship would lead me to another role as originator and series producer of a television series on U.S. foreign policy in this century. Polly Kosko of South Carolina ETV gave me indispensable encouragement. I also wish to thank members of the production team and co-production company who through their efforts have contributed to this book. For photographic research I am grateful to Susan Hormuth and especially to Shirley Green. Also helpful were the academic consultants for the project, including David Calleo,

Robert Divine, Walter LaFeber, Walter Laqueur, and Donald Cameron Watt.

I am very grateful to my typists, Dorothy and Katherine Kallivas; to the librarians at various archives where I have worked; and to friends with whom I stayed on my research trips. I also wish to thank my editors, Robert Wright, Debra Elfenbein, Stephanie Gunning, and especially Hugh Van Dusen, for their loyalty and patience. Timothy Dickinson and Robert Divine have read the manuscript and offered many helpful suggestions—but of course they do not necessarily agree with all of its interpretations—and any objective errors are my own responsibility. Finally, by far the most important contributor to my work—as an authority on its subject and as a loyal friend—has been John Ranelagh, to whom this book is dedicated.

JOHN TAFT
Washington, 1989

But Time, a taper guttering,
Drops in a slow decay,
And Youth, a white moth fluttering,
Blows with the wind away;
And walls and towers made of hands,
And faith, and roundelay,
And laughter, and red fallow lands,
Pass like the withered spray.

And certitude grows rank with ease,
And idols turn to mold,
And passion's cup holds bitter lees,
And pale, soft hands grow cold;
All shimmering reality,
The world that shines and seems,
The earth, the mountains and the
sea,
Are shadows of old dreams.

From the class-day poem at Yale College
by Archibald MacLeish
June 21, 1915

All bad poetry springs from genuine
feeling.

Oscar Wilde, 1894

Prologue
A Philadelphia Story

During the presidential campaign of 1916, an American journalist by the name of William Bullitt came home from Europe to
publish his views about World War I. The United States was
neutral and aloof from the conflict—after two years of transatlantic slaughter—with President Woodrow Wilson running for
re-election on a peace platform. According to candidate Wilson,
this war of England, France, and Russia against the German
Central Powers was none of America's official business. Much as
he admired Woodrow Wilson, young William Bullitt was inclined to disagree.

Recently married in Philadelphia, Bill Bullitt and his wife had
taken a working honeymoon to Central Europe as guests of the
German High Command. Their trip included visits to occupied
Belgium, an airplane tour along the Russian front, and talks with
important *Reich* officials in Berlin. Although the Germans tried
to be hospitable, they could not win over Bullitt. He left with a
feeling that American intervention against Germany was probable and, perhaps, necessary for a lasting peace. This would be
not a war against the German and Austrian empires so much as
a war for "liberal" and "progressive" ideals.

* * *

The date 1916 deserves a place in American political history. It was then that many Progressives like Bullitt began using the word "liberal" to describe their aims, although "Progressive" was really a better label for them. A reform movement since the turn of the century, progressivism had sprung from two political traditions. One was that of certain mugwump Republicans after the Civil War—genteel reformers like Henry Adams and his friend Samuel Bowles, who wanted to combat civic corruption by restoring the virtue of their eighteenth-century ancestors. Another was the Democratic populism of William Jennings Bryan, who fought the growing power of big corporations and banks by applying political pressure from below. However disparate their roots, Progressives had a common purpose in the moral regeneration of urban life. They pushed for a return to fundamental values, which were to be found either in the countryside or in a distant American past.

Beyond that, it is hard to find a common theme to the Progressive movement, which after 1900 became a vast, bipartisan event. Progressives tended to believe in laissez-faire economics and neutrality toward Europe. While many of them had supported the Spanish-American War, they generally opposed U.S. government intervention both at home and overseas. More seminal perhaps were the later stages of progressivism, when the movement produced an important new branch that questioned both of those beliefs. Young intellectuals like William Bullitt believed that an activist central government would help to fulfill America's promise to its citizens, and perhaps to the entire world.

Led for the most part by middle-class professionals and writers such as Bullitt—some of whom founded the *New Republic* magazine—this group of Progressives was not linked with either of the main political parties. They had a personal tie to Theodore Roosevelt, a Republican Progressive, and many of them backed his third-party bid for the presidency in 1912. But when a Democrat, Woodrow Wilson, took control of the White House in 1913, they remained uncertain which party to support.

The outbreak of a European war in 1914 caused even greater uncertainty by diverting their attention to foreign affairs. Dean

Acheson once said that in his time at the Groton School, Yale College, and Harvard Law, being a "liberal"—or a Progressive—was all "quite simple and rather innocent. One was a liberal if one was sympathetic to labor unions, employers' liability, direct election of United States Senators, the federal graduated income tax, maximum hour and minimum wage legislation for women, and if one read the *New Republic.*" In reality, things were more complicated during World War I. Most of those reforms had been achieved, and the *New Republic* Progressives wanted a broader, deeper program that might also include international changes. Instinctively pro-British, they could see faults on both sides in the European war. And yet their proposals were still quite tentative and vague.

Bill Bullitt belonged almost by birthright to the *New Republic* crowd—young Progressives who wanted centralized reform, and who felt a keen interest in the European war. He shared with many of them the same comfortable, private school past. Their struggle with the establishment sometimes began as a struggle with their parents, and Bullitt, from one of the most prominent families in Philadelphia, was an example. His background may have been more international than most. In fact, that much was impressed upon him from within an hour of his birth in 1891. Great-Aunt Grace Gross—later Lady Osler—had shown up for the delivery. Finding what she thought was an empty chair, she sat down and nearly squashed Bullitt to death, whereupon he was taken on a visit to Aunt Alice, duchess of Assergio, in Rome. Vacations to Europe were frequent thereafter, giving Bullitt a command of three languages, but his interest in foreign affairs arose from more than just a cosmopolitan childhood. Like others of his generation, he came to regard an outward-looking involvement in world events as an aspect of his nationalist, interventionist economics. Diplomatic neutrality toward Europe seemed the creed of conservatives and older Americans, especially the self-satisfied rich.

While the self-satisfaction of Bullitt's family was considerable, he began fighting back at an early age. Among all of his claimed ancestors, one of his favorites was Fletcher Christian, hero of the

Bounty mutiny against a cruel British tyrant, Captain Bligh. Another favorite was Patrick Henry, the Virginia revolutionary who demanded that the British "give me liberty, or give me death." And not surprisingly, young Bullitt greeted the Spanish-American War as a struggle for freedom led by an American liberator, Colonel Teddy Roosevelt: "I had pictures of the poor Cubans tacked up in my room, as well as one of Teddy Roosevelt. I thought nothing would be smarter than to go out and shoot down two or three Spaniards, because they were so wicked." A few years later, on the day of departure for a first year at Groton, Bullitt sat on his baggage and refused to move. What was the matter with little Billy? "Every Groton feller I know is a snob," he said with a pout, and so Bullitt ended up at a local prep school instead. That was the first in a series of gentlemanly rebellions against the Philadelphia establishment. His struggle, along with the Progressives', remained for the most part an inhibited one, a question of compromise rather than violent revolution.

He had no objection to attending Yale, for example, though he did continue his anti-snobbery campaign and dropped out of the Harvard Law School in 1914. Lawyers, he decided, were no better than crooks. The outbreak of World War I in Europe found him moving across the continent even faster than the Germans—from Moscow to Berlin and then to Paris in time for the Battle of the Marne. Bullitt's reactions to it all were contradictory. In a fit of romantic *élan* he tried to join the French Army, but the violence also inspired in him a pacifist desire to end all war. One way of doing that seemed to be a career in journalism. Reporters in Europe were influencing events, sometimes taking part in them, and journalism was a common outlet for American reformers. Muckraking writers like John Reed and Lincoln Steffens would soon form friendships—if not comradeships—with Bullitt; and polemical writing always remained his metier, through many an effort to change occupations. Rejected in Europe as a soldier and a war correspondent, he consented to return home and begin on a local newspaper, collecting stories in the Philadelphia slums.

* * *

Bullitt's political odyssey over the next three years was a typical one. His Progressive friends moved with him, from a distrust of Woodrow Wilson to a zealous support for the President's call for war in 1917. For many of those young men, Wilson's crusade would be the most formative experience of their lives. And its effect on them would help change history when they came to power three decades later.

The apparent aims of Wilson before he took office had been anathema for most Progressives like Bullitt. His economic policy seemed "liberal" in the classical sense of that word—meaning individual freedoms, local autonomy, anti-trust legislation, and non-interference in competitive business. But the *New Republic* Progressives, while accepting the usefulness of free enterprise, favored elements of what in Europe might be called "social democracy." They wanted federal regulations to protect workers and consumers, to help the weak against the strong; and this meant an active, nationalist government run by humane intellectuals like themselves. Large-scale industry, they believed, would help raise living standards and encourage national unity if it were regulated by a strong federal government.

Slowly, grudgingly, the *New Republic* crowd came around to the view that Wilson agreed with them on most domestic issues. He had, after all, been an innovative president of Princeton University—where he tried to fight snobbery by closing the "eating clubs"—and his first two years in the White House were a great period of centralized reform. Then he moved farther left in 1916 with another spate of reform legislation, such as government help to workingmen and farmers. At the same time, Wilson appointed Louis Brandeis to the Supreme Court and quietly wooed the *New Republic* with talk of a "new liberalism." That phrase had a nice ring to it. It delighted Messrs. Reed, Steffens, and Walter Lippmann, who supported the President for re-election and took up the liberal Democratic cause as their own.

On the war issue, Wilson's peace platform held less attraction for some of these New Liberals. An activist government, they felt, should be more active internationally. Wilson seemed to prefer a passive stance, and he boasted of having "kept us out of war"—even his effort to mediate an armistice was dropped in

1916, when Germany stopped sinking U.S. ships that were trading with England. Despite his diplomatic tilt toward England and France, it was clear that Woodrow Wilson had strong doubts about joining the European war.

Meanwhile the gradual shift of attention from domestic to foreign affairs was raising Bill Bullitt to greater prominence in the movement. Time spent in the Philadelphia slums may have strengthened a certain humane impulse in him, but Bullitt's expertise was wasted until he began writing editorials on foreign policy. In 1915, he had started a lively correspondence with Walter Lippmann, who was an editor of the *New Republic* and about the same age as Bullitt; Lippmann only regretted that they could not see more of each other, "because of the extra work which the international situation creates for us." At first Bullitt had toyed with pacifist solutions to the European war, such as a meeting of neutrals to encourage peace by moral example. Finally, in 1916, he faced up to the practical implications of his idealism.

Many New Liberals took great pride in their toughness and practicality. Like all good bourgeois, they felt idealism led nowhere without some pragmatic compromises along the way. Perhaps the ultimate pragmatic compromise was a war against Germany. Only thus could America have influence on the peace, and after Germany's defeat America could reform the Allied empires as well. Bullitt suspected, in any case, that America's loans to England would drag it into the conflict. On returning from his European honeymoon, he announced that the United States ought to build a thousand airplanes and a thousand destroyers. The German Empire was an aggressive military machine: it bore most of the blame for the war, and there was talk in Berlin of renewed attacks on American shipping by German submarines. In a *New Republic* article, he conceded that the "liberal" Germans were still in power, but on "the day conservative Germany overcomes liberal Germany, sinking without warning will be recommended and we shall be drawn into the war." America's New Liberals believed that war was likely, and that Wilson presently would accept it.

They were right. After his re-election, Wilson launched another effort to mediate peace and both sides feigned an interest; then, in early 1917, Germany suddenly recommenced sinking U.S. merchant vessels and the President felt obliged to call for war. He found strong congressional and popular support for this move, which ended a century of American neutrality in Europe's imperial disputes. At the same time, he continued to cultivate a friendship with New Liberal writers, having taken his slogan "peace without victory" out of an issue of the *New Republic.* When he sanctioned a League of Nations to maintain peace after the war, both Walter Lippmann and Bullitt responded with elation. "I believe he, who is our President, is a great man," declared Bullitt in a Philadelphia speech. Moreover, "we are entering this war for one purpose and one only—that better international *mores* may be established on the earth."

Bullitt was getting a little carried away, but then so were a lot of New Liberals in 1917. Wilson's rhetoric had an intoxicating effect on young people. Riding a tidal wave of political expectation, Bullitt and Lippmann moved down to Washington, now the center for a mobilization of labor and industry. No longer the sleepy southern city of one year before, the capital was becoming what the New Liberals wanted it to be. A foreign war, by giving rise to central economic regulation, might bring about new economic reforms at home.

The Fitzgerald-Hemingway generation is thought to have responded courageously to World War I. However, not all those who supported the cause tried to join up as soldiers. Some were too young, others felt too old. The experience of Bullitt's contemporaries ranged from sheer war profiteering by young millionaires, such as Averell Harriman, to death or dismemberment in battle. Robert Lovett and James Forrestal joined up with a daredevil outfit, the Naval Air Service, and there was one undergraduate whose behavior almost fit the ideal. When war was declared in his sophomore year, David Bruce dropped out to enlist as a buck private, not taking a Princeton degree until they gave him an honorary one forty years later. It was cases like this that gave rise to a myth.

William Bullitt's own war effort was more influential, if not so heroic. While David Bruce went overseas to a string of promotions, Bullitt tarried in the capital. His social background served him well as a Washington reporter. He and Colonel House, the President's right-hand man, had already met at a summer resort, and soon the Colonel was slipping him news scoops in exchange for advice on Europe. Secretary of State Lansing also was ready and willing to make use of these young reformers. After a few months, Bullitt accepted a State Department position, offered to him in lieu of military service.

A feeling of commitment to progress can animate a bureaucrat, especially in wartime. Bullitt worked long hours and slept hardly at all. He already was one of those manic types who can never sit still or shut up—not a workaholic, but always agitated about something. At age twenty-seven, he had an adolescent temper, egotistical and romantic, with a way of making close friends, feeling betrayed, and then regarding them as enemies forever. Beneath his red face and balding head, Bullitt displayed a great athletic vitality, and it goes without saying that he was charming and brilliant too. Having rejected social snobbery, he let his self-esteem come out in the form of intellectual vanity.

His new job at State was to analyze information from Central Europe, which he set about doing with a liberal bias.[1] Bullitt still thought that he could widen the split between conservative and liberal Germany. German liberals and Social Democrats held ideals similar to his own, especially on international issues. The "better" sort of Germans might help to redeem Central Europe after the war, for theirs was the movement of the future. All they needed for success was a generous peace. Bullitt passed on these ideas, along with the latest political data, every week to the White House. And the White House accepted them readily, to the point of inserting the German Social Democrats' own criticisms of their government into President Wilson's speeches. However, Bullitt and the *New Republic* crowd also were urging a positive theme for Wilson's propaganda—something to reassure the better Germans that America did not share the aims of European imperialists, that Wilson wanted a peace based on internationalist liberal principles.

Liberal principles. The term was, and is, a little vague. Woodrow Wilson had already stood domestic liberalism on its head, so what did *international* liberalism mean to him and his followers? Wilson had spoken often on the kind of world he wanted after the war, on his desire for the democratic redemption of mankind. But he made his clearest statement in early 1918, when he issued a fourteen-point plan for an armistice. This was his most positive offering—written with the help of Walter Lippmann, among others—and it did help to shorten World War I.

Every European knows the story of Wilson's Fourteen Points, how utopian they were and how they never were carried out. However utopian, perhaps they were useful as basic principles; and most of them, at any rate, have been accepted as desirable. The proposal had a few simple goals: democracy, freedom of the seas, arms reduction, universal free trade, an end to imperialism, and a League of Nations to enforce the system. These ideas descended from nineteenth-century liberalism, with its faith in free enterprise and national autonomy. What was novel in Wilson's program, what tied it directly to New Liberalism, was the League of Nations. "At the pinnacle of liberal belief in domestic affairs stood the trade union movement; in foreign affairs, the League of Nations," Dean Acheson assures us, and the League certainly was a natural cause for New Liberals. It implied that humankind and the U.S. government had a duty to protect countries not only against aggression, but against any injustice—just as the New Liberalism meant defending labor against big business.

A postwar League to Enforce Peace already had been backed by both political parties. As envisioned by Wilson, however, the League would function as more than just a legal framework. It meant that liberal ideals—including the old mugwump ideals of free trade and anti-imperialism—might now be encouraged by the United States all over the world. A league of democracies, dominated by America, would provide a rationale for U.S. interference overseas that did not look cynical or imperialistic. Its adoption by many younger Progressives also gave it a special dynamism, an aura of being part of their idealistic mission.[2]

Idealistic as the Fourteen Points appeared, President Wilson had a tough side to him. For all of his high moralism, he could be a cagey and compromising man. In order to push his reform legislation through Congress, he had engaged extensively in political patronage. And lying he considered a regrettable necessity, at least when done in the national interest. Nor did he scruple to use force against weaker countries when they broke his self-serving rules of good liberal behavior. He was ready to guarantee the preservation of the Austro-Hungarian Empire; and in Central America he imposed U.S. hegemony by armed force more often than any other President, before or since. Unilateral intervention was the underside of Wilson's internationalist liberalism, an unpleasant but integral part of the game.

Walter Lippmann, for that matter, was shrewd enough to realize that a universal league could not uphold peace on its own. Nation states were far too self-centered to rely on a world government for security; regional alliances and a balance of power would be necessary. After all, Americans had slid into war partly because they considered a British Empire to be more in their interest than a German one—Lippmann himself had warned that a German victory would endanger "the Atlantic community." Still, the New Liberals disliked unilateral force, and they believed that an internationalist liberal system must be set as the goal for a League of Nations. Lippmann and Bullitt relied upon President Wilson to do exactly that.

Bullitt's hero worship of the President seemed almost reasonable in early 1918. The call for a liberal peace was putting conservatism and snobbery on the run everywhere. Woodrow Wilson had captured the hearts of the laboring poor, especially in foreign countries. One bizarre development in Europe, one very anti-liberal event that confused people like Bullitt, was the Bolshevik Revolution. Wilson had issued his Fourteen Points partly to co-opt the new Soviet government. His point number six promised that "the treatment accorded Russia by her sister nations in the months to come will be the acid test of good will." With this sentiment Bullitt heartily agreed, thinking that the Bolshevik regime—so anti-imperialist and unsnobbish—reflected the dawn of a worldwide spiritual rebirth. He could not resist jotting down a piece of bad poetry—a piece from Wordsworth that described Bullitt's favorite era, the late eighteenth century and French Revolution, when

> Bliss was it in that dawn to be alive,
> But to be young was very Heaven! O times,
> In which the meagre, stale, forbidding ways
> Of custom, law, and statute, took at once
> The attraction of a country in romance!

Behind all their talk about terrorism and class warfare, the Bolsheviks might be good liberals.

The confusion was understandable. Communism was an unfamiliar beast. There was a lack of reliable information coming out of Russia. The *New Republic* had some awareness of the real nature of Bolshevism and said so, but few young liberals could entirely resist it. How could you resist any new government in Russia, after that awful czarist despotism? Bullitt bombarded Colonel House and the President with a series of memos, begging them to announce their sympathy with the goals of the Soviets: "Trotzky is a good deal ahead of us in the march toward world liberalism, but he is marching in our direction, and we must support him or Nihilism will follow." Wilson and the Secretary of State felt no such comradeship with Lenin and Trotsky. The President took care to make his promises vague, extending them out of a practical desire to keep Russia fighting with the Allies.

Unfortunately, Wilson's promises failed to impress the Russians. With their country in a shambles and facing the prospect of civil war, Bolshevik leaders could not have held off the German Army for long, no matter what their intentions. And it soon became obvious that they wanted a separate peace. In response, several West European statesmen decided upon a more drastic solution, making plans for an Allied invasion north and east of Petrograd. This, they claimed, would weaken the Bolsheviks and help other Russians to go on fighting Germany. The idea was naive, but then so was the reaction of many American liberals, who were horrified by any thought of armed intervention in a country struggling for freedom. To Bullitt, the whole scheme came as an imperialist outrage typical of French and British conservatives; the President must speak out against it or "his position as moral leader of the liberals of the world will be lost." With somewhat less fervor, the *New Republic* made a similar plea. The Bolsheviks could not be defeated anyway, and to interfere in Russia might embitter them against the West; only goodwill, trade, and economic assistance would keep Lenin from going to extremes.

And so it was with a sizable group of Wilson supporters, from Justice Louis Brandeis to the young muckrakers. While most of them stopped far short of embracing Bolshevism, there were some exceptions even to that. The poet-journalist John Reed, having been in Petrograd during the Bolshevik coup, was overwhelmed by its atmosphere of cataclysm and romance. He converted to communism, came home to write a book about it, and in a memo to Bullitt added his voice to a liberal chorus against intervention. Forwarding this memo to Colonel House, Bullitt tacked on a personal suggestion: a government board should be created to execute a more sensible policy toward Russia. In another message, he proposed that the chairmanship be given to Justice Louis Brandeis, for Brandeis was "passionately interested in Russia and the Revolution."[3] None of Bullitt's advice on this subject made much impact. A German-Soviet peace treaty was signed and Wilson finally agreed, largely to keep an eye on other invaders, to follow France, England, and Japan with his own military intervention.

The ensuing scuffle in Russia, a sideshow to World War I, had little significance in itself. The U.S. invasion force was weak, it accomplished nothing, and while it annoyed the Bolsheviks, they would scarcely have been less hostile to the West without it. Yet the story remains important for the impression it made upon the more purist liberals, because of a myth it created which was not dispelled until after the next world war—if then. It seemed at the time to be Wilson's first betrayal of his war aims, a departure from liberal purity with no practical justification.

Germany had helped put the Bolsheviks in power as a way of weakening Russia and getting it out of the war. Perhaps the only reason why Germany did not then remove the Bolsheviks was its concern with other matters, especially the Western Front. The separate peace with Russia had freed enough German resources to permit a huge offensive in France, involving millions of troops and some fearsome new weapons. As it turned out, they were not quite enough to win the war. The offensive bogged down and, after an Allied counterattack, German morale collapsed. Soon a reformist group in the *Reich* government took control—liberals and Social Democrats for the most part, one of them an old beer-drinking friend of Bullitt's. They asked for a peace treaty based on Wilson's Fourteen Points.

Bullitt could take legitimate pride in this result. The propaganda war, which had helped to undermine German and Austrian morale, was based partly on his advice. He knew what appealed to liberals in Central Europe and he understood, when the Social Democrats took control in Berlin, how to deal with them. It came as no surprise when Germany sent its armistice offer to America, rather than to the English or French, who wanted to impose much harsher terms on the enemy.

And President Wilson responded wisely to the offer. He delivered an oration in Congress and at the Metropolitan Opera House, clarifying his Fourteen Points and stressing the need for a just peace: German militarism was wicked, yes, but the treaty must be reasonable. He forced the Allies to accept a surrender from Germany that was based, at least nominally, on the Fourteen Points. His evident firmness, and the whole euphoria of winning a war, so swept up American liberals that they forgot most of their doubts. True, the war effort in America had caused some terrible abuses of civil liberty, and there was that sordid business of U.S. troops in Russia; but all of these old problems would disappear now that the fighting was over.

Most liberals, in their euphoria, failed to notice some tough new problems. With Germany defeated, Wilson had far less bargaining power in Europe—already he was diluting the Fourteen Points in order to satisfy England and France. And he also had less bargaining power at home, after the Democrats' recent loss of their majority in Congress. By late 1918, internationalist liberals represented a depleted force in the United States, for most Americans hated Germany with a passion. President Wilson himself often fretted about this. The ugliness of American war hysteria once caused him to burst out crying in Bullitt's presence. Clearly, popular support for a generous peace was receding day by day.

Wilson's outburst in front of Bullitt showed another liberal weakness: so pragmatic in many ways, President Wilson had been more caught up lately in his own emotions and rhetoric. Always he had believed that God created America to save mankind. Now his habit of preaching to foreign peoples over the heads of their governments was being applied even to the Allied nations. A meliorist faith in moral progress and the power of persuasion—both of them American liberal traits—was growing a little too strong in the President's mind.

One way, perhaps, to stop Wilson from harming himself was to stay very close to him, which Bill Bullitt proceeded to do. Bullitt never could be happy just backing a cause—he wanted to be physically on location, in the thick of things. He had traveled to Germany in 1916, then to Washington in 1917, and now in 1918 he decided that it was time to follow Woodrow Wilson to the Paris Peace Conference. Colonel House, ever agreeable, provided jobs on the American delegation for him and some other liberal intellectuals—including James Shotwell, a professor of medieval history. Another member of the delegation would be Lieutenant Adolf Berle, a *wunderkind* and protégé of Brandeis who was the youngest student ever to graduate from the Harvard Law School. And not surprisingly, this American group had a counterpart in the British delegation. Young mandarins-on-the-make like John Maynard Keynes and Harold Nicolson, for all their appearance of worldliness, also admired President Wilson. "In the main tenets of his political philosophy, I believed with fervent credulity," Nicolson has written. "In spite of bitter disillusionment I believe in them today." European liberals went to Paris with some different problems and the same general purpose.

No doubt, the Fourteen Points inspired young Americans more than anyone. Perhaps it is odd that they followed Wilson with such a religious zeal. After all, the tenets of his philosophy

were quite mundane: the promotion of free trade and investment, economic aid, democracy, national independence, and
multilateral institutions like the League. Nevertheless, many
young liberals accepted it like a creed. Typical was a Foreign
Service officer named Sumner Welles, who believed that, by
Wilson's program, "the errors of the past were to be valiantly
corrected; that human wrong would be righted; that the self-
determination of peoples would end oppression; that human
freedom and individual security would become realities; that
war in this new dawn breaking over the earth, was now a nightmare of the past." And all of this would be inaugurated by
Woodrow Wilson himself—in Paris.

I

Man of the World

1918–1940

At the end of 1918, during Woodrow Wilson's triumphal tour
of Western Europe, the trauma of World War I was momentarily
forgotten. Europeans greeted Wilson as a prince of peace who
would bring serenity and calm to the world. Always it was the
working classes that cheered him loudest, even in cynical Paris.
A working-class American, Robert Murphy, remembers having
"stood with the French crowds who gave the American messiah
a tumultuous welcome as he drove in an open carriage down the
Champs-Elysées." That was how it sounded, anyway; in truth
what the crowds were cheering was their own better nature.
Wilson symbolized for them what was clean and decent in the
Allied cause, but European workers had an indecent side as well.
While cheering for President Wilson, they counted on other
politicians to do some dirty work at the bargaining table.

The Paris Peace Conference came together slowly, rather like
an international arts festival or the Olympics. Scattered in hotels
and embassies throughout the city were the headquarters of a
dozen countries. At American headquarters, in the Hotel Crillon, the first of Wilson's retinue to arrive were Professor Shotwell and William Bullitt.

Things had not gone well for Bill Bullitt on the boat trip over.
Much of the journey was boring, with the President rendered
incommunicado by a bad cold. Worried about the silence from
above, Bullitt decided to put an end to it—his chief had to be

watched carefully and kept in line. One night he cornered the President by sitting next to him at a movie. There was a mutinous mood on board, he warned Wilson, because the intellectuals felt "entirely left out of the game." Couldn't the President hold a meeting to explain his strategy? Wilson did so, but the meeting revealed only his ignorance of Europe and the vagueness of his plans. Even on the League of Nations, he spoke in loose generalities.

Confusion mounted on arrival at the Hotel Crillon. President Wilson cut himself off again and left for his tour of the continent. Without any guidance, American delegates still had plenty to keep them busy, so Bullitt went back to collecting information on Central Europe and passing it on to Colonel House. His main concern now was the Soviet threat. Lately he had grown more and more ambivalent about Bolshevism—perhaps it did not represent a progressive step after all, at least not in the more civilized countries west of Russia, where liberalism and social democracy had a good fighting chance. Bullitt reported with alarm on the political upheavals in Germany, Budapest, and Vienna. Hoping to encourage moderation, he urged Wilson to promise aid only to democratic countries. He hoped also that Wilson's popularity with labor could be used to ward off extremism, and to pressure Allied leaders to go along with the Fourteen Points. As always, the best antidote to trouble appeared a soft, Wilsonian peace.

When the peace conference opened in mid-January 1919, it remained uncertain whether Woodrow Wilson himself would perform like a good Wilsonian. At this point he found some of the *New Republic*'s views quite unorthodox. His continued isolation from Bullitt and the liberal crowd was another bad sign. He seemed determined to negotiate the treaty all alone, not trusting even Colonel House. This kind of treatment prompted Walter Lippmann to resign from the delegation, and Bullitt also felt an urge to leave town. Paris did provide a good social life. Because he knew members of every delegation, Bullitt's hotel room at teatime functioned somewhat like a diplomatic salon. His beautiful wife dazzled everyone, and there were amusing dinners with exotic people like Lawrence of Arabia and Prince Faisal, complete with their Bedouin outfits. Later in the evening, Bullitt could entertain in his room resplendent in pink silk pajamas. However, his diplomatic ideas of reconciliation with Russia and Germany failed to dazzle President Wilson, and that was what really mattered.

Despite Bullitt's frequent urging, Wilson refused to send any American workingmen to the Socialist International in Switzerland, a general convention of Socialist parties. Finally Bullitt went as an observer and came back very enthusiastic. Along with most young liberals, he exaggerated the virtue and solidarity of the oppressed classes. The Socialist parties had denounced Bolshevism, he reported happily, and they "showed an almost pathetic confidence in President Wilson. Speaker after speaker praised the President and insisted that the masses of Europe must stand behind him." Bullitt ignored some ominous trends, such as the pervasive hostility directed toward German Social Democrats. That was the indecent side of European labor.

The Socialist meeting encouraged Bullitt's desire to do some more traveling, to go east and see for himself what was happening in Russia. Allied troops were still stationed in Siberia and north of Petrograd; the Russian civil war was in full swing. Paralyzed by conflicting pressures, Allied leaders could find no answer to the Bolshevik question. Some of their constituents said that communism should be accepted in Russia and perhaps given aid, while most wanted to destroy it. The Bolshevik terms for a cease-fire remained equivocal and unclear—and anyway, with so little information, it was hard to know if any group held real power in that part of the world. When Colonel House suggested sending a secret investigative mission to Moscow, President Wilson and the British prime minister, Lloyd George, did not object. Taking no chances, they left all arrangements to subordinates and gave no written approval. The whole mission, so delicate and controversial, might have to be repudiated.

Colonel House's choice of Bullitt to head a secret mission was foolish but predictable. Bullitt for many months had been pestering Wilson to do something about Russia, to withdraw U.S. troops and make contact with Lenin. The Socialist International was sending emissaries to Moscow, which seemed the best way of taming Bolshevism on its home territory—isolating it, as the French government wanted, only would make it more stubborn and violent. Of course, Bullitt was delighted to be given what appeared an important task. He obtained, from Lloyd George's secretary and from Colonel House, a list of terms to offer Lenin as a basis of peace in the civil war. Then, in late February, he left quietly for Moscow with a group of three associates, to tame the Bolsheviks.

Among the group chosen by Bullitt was Lincoln Steffens, the muckraking journalist and old mentor of Walter Lippmann. Steffens remembers that Bullitt also brought along a male secretary, apparently just "to play with. On trains and boats they skylarked, wrestling and tumbling like a couple of bear cubs all along the Arctic Circle. A pretty noisy secret mission we were, but Bullitt knew just what he was about; nobody could suspect us of secrecy or importance." The Bolsheviks, however, took the group seriously enough to send Bullitt on to Moscow for a talk with the Chairman himself.

Secretary of State Lansing was hoping that a trip to Russia might cure Bullitt of Bolshevism, but in fact it did nothing of the sort. Soviet officials made an excellent impression on both him and Steffens. Perhaps as liberals they felt reassured by the fact that Lenin, among all his revolutionary duties, found time to read the *New Republic*. "Lenin was impatient with my liberalism," Steffens noticed during an interview, "but he had shown himself a liberal by instinct. He had defended liberty of speech, assembly, and the Russian press for some five to seven months after the October revolution which put him in power." In other words, Lenin held out as best he could against the left wing in his party. Then he repressed his liberal instincts.

Actually, Lenin despised Western liberalism. But he always managed to be friendly with foreign visitors, and he struck Bullitt as reasonable—almost as a conservative, really, in the Soviet context. Lenin knew that the Soviets would have to make some big concessions if they expected to win over France; and it is true that he wanted to stop the Russian civil war by means of a compromise with the West. In the end he accepted almost all of

Bullitt's proposals. Lenin would give up any territory not already held by the Bolsheviks. In exchange, the Allies must refrain from supporting his opponents in the civil war and provide
food aid to his regime. This offer, the most generous he ever
made to the Allies, was in one sense disingenuous. Lenin reckoned that without Allied help, the counterrevolutionary forces
in Russia would collapse.

Bullitt returned to Paris in a typically enthusiastic and upbeat
mood—surely this treaty was so good that even France would
accept it. Coining one of the most famous clichés of Western
Marxism, Lincoln Steffens told everyone, "We have seen the
future, and it works," and Bullitt was inclined to agree: he reported that in Soviet Russia, "the terror has ceased" and the
trains "run on time."[4] Yet for all of his optimism, an array of
forces and circumstances were gathering to thwart Bullitt. For
one thing, his politics became a matter of public debate. The
U.S. trade union chief, Samuel Gompers, had shown up in Paris
and denounced him as a Communist sympathizer, a radical
whose presence at the international Socialist meeting was an
affront to American labor. Wasn't it a disgrace that "faddist
parlor socialists" like Bullitt had more influence at the peace
conference than genuine workingmen? This attack typified the
kind of working-class obstinacy that so often has undermined
the political intelligentsia, especially in America. Bullitt's acceptance of the Bolsheviks had considerable support from labor
leaders in Europe, and almost none at home.

Middle-class conservatives were more obstinate now, too.
The great Red Scare was building up in England and the United
States, producing a strong upsurge of resistance to any compromise with Bolshevism. Anti-Bolshevik forces suddenly seemed
to be winning the civil war; the Paris Peace Conference, in any
case, had turned to other matters. Efforts by Lloyd George and
the French to abandon the Fourteen Points, at Germany's expense, were wearing down Wilson's physical health to an alarm-
ing extent. The President suffered a series of headaches and
soon took to his bed with what he called "Turmoil in Central
America," meaning indigestion and the flu; he began yielding to
the Allies on some crucial issues. Under these circumstances, a

controversial proposal on Russia from a callow young envoy sounded like too much to be bothered with. Wilson had enough differences with England and France as it was, not to mention the American conservatives. So, once again, he postponed further action on Russia and ignored Bullitt's suggestions.

For Bullitt, this was the final straw in a cumulative series. With a mixture of outrage and near panic, he began accosting people all around Paris, complaining of his treatment, predicting disaster. If the Allied leaders did not soon come to their senses, a Red tide would sweep over Europe. Lawrence of Arabia heard his story and so did Harold Nicolson, who listened politely and said nothing. British liberals wanted to cooperate, but they felt a commitment to the British Empire and an uncertainty about Bolshevism. Bullitt felt no uncertainty at all. He insisted that the President absolutely must make peace with Moscow so as to retain the loyalty of the European masses, aye, so as to retain the loyalty of Bullitt himself. It was clear to his colleagues that Bullitt wanted to do something rash, something very silly, but no one could tell what. He made some noises about turning Bolshevik and swept off to the Riviera on an infuriated vacation—then swept back a week later, still officially a member of the U.S. delegation.

In the calamitous event, Bullitt's anger proved to be not so very different from that of many Wilsonians. When the final treaty draft emerged from the peace conference, the liberal camp reacted to it with a collective sense of outrage. Herbert Hoover received his copy at 4:00 A.M. and was horrified at its harshness. Unable to sleep, he went out for a walk and soon ran into a group that included John Maynard Keynes. "It all flashed into our minds," Hoover recalled, "why each was walking about at that time of the morning."[5] Theirs was a fairly standard reaction. Bullitt was only more colorful and extreme than the others, only a few steps ahead of his enlightened comrades.

Much has been said about the disgrace and stupidity of the Versailles Treaty, some of it exaggerated. The League of Nations Covenant, however imperfect, was a hopeful start; and it would have been difficult for the Allies to improve upon their new boundaries in the Balkans. Still, when it came to Central Europe, they went disastrously wrong. Germany—not Russia—was the acid test of Allied goodwill, a test which the best of them failed. The treaty handed over vital areas of Austria and Germany, with German majorities, to neighboring countries; it confiscated almost every movable form of property that Germany possessed; it made provisions for indemnity payments known to be about ten times more than Germany could afford. These terms were imposed without negotiation, and the German Social Democrats who accepted them were seen as traitors by a large portion of their compatriots. Undoubtedly, the Versailles Treaty was an important element in the rise of Adolf Hitler, who could blame the Social Democrats for Germany's humiliation.

Strangely enough, Bullitt and his friends pinned the blame for this disaster on Woodrow Wilson. Perhaps their attitude arose from a feeling of betrayal. You had to expect a certain amount of narrow-minded greed from the European premiers, but Wilson had made all those wonderful promises. More irritating, he presented the treaty to Germany as though it embodied his high, moralistic ideals. Many of the liberals thought he should have used force to get his way with the Allies. Walter Lippmann wrote several months later to Bullitt asking, "How did you and I ever have any faith in the Wilson administration? I mean any faith?" In their faith, they had failed to notice that Wilson had no real clout at the peace conference. France and England no longer needed the American Army; and there was little support for a liberal peace in any Allied country. When the treaty became public in early May and Wilson refused to consider any changes from the younger delegates, they met one evening at the Crillon to determine a response.

It was a melodramatic occasion. Of course Bullitt dominated the proceedings, although some other notables such as Adolf Berle and Christian Herter were present. Lincoln Steffens remembers that he was "the only older man there to see that significant scene; all those conscientious, high-bred, mostly rich young gentlemen and their wives, who wanted to do right and had to decide then and there whether to sacrifice their careers, as they honestly believed, by an open challenge to the wrong done by their government." Bullitt and Lieutenant Berle intended to resign in protest, but most others refused to do likewise; they were indeed hesitant to endanger their careers, and reluctant to turn on Woodrow Wilson in public. Contemptuously, Bullitt snatched up a bouquet of flowers, flinging yellow jonquils at the cowardly. To each of the courageous—including himself—he awarded a red rose. By comparison to that performance, his resignation a few days later came as an anticlimax. Most people, if they paid any attention at all, dismissed his resignation letter as pro-German and Bolshevik. It finally seemed to dawn on Bullitt that, whatever Socialist leaders might say, even the working classes felt a bitter hatred for Germany.

Nevertheless, Bullitt had his revenge on President Wilson. Republican politicians in America who cared little about the harshness of the Versailles Treaty were attacking it on other grounds: those clever Europeans intended to use the League of Nations to entangle us in their quarrels, to trick the United States into defending their empires; the treaty might even amount to a surrender of U.S. sovereignty. Isolationist conservatism was on the upswing and Senator Henry Cabot Lodge, Sr., eager to delay ratification and embarrass Wilson, held extensive hearings on Capitol Hill. When—on Walter Lippmann's urging—Republicans called in Bullitt to testify as their last witness, he again provided a suitable climax for the occasion. His story of the secret mission to Russia, and the subsequent cover-up by Wilson and Lloyd George, created a stir; but what really astonished everyone was his report of some secret parleys and conversations held in Paris. The Secretary of State, said Bullitt, considered much of the treaty "thoroughly bad" and the League of Nations "entirely useless. The great powers have simply gone ahead and arranged the world to suit themselves." So embarrassing was this testimony to the administration that it played a significant part in Congress's failure to ratify the Versailles Treaty.[6]

It was not without a little private melodrama that Bullitt had spoken out so freely. On receiving the subpoena, he had "wrestled" with himself for hours in an anguished frenzy of soul searching and indecision. He warned his wife that telling the

whole truth meant an ignominious banishment from Philadelphia society for fifteen years; then, no doubt, he would be vindicated, but she would meanwhile have to share the exile with
him. His ignominy began with a storm of abuse from the American newspapers: Bullitt was a secret Bolshevik, a spoiled tattle-
tale, a disgrace to his profession as a journalist. Red Scare politicians labeled him a leftist infiltrator and the London and Paris
press flayed him as well. Under questioning in the House of
Commons, Lloyd George denied all responsibility for the Bullitt
mission to Russia—his secretary dismissed this effort to implicate the PM as nothing but a "tissue of lies." Only the German
newspapers and a few liberal magazines like the *New Republic*
came to Bullitt's defense.

In Washington, the entire fiasco elicited a loud silence from
the Wilson administration. It caught Wilson himself at a bad
time, less than two weeks before he suffered a paralytic stroke
that crippled him for life. Isolated in the White House, he
refused any compromise with the Senate over the treaty, and the
Republican landslide gathered force. Not all young liberals, by
any means, took pleasure in Wilson's downfall. Dean Acheson
arrived in Washington during the month of Bullitt's testimony
and observed the consequences from close by: "In the circle in
which we moved depression and bewilderment deepened. Justice Brandeis, whose law clerk I was, brushed aside attempts to
draw him out, giving the impression that things were so much
worse than could be imagined as to be beyond discussion. We
went on with our work and our lives, as I imagine people did in
Rome in the fifth century with the defenses of the frontiers
crumbling. A year passed; the depression grew; the forthcoming
election, a bad prospect, turned into a horror in fact. A sack of
the city by the victorious barbarians appeared a certainty. It
was."

So the Versailles settlement encouraged a split in internationalist liberal opinion that would persist through the century. While
Bullitt and some of his friends felt betrayed by Woodrow Wilson, other liberals felt betrayed by Bullitt. Dean Acheson typified the majority of young liberals who remained loyal to the

President—after all, Wilson's domestic reforms had to be pre-served, and one recoiled at the thought of a pack of Republican yahoos taking over the government. Mistakes in the peace treaty might be corrected later, as Wilson suggested, but even a bad treaty seemed preferable to an onslaught of anarchy and Bolshevism in Europe.

That viewpoint was reflected in the efforts of Herbert Hoover and John Foster Dulles, the latter a financial adviser to the U.S. delegation. Hoover was undaunted by his own failure to per-suade Wilson to soften the treaty. He wrote to the President that the United States should try, "in a definite and organized man-ner," to ensure that enough credits were extended to Europe. He and Dulles suggested a committee of government officials "to determine the broad policies to be pursued in economic assistance," as well as a postwar recovery plan. Believing that Europe could recover through American credit creation, they accepted the treaty reluctantly as better than nothing.

For an impatient purist like Bullitt, on the other hand, a docu-ment so evil as the Versailles Treaty just had to be repudiated, no matter what the side effects. Woodrow Wilson should have fought it like a man. As for Bolshevism, appalling as it might be in a Western country, it appeared a positive step in remote and exotic Russia. Indeed, it *must* be a positive step if the Western establishment opposed it—any official terrorism or intolerance in Soviet Russia must be due to Western hostility. The funda-mental meliorism of liberal thought, a belief in human reason and moral progress, made it hard to regard any revolution as a step backward.

A feeling of optimism about the human race, unusually strong in Bullitt, served as the binding force among these young Ameri-can liberals. Their differences were trivial compared to what united them. Most liberals still agreed on the basic ideals re-flected in Wilson's war program—free trade and investment, economic aid, national self-determination, and multilateral or-ganizations such as the League—which most Republicans tended to view with distaste. Behind these ideals lay a certain moral earnestness, a missionary faith that made isolationism look like an abandonment of duty. American liberals had an obligation as gentlemen to elevate the masses of the world. Though Bullitt and others talked often during the 1920s about their "disillusionment," in fact they were just momentarily discouraged. Liberalism was the natural goal of all human progress; and the United States remained the most hopeful agent for achieving that goal. Under a better set of leaders, and a better set of circumstances, American liberalism could resume its ministry on an international scale.

That kind of self-assurance was disappearing fast among liberals and Social Democrats across the Atlantic. For America the war had been a short, glorious romp to victory; for the Europeans a prolonged and horrible slaughter. Their nerve was unsteady and optimism gave way to irony. The Versailles Treaty came to British liberals as a misfortune, but hardly as a surprise. John Maynard Keynes, who had resigned from his delegation, published a book denouncing the treaty less for its wickedness than for its stupidity: what Europe needed was economic unity and a program of financial help from the United States. Keynes wrote plaintively of President Wilson that "his thought and his temperament were essentially theological not intellectual, with all of the strength and weakness of that manner of thought, feeling, and expression. It is a type of which there are not now in England such magnificent specimens as formerly." There were numerous specimens among American liberals—such as Bullitt himself, who described Keynes's book as a "moderate, practical and Christian" remedy for the Paris disaster.

No doubt, the word "Christian" would not have occurred to most English intellectuals, for religious morality struck no fire in them. European liberals were ironic, secular, and defensive, while in the United States a dose of theology, and of genuine feeling, gave to liberalism a continued strength and self-confidence. The Americans believed in God, and therefore in themselves.

This is not so much a story of William Christian Bullitt as a story about the internationalist liberal movement in which he sometimes participated. Yet his long period of "exile" was quite representative. It corresponded with the twelve-year exile of liberal Democrats from the government, between the Republican invasion of 1921 and Roosevelt's New Deal. It was similarly empty and non-political. Bullitt lingered for a while in New England, living the life of a gentleman farmer, and in New York, editing movie scripts. Then he left once again for foreign parts.

The expatriate phase of Bullitt's life has a slight air of farce about it. With a *rentier* income behind him, his trip into the counterculture could never have been more than a good act. He played the part with diligence. In New York, his first marriage dissolved when his wife ran off with another man; and in Europe, he took up with Louise Bryant, the widow of his old Communist friend, John Reed. Consummating a spectacular romance, Bullitt and Bryant went to live in a palace on the shores of the Bosphorus. They soon were married; she gave birth to a daughter; he wrote an off-color novel about Philadelphia; and all seemed well until at length she became seriously ill, at which point their passion fell on very hard times. Aggravated by alcohol and drugs, Bryant's illness drove her to some wildly eccentric behavior. So Bullitt got a second divorce in 1930, pleading "general indignities."

He never married again. But amid all the indignities, Bullitt had taken solace from some love affairs and enjoyed the company of celebrated people. He was accepted as a fellow writer in Paris by Ernest Hemingway and the lawyer-poet Archibald MacLeish; he was given psychiatric help in Vienna by Dr. Sigmund Freud. The doctor, unfortunately, shared a dangerous and debilitating obsession with his patient. "Your Woodrow Wilson," Freud opined in 1926, "was the silliest fool of the century, if not of all centuries. And he was probably one of the biggest criminals—unconsciously I am quite sure." On the strength of this hatred, Dr. Freud and Bullitt became close friends and spent two years collaborating on a psychological study of President Wilson.[7] It was two years foolishly wasted; in fact Bullitt's meandering might have continued indefinitely, had it not been for a liberal renaissance back home after the 1929 stock market crash. The Great Depression came as an opportunity for our protagonist, providing him at last with a steady job.

Even before the Great Depression, not everything had been

darkness and barbarism in American politics. The 1928 presidential campaign had transformed Governor Al Smith into a folk hero for such party stalwarts as Dean Acheson. And Acheson's schoolmate, Averell Harriman, converted to the cause that same autumn, a latecomer to liberalism whose conversion was rather tentative. As a business tycoon, Harriman could not help noticing the dismal economic consequences of America's isolation—of its protectionism, of its insistence that Europe should repay all war debts. "I became a Democrat," he recalls, "among other things because I began to realize how right Wilson was about America's post-war role and how wrong the Republicans were." Other internationalists—mostly northeasterners of Anglo-Saxon descent, like Acheson and Harriman—tried to keep the Wilson program alive in political clubs and pressure groups. Still active in the movement was Professor James Shotwell, who helped organize the Council on Foreign Relations as a bipartisan shrine of Woodrow Wilson's legacy. Some of these foreign affairs buffs were not anti-imperialist, or even liberal, so much as they were concerned Americans who wanted to avert a European catastrophe that might involve the United States.

Nor were they exclusively Democrats. The Republican elected President in 1928 was Herbert Hoover, who appointed Henry Stimson his Secretary of State. Stimson was an internationalist liberal, and Hoover never ceased to consider himself a Wilsonian. As Commerce Secretary for seven years, he had tried to help Europe by encouraging American credit expansion and private loans—a series of ad hoc rescue plans were launched. But the opposition of other Republicans always made an aggressive policy difficult for Hoover. And the onslaught of the Depression put an even stricter limit on U.S. action abroad.

The Democratic Party seemed to offer more hope. When in 1932 the Democratic campaign appeared a foregone success, internationalist liberals heard the call with a renewed sense of ambition. Franklin Roosevelt sounded quite emphatic about the need to revive old Wilsonian ideals, to resurrect "plans like those of 1917 that put their faith once more in the forgotten man at the bottom of the economic pyramid." Earlier he had urged American membership in the League of Nations and suggested that the United States forgive all of Europe's war debts. Perhaps Roosevelt would begin again where President Wilson had left off.

In practice it was not nearly so simple. From the point of view of a neo-Wilsonian and an internationalist, this liberal revival suffered from one serious drawback: it was almost entirely a domestic affair. When he spoke of Wilson's plans for 1917, Roosevelt meant only the plans for economic mobilization. Wilson's plans for 1918—to make the world safe for democracy on the basis of the Fourteen Points—would just have to wait awhile longer. In the depths of a depression with unemployment at 25 percent, economic mobilization sounded like a good idea to the American people, but they were more isolationist than ever. Changing his earlier tune, Roosevelt denied any intention of joining the League of Nations. Only on free trade did he remain a better internationalist than Hoover, and he seemed to agree with the verdict that World War I had been a swindle. Arms manufacturers and clever politicians in Europe had tricked us into abandoning our neutrality to fight someone else's war. The United States would not make that mistake again.

Whether true or not, such a harsh verdict ignored some harsher realities. The outside world, rather than being safe for liberal democracy, was deteriorating in much the way Bullitt had predicted it would. A Bolshevik tide had not swept over Western Europe, as feared; but now there was a new menace in the form of Adolf Hitler and Imperial Japan, and none of the democracies appeared willing to resist it. For all their disappointment, a number of internationalist Democrats wanted a place in the nationalist New Deal, just as they had flocked to Woodrow Wilson in 1917. Perhaps they sensed that under a Democratic administration one at least could hope for a substantive change in American foreign policy. International reform and involvement were a natural result of domestic liberalism. That of course had been the pattern of Wilson's presidency and, with enough encouragement, it might become the pattern of Roosevelt's presidency, too.

* * *

When he came back from Europe to rejoin the Democrats, William Bullitt wanted very badly to be made Ambassador to Paris, one of his childhood dreams. However, he was not yet a born-again Wilsonian. Far from it. He clung to most of his old resentments; and he thought that he knew too much about Europe to swallow any program for international reform. The United States could do little to help out England and France—even if England and France deserved any help, which was doubtful. At the same time, Bullitt remained a liberal reformer at home, with a few loyal friends close to Roosevelt who could make the requisite introductions. After giving him some free-lance work, Roosevelt hired him finally for a minor State Department position, the same one Bullitt had held fifteen years before.

This time around he managed to get promoted, working his way up slowly to an intimate friendship with the President. Although Roosevelt had gone to Groton as a boy, he did not approve of snobbery, and both he and Bullitt took an almost buccaneering approach to international relations. Diplomacy for Roosevelt was largely a matter of informal contacts with foreigners, avoiding the State Department, and gathering as much power as possible into his own hands. The Foreign Service he regarded as a society of pompous drones—to get rid of them was difficult, but at least you could get around them on some issues. Over the next seven years, the President's chief instrument for circumventing State on European issues was Bullitt—a New Deal enthusiast, not at all pompous, brimming with energy, and entirely at ease in chatting with European officials. A love affair with Roosevelt's secretary may have confirmed his status, but Bullitt also developed an intellectual bond with Roosevelt. The President's policy on Europe came largely from Bullitt's advice, advice which began as isolationist and then moved quite suddenly in the other direction.

In his freebooter status, Bullitt played a conspicuous role right from the beginning of the New Deal. Long before the inauguration, Roosevelt sent him on a secret mission to discuss the repayment of World War I loans with European governments. As usual, the secret leaked out, causing a furor in the press: Bullitt wanted to release England and France from their debt obligations to America, and he had no right to represent the United States anyway. Several isolationist senators became so exercised about it that they tried to have Bullitt arrested.

Hardly surprising, perhaps, that Bullitt came to symbolize for the Republicans all that was dangerous in New Deal diplomacy. After the Great War, isolationists of both parties could not trust certain Democrats when it came to foreign affairs. At this point their suspicions of Bullitt were unfounded, for he had no more desire than Roosevelt did to compromise with Europe on the matter of war debts. He supported the New Deal policy of reflation and monetary independence; and when the International Economic Conference in London ended in failure, Bullitt did not particularly mind. "I am more than ever convinced," he wrote to Roosevelt from England, "that we can do little in Europe and should keep out of European squabbles and that our future lies in the Americas and the Far East." President Roosevelt agreed—and his refusal to provide any economic leadership encouraged a further drift into protectionism all over the world. During the 1920s, the United States at least had made some effort to keep the international economy going. Except for some bilateral trade agreements, that effort now was abandoned, and economic reform had to wait another decade.

There did remain one loose end on the edge of Europe, a left-over problem of World War I that continued to intrigue Bullitt. The Soviet Union now was recognized by almost every important country except the United States. Worried about Japanese expansion in the Far East, the President decided early on a détente with Russia; and the Russians, who felt directly threatened by a Japanese invasion, were no less eager for an understanding. A few bilateral disputes—such as unpaid Russian debts and Bolshevik agitpropaganda in the USA—would have to be settled first, before any formal act of recognition. At least, it would have to appear as if they were settled. Anti-Communist snobs in the State Department could be evaded by an informal, direct approach, by a quick and quiet negotiation with Foreign Commissar Litvinov. "If I could only, myself, talk to one man representing the Russians, I could straighten out the whole question," Roosevelt declared. His personal agent took the form of Bullitt, who involved himself in the *démarche* by sheer bureaucratic aggression. The effort paid off handsomely. When an agreement was reached with Litvinov, leaving vague the matter of unpaid Russian debts, Bullitt was rewarded with the new ambassadorship.

Naturally, the appointment came as a personal triumph. During his short visit to Moscow to present credentials, the Soviets overwhelmed Bullitt with flattery and friendship: Chairman Lenin, they said, had liked him immensely back in 1919; and Joseph Stalin, who was very worried about Japan, went so far as to plant a loud kiss on Bullitt's mouth. The United States responded in similar fashion, for most conservatives now had no serious objection to recognizing Russia. In Philadelphia, a group of businessmen invited Bullitt to come and give a speech, which invitation he accepted with surprising grace. "To be honored thus in my own city, a stone's throw from the house in which I was born, is a unique pleasure," rejoiced Bullitt, and he obviously meant it. "We Philadelphians are peculiar. Wherever we may travel, Philadelphia goes with us and remains the center of our world."

So when he went back to Moscow one month later, Bullitt took with him the approval of Philadelphia. He also took with him, as it were, a woman who was his mistress. But with a new sense of propriety he kept her in the background, away from photographers and the perhaps all too distant American eye.

The New Deal view of State as a bunch of air-headed fops still had considerable justification at the time Roosevelt took office. Even so, with regard to the diplomatic staff at Moscow, it distorted the real picture. Ambassador Bullitt picked out one of the most interesting crops of Foreign Service officers ever to run a U.S. embassy, and at an interesting moment in Soviet history, a time of rare relaxation and tolerance. The Stalinist Terror would recommence a year later, but in Moscow of 1934 Communist Party members mixed openly with foreigners. As Bullitt reported to Roosevelt, Soviet officials appeared quite bored by ordinary envoys; "on the other hand, they are extremely eager to have contact with anyone who has first-rate intelligence and dimension as a human being. They were, for example, delighted by young Kennan who went in with me." Young George Kennan's fondness for "unofficial" Russians was intensified in this period to a degree from which he never fully recovered. Not that his relations were confined to intellectual talk; with characteristic gusto, the ambassador arranged polo matches, baseball games, and all-night parties with the natives, turning the American Embassy into a social center for his own diplomatic staff.

Third Secretary Kennan could not agree with Bullitt's optimism about official relations. The American staff in Moscow had been chosen for its objectivity and expertise; but Kennan had opposed recognizing Russia, and he predicted from experience that the Bolsheviks, sooner or later, would evade most of their agreements. At this stage in his career, he still had a relatively open view of the world. Princeton University had not etched upon his mind "anything very much in the way of settled opinions, conclusions, or certainties in the field of public affairs. I can recall experiencing, as a fresh college graduate, the promptings of a vague Wilsonian liberalism; a regret that the Senate had rejected American membership in the League of Nations; a belief in laissez-faire economics and the values of competition; and a corresponding aversion to high tariffs." This mild Wilsonianism may have arisen from a certain sentimentality. Too young to go to war in 1917, Kennan was lured later on to Princeton by an F. Scott Fitzgerald novel, and he always felt a vicarious nostalgia for that earlier era at the Ivy League. He admired the zestful idealism of Bullitt's generation, writing much later of the *New Republic* liberals that "they were able to muster among them a catholicity of interest, a depth of perception, a seriousness of concept, a tolerance, and a good taste that placed their collective effort in the foremost ranks of English language journalism of all time." Without ever accepting the internationalist liberals' world view, Kennan went along with them as an occasional fellow traveler. His opinion overlapped with theirs at particular times and on particular issues—like Russia. After World War II his grim assessment of Stalin's aims, and his eloquence in expressing it, would be used by the U.S. government to remarkable effect.

From the time of their first meeting, George Kennan suspected that his boss was too impatient to achieve even the minimum in Russia. The new ambassador arrived with some of his bourgeois fantasies still operative. "After all," Bullitt exclaimed, "the President, Jack Reed, and I are of the same American strain"—meaning that they were aristocratic, eighteenth-century rebels who could get along with the Bolsheviks, a fantasy that the Russian government tried to encourage for a while.[8] In order to frighten Japan, Soviet officials fêted Bullitt and made a good deal of noise about Soviet-American friendship. This concealed a basic disappointment, for the United States was too firm in its isolation to make any practical offers of help; Litvinov asked several times for a mutual defense pact, which Bullitt refused. Then suddenly the Soviets, a few months after their détente with America, decided that a Japanese invasion no longer was at hand, and they lost all interest in cultivating the U.S. ambassador. They reneged on some minor promises and backtracked on a major understanding, joining the rest of Europe in a refusal to repay any American debts. After the initial big kiss, Bullitt never met Stalin again.

Already a lonely man, Bullitt was made even lonelier by this rejection; he returned often to America on errands or sick leave, spending less and less time on post. Running through his messages to Franklin Roosevelt were two emotive themes, one of them a strong affection for the President and first family, amounting almost to hunger for love. Bullitt's statement that "you are an angel as well as a President" gives the gist of his feelings, oddly similar to that old adoration for Woodrow Wilson. He once said that Roosevelt was almost like Jesus Christ—and he wrote to the President in perfect sincerity, "I should like to hear the sound of your voice and be with you for a few days. I don't like being so far away from you." A delicate and dangerous influence was beginning to take hold of our protagonist once again.

Another theme in Bullitt's letters, related to his homesickness, was a heightened contempt for things European and a firmer support for American isolation. Once an object of Bullitt's scorn, America during the 1930s seemed more and more an island of political virtue in a totalitarian swamp. Roosevelt was doing great things at home and should stick to that. Quick visits to Berlin and Paris convinced Bullitt that war was coming. The French attitude was that "it is only natural that the United States, in view of the fact that its sole harvest from the last war was a crop of disillusionment, should remain completely aloof." As for Nazi militarism, "the present Nationalist movement in Germany has, in my opinion, been inevitable since the terms of the Treaty of Versailles were imposed." In Moscow, the full horror of Stalinist rule became increasingly clear to him as Russian friends and acquaintances were quietly arrested, never to be seen again except maybe in a show trial. His ambassadorship was brought to a head when some American delegates attended a local Communist International meeting, in violation of Soviet agreements not to encourage anti-U.S. propaganda. Bullitt responded to this with a propaganda campaign of his own—reducing the embassy staff and criticizing the Soviet government in front of journalists. He also urged the President to make a public protest, just short of a rupture in diplomatic relations.

Bullitt's total rupture with communism was among the great disillusionments of his life. This time it was not just a single politician that he turned against, such as Woodrow Wilson, but a whole political movement. The Russian Revolution, instead of being a step forward, was the most dangerous threat imaginable to his liberal ideals; even the Nazis, who hated liberal democracy, lacked the long-term potential of Soviet power and propaganda. Another thought occurred to him: if Hitler started a world war, then Russia would have a chance in the general chaos to establish a Communist federation over most of Eurasia. By comparison with that alternative, the old pre-war empires in Europe did not look so bad after all. This new-found loathing of the Bolsheviks had a moderating effect on Bullitt's radical views, turning him back toward the mainstream of internationalist liberalism.

One might suppose that his rupture would have led Bullitt to advocate an American alliance with England and France, so as to prevent a world war from which only Russia could profit. But he did not go that far—yet. American public opinion, he well knew, made such a strategy impossible. And he retained a mistaken hope that Hitler could be deterred from war without American involvement.

Before leaving Moscow, Bullitt wrote one of those prophetic valedictions at which he excelled, analyzing the nature of Soviet rule and its challenge to Western liberals. He tended to agree with George Kennan that the Stalin regime had inherited some of its worst traits from czarist Russia, which the Bolsheviks had grafted onto the teachings of Karl Marx. The combined effect of Russian Marxism and Leninist tyranny presented a complex problem to the West, a problem that must be met with both flexibility and firmness. In making this analysis, Bullitt was a liberal way ahead of his time. The liberal moderates saw other, more pressing problems to cope with in Europe and Asia; and many New Deal radicals hung onto the illusions of 1919, knowing little about Soviet Russia and blaming the latest difficulties on Bullitt's fiery temper. Eventually he was replaced in Moscow by Joseph E. Davies, an ambassador who did not take communism so much to heart.

William Bullitt made his final departure from Russia in the spring of 1936, more eager than ever to do some political work for the Democratic Party. President Roosevelt's re-election bid that year held far greater excitement for him than the dreary spectacle of Europe. He spent the summer as a campaign speechwriter and accepted the job of "reforming and regenerating" the Foreign Service—one of several New Deal attempts to abolish right-wing degeneracy at State. Unfortunately, with the mood of the country so xenophobic, the New Deal did not even attempt to reform and regenerate American foreign policy. Congress, after allowing some free trade agreements, had gone and passed the Neutrality Act—a law designed to keep Americans from any direct economic interest, or any political favoritism, in any foreign dispute. As long as Congress took that attitude, Roosevelt had no choice but to follow Bullitt's advice and campaign once again on an isolationist platform.

This platform looked good to the average voter, whose isolationism had intensified along with Ambassador Bullitt's. While a large portion of isolationists were conservative, they were a broad coalition that included most New Dealers. Many of them were liberal purists who wanted no truck with Europe except in the framework of a "one-world" government—or who believed, like Bullitt, that America should stick to domestic reform. There also existed between the wars a popular ignorance and suspicion of foreigners. Whatever lay behind it, isolationism stayed so strong that it would not be destroyed even by another world war.

Two months before election day Bullitt was made Ambassador to France, now the one foreign post he really wanted, a post where his contacts in Europe might make a substantial difference. Using France as a home base, he could report by telephone to Washington on conditions all over the continent. Moreover, his arrival in Paris was greeted with a show of genuine enthusiasm: the new Popular Front government had some rough similarities to the New Deal, and Bullitt came over as a close friend of France as well as of Roosevelt. His daily red carnation delighted French officials. And when the Democrats won by a landslide in America, no one was more pleased than the French premier, who gave Bullitt a kiss of congratulation rivaling even that of Stalin.

One of the first things Bullitt did at the Paris embassy was to seek out fresh talent from among the "white spat brigade," as he called it. Though he found the pickings meager, he quickly discovered a bright consular officer named Robert Murphy: here was a man who after fifteen years in the State Department still retained some midwestern qualities. The very name Bob Murphy must have sounded reassuring to Bill Bullitt—it reflected the proper New Deal image of tough, cigar-chomping earthiness—and Murphy shared an important crony with the ambassador in Jim Farley, the Democratic Party boss and former lieutenant of Al Smith. It just so happened that Bob Murphy, despite his name, was neither a convinced liberal nor a convinced anything else. Over the next four years in Paris he was elevated to second-in-command at the embassy, and to higher honors afterward. But what Murphy liked was to keep the American ball rolling or to clinch a deal, without a lot of worry about basic principles.

Murphy and his colleagues were prodded by Bullitt to make

contact with as many important Frenchmen, in and out of the government, as they could get to know—and the ambassador bent himself to the same task. He nevertheless did a surprisingly poor job during his first two years in France, judged by the already low standard of Roosevelt's ambassadors. Until the Munich crisis, Bullitt continued to downgrade the danger of Nazism and was opposed to American involvement even if a war *did* break out. Because of his friendship with the highest French officials, he had as much information as a diplomat could ask for, and he drew some strange conclusions from it. In a sense, Bullitt reverted to his old role as reporter or columnist, groping his way from one problem to another and occasionally advancing a crackpot solution. His peculiar logic was set forth in a book by Bertrand Russell, a book which he recommended to the President as "a brilliant analysis of the present international situation. Bertrand (who is in many ways an ass) holds as the one hope of the world the possibility that the United States will stay out of war in the Far East or in Europe and will have, at the end of the holocaust, a civilization intact and sufficient strength to pick up the pieces and put them together again." That was not a very constructive suggestion, though it had a strong influence on President Roosevelt. Such views may also have had an influence on Adolf Hitler, whose minions were decoding most of Bullitt's cables.

The essential threat to Europe, so far as Bullitt was concerned, was Russian communism. As he wrote to Roosevelt, the European peoples "have the alternative of submerging their national hatreds and national prides sufficiently to unify the continent or of destroying themselves completely and handing Europe over to the Bolsheviks." Ambassador Bullitt therefore directed his efforts toward a Franco-German reconciliation that would keep the Soviets safely in their place. A long talk with Feldmarshall Goering persuaded him that it might be possible to appease Hitler by allowing German domination of Eastern Europe. Harkening to the experience of World War I, he told Roosevelt that the French "wish today that they had followed Wilson and written a real peace instead of the Treaty of Versailles." He gave repeated warnings in Paris that America would not intervene in this war, but his warnings never were quite accepted by French officials, who saw Roosevelt as a last hope. "You are, in other words, beginning to occupy the miracle man position," he wrote to the President. "And I am strongly reminded of the sort of hope that for a time was reposed in Woodrow Wilson." Roosevelt must not repeat Wilson's mistake of being drawn into war, nor be tricked into any hint of a commitment; this only would mislead France and create a worse bitterness.

If Bullitt seemed bogged down by the lessons of World War I, then in his diplomatic style he sometimes went right back to the eighteenth century. He rented a small château in the park of Chantilly, where he held occasional hunting parties for stag and deer. His social life in the city, often lavish and unconventional, covered the entire spectrum of French politics, including Communists and Fascists alike. He also kept a few mistresses, just to do things right. And to annoy the stuffy British, he consorted with that perfect aristocratic rebel, the ex-king of England and duke of Windsor; British diplomats worried that he was having an affair with the duchess and tried to get him recalled. Of course, a hearty hatred of England was in the oldest tradition of American ambassadors to France, and Bullitt had hated England heartily ever since the Boer War. Now he suspected that the British official classes were trying to undermine his efforts at a Franco-German détente, so as to keep Europe divided in their customary manner.

Sad to say, there were some other eighteenth-century backdrops to Bullitt's ambassadorship: a seclusion from the common people, bickering intrigues in the Paris government, a general sense that something was rotten in the state of France.

In the months leading up to the Munich crisis, Bullitt's view of Adolf Hitler achieved a gradual clarity. His dark isolationism began alternating with flashes of partial insight—at one moment he urged France to compromise with the Nazis, at the next moment he wanted Roosevelt to convene a general peace conference. Then when France and England caved in at Munich, virtually handing over Czechoslovakia to Hitler, he understood at last what must be done. Another European war was unavoidable, and America must provide arms and moral support to the democracies.

Bullitt went right back to Washington and said as much to Roosevelt, who had been thinking along these lines already. The nub of the problem no longer was Russian communism, it seemed, but rather English and French military weakness. All of the energy he had put into preventing U.S. involvement, Bullitt now put into obtaining American airplanes for France. The best purchasing agent, he told Roosevelt, would be one M. Jean Monnet, "who, as you know, has been an intimate friend of mine for many years, whom I trust as a brother. Monnet organized and directed the Inter-Allied Maritime Transport Council; the wheat and shipping pool and all the vast other Inter-Allied organizations during the war when he was only a man of twenty-eight. He then became Under Secretary of the League of Nations." No question about it, if there was such a person as a French Wilsonian before World War II, that person was Jean Monnet: rich banker and Social Democrat, anti-Communist and economic regulator, critic of the Versailles Treaty. National prides and national hatreds left Monnet cold, and a European federation struck him as simple common sense. It was a peculiarly un-French set of attitudes.

Jean Monnet's common sense was overwhelmed in 1939 by political passions on either side of the Atlantic. His first problem was the U.S. Neutrality Act, which prevented the sale of American arms to any belligerent country. When Ambassador Bullitt appealed to Congress for changes in the act, he succeeded only in angering isolationists, both Democratic and Republican—all their old suspicions of him were now confirmed. And their suspicions of Franklin Roosevelt were confirmed as well, for the President went public in his support for the European democracies at about the same time. With enormous difficulty, President Roosevelt did obtain some modifications in the Neutrality Act, but this meant little to a foreign country that may have been past any kind of outside help. By 1940, the French could not even make effective use of what airplanes they had. Their defense effort proved so feeble and disorganized—and Germany's attack so well prepared—that they were vanquished by Hitler's *Wehrmacht* after six weeks of fighting.

One obvious sign of weakness in France was the emotional bond between its leaders and a foreign diplomat, William Bullitt. Cabinet ministers became ever more intimate with him as their fear of Germany increased—and, predictably, Bullitt's own behavior lost a certain element of modesty and restraint. When the *Wehrmacht* began closing in on Paris he descended to his wine *cave,* now a bomb shelter, and refused to go south with the fleeing French government: never had a U.S. representative fled Paris, no, not even during the Reign of Terror and the Commune. Sometimes the idea of dying in Paris, at the hands of a Communist or Fascist mob, seemed to fascinate him—he left orders that he should be buried in Philadelphia—but he also wondered what might happen if he lived through it all. The Germans, he suggested to Roosevelt, will "prevent me from having contact with anyone. Probably I shall have to transact all business through Bob Murphy, the Counselor of the Embassy, who is a corker. Under those circumstances, I could certainly be of more practical use running that Department in Washington than here."

The German Army set up headquarters at the Hotel Crillon, next door to the U.S. Embassy, and treated Bullitt with perfect propriety. Nevertheless, the ambassador felt cut off from his higher duties back home. Leaving Robert Murphy behind as chargé d'affaires at Vichy, he returned thence to the United States, horrified at the extent of France's demoralization and defeat.

History plays the strangest tricks on people. For William Bullitt, the collapse of France should have signaled the beginning of a meteoric Washington career. As the war drew closer to America, other interventionists with similar views were moving onto the center stage. All of the right pieces were falling back into place, in Bullitt's own mind as much as in the U.S. government. Germany had to be defeated and America's involvement was inevitable; the good old cause of 1918 would be revived, this time with no illusions about Russia and no back talk from England and France; the United States would be stronger and more realistic now, without abandoning its liberal ideals. And yet Bullitt, instead of being given an important role in this revival, was pushed aside by the Democratic administration—a few years later he and President Roosevelt parted company almost as enemies.

Their falling out developed slowly. Because the pacifist-isolationist sentiment ran so high, Roosevelt could not speak openly against it during the 1940 presidential campaign. He counted, therefore, on people like Bullitt and Averell Harriman to function as advocates for rearmament. In a Philadelphia speech, Bullitt asserted that the dictatorships—meaning Soviet Russia as well as Germany and Japan—would bring war to America whether America wanted it or not, and he repeated this theme in other parts of the country. Meanwhile, as the months dragged on, he was denied any sort of promotion in the foreign affairs hierarchy. After Roosevelt's re-election, Bullitt touted a new program of "lend-lease" aid for England; and to Averell Harriman, who was running the program in London, he wrote that the President was "waiting for public opinion to lead and public opinion is waiting for a lead from the President"; but what Bullitt himself was waiting for was a more influential job. He went occasionally to the White House and traveled on special missions, and still there was no place for him in Roosevelt's inner circle. This was the President's usual method of removing people whom he did not wish to fire.

Roosevelt had an ample pool of talent to draw from. One important reason for Bullitt's decline was the ascent of other public servants, some of them more competent than he—not just Harriman, but two other old Grotonians. In the summer of 1940, Dean Acheson had helped arrange the transfer of American destroyers to England, and then he left his law practice to join the State Department. At the same time, Under Secretary of State Sumner Welles began trespassing on Bullitt's territory as chief adviser to the White House on European affairs. And Adolf Berle, another specialist in Latin America, was making himself increasingly influential as Assistant Secretary of State.

Furthermore, much of the clout in foreign policy was shifting to the War Department. Bullitt had hoped to become Secretary of War in 1940—but the President instead appointed Colonel Henry Stimson, the Republican internationalist who had been Hoover's Secretary of State. Along with Colonel Stimson came Robert Lovett and James Forrestal, taking charge as Assistant Secretary for Air and Under Secretary of the Navy, respectively. And as his personal assistant Stimson also brought in John McCloy, a New York lawyer who was familiar with Europe. These people had known each other for many years in Wall Street banking and law, forming a new Washington network from which Bullitt was excluded.

Although William Bullitt usually overreacted to any kind of exclusion, his failure to take this one with patience and good grace soon led to a permanent downfall. Already President Roosevelt had grown tired of his egotism, his refusal to sit still and be quiet, which in Washington gave off a downright evil smell. Bullitt fell to making nasty remarks about those who outranked him. Several State Department officials were "criminals," in his view; Dean Acheson ought to be fired and so should Adolf Berle, that old companion of the red rose in Paris who was now nothing but a "shifty, smart, little person." When Bullitt spread around a rumor that Sumner Welles was a secret homosexual—forcing Welles to resign in 1943— Roosevelt decided that the former Ambassador to France could be tolerated no longer. He summoned Bullitt to the White House and said he deserved to go to hell for "betraying" a fellow human being. Furthermore, the President wished never to see him again.

Like the poet Wordsworth, who was disillusioned by romance, Bullitt found himself condemned to a pointless longevity. Always in search of new adventures, he ran for mayor of Philadelphia in 1943 and lost. The next spring he became chief of psychological warfare in the Free French forces under Charles de Gaulle, winning a place in the Legion of Honor. But he survived those experiences by twenty-two deadly years—a tiresome, talkative, and somewhat irrelevant figure. Meanwhile, his decline formed a distant backdrop to the internationalist liberal revival, a revival that would move along with accelerating success through the decade of the 1940s.

II

Waging Deals

1940–1944

The wartime diplomacy of Franklin Roosevelt presented a further puzzle and a further challenge to the internationalist liberal movement. While the revival of Wilsonian ideals gained momentum—in private groups, as well as in government—the President himself continued to hold them at arm's length. And rather than subordinating the war effort to political or economic goals, he did something quite different. In his agreements with Allies, Roosevelt used diplomacy as a weapon for military success, not long-term solutions. What Roosevelt wanted was the "unconditional" surrender of Germany and Japan—as quickly and cheaply as possible, and without much concern for a postwar settlement. In one respect this method was vindicated, for American casualties were indeed low and the victory was cheap. The United States came out of World War II more prosperous than ever before.

Still, it is hard to say why President Roosevelt put off so many political decisions. He was as slow in planning for peace as in joining the war. Despite his doubts about the use of a Universal League, he did agree with the other points of Woodrow Wilson's program, and with the whole idea of American involvement in world affairs. Perhaps his good sense of timing was at work once again, as it always had been during the New Deal: isolationists felt resentful and humiliated, especially after Pearl Harbor; the President saw no point in giving them another target until he knew the time was right. Of course, the Fourteen Points had served as good propaganda during World War I, and Roosevelt could not completely ignore the question of what Americans were fighting for. He made some vague speeches about the four freedoms—the freedoms of speech and worship, the freedoms from want and fear—and he spoke out for economic reforms and national autonomy. He even permitted the secret discussion of postwar plans by committees in the State Department. However, this was mainly to keep State busy, while America won the war.

For the most part, State Department officials had no influence on the strategic choices. True to his long distaste for the Foreign Service, Roosevelt maintained a second foreign office in the White House, and occasionally in his own bedroom. When he was not actually meeting with Allied leaders, he conducted much of his business through special envoys—trusted henchmen like Robert Murphy, Harry Hopkins, and Averell Harriman, who had orders to arrange what was needed for a cheap victory. U.S. ground fighting was to be kept at a minimum, so as to cut the loss of American lives. In effect, that meant giving military help to England, France, Russia, and China in the form of basic commodities and Lend-Lease equipment. It also meant making ad hoc arrangements for the rule of liberated areas by Communist cadres and by old-fashioned imperialists. If these arrangements had a way sometimes of becoming permanent, then at least they kept America's Allies happy and brought the war to an inexpensive end.

Roosevelt's pragmatic style during World War II achieved its purest expression in the Vichy story. After the fall of Paris in mid-1940, the invading Nazis had allowed a segment of France to remain independent, with its capital at Vichy—though perhaps "independent" is not exactly the right word. Assisted by some French right-wingers and military men, Marshal Henri Philippe Pétain set up a new government in Vichy the ambiguity of which made for confusion in the United States. Was "Vichy France" a Fascist regime under Nazi control, or was it secretly pro-British? Was it totalitarian, or was it merely authoritarian?

A group of news reporters put those questions to Ambassador
Bullitt on his return to America, and he sought to reassure them.
"I don't know if it is right to call it a fascist state. Marshal Pétain
has a tremendous reputation, and he is thoroughly honest and
straightforward." Nor would it make sense to close down our
embassy at Vichy, where Bob Murphy remained in charge with
a few other U.S. diplomats.

Up at his manor in Hyde Park, President Roosevelt heard
about these remarks with a blend of skepticism and annoyance.
Marshal Pétain, he believed, was a shrewd old peasant who had
managed to seduce Bullitt, and who was not averse to collaborating with Adolf Hitler. Even so, Roosevelt could see no
sensible alternative to recognizing Vichy France. The Free
French Committee of Charles de Gaulle, exiled in London,
never was regarded as a serious option. De Gaulle did not appear to represent more than a small number of Frenchmen and,
besides, there were practical advantages to remaining at Vichy.
Fascist or not, Marshal Pétain must be pressured to keep his
distance from Hitler, to refrain from outright collaboration; and
American diplomats, in the process, might pick up some useful
intelligence. These considerations persuaded Roosevelt to
maintain the U.S. Embassy in France, where he sent a new ambassador after six months of delay.

As for the nature of Pétain's regime, all doubts were fully
justified. The dismal state of French politics was reflected clearly
in Vichyite attitudes. Marshal Pétain claimed that the moral
corruptions of the Third Republic had brought about the defeat
of France. However, the defeat also was caused by a deep cynicism toward democracy, and by a hostility to it among French
Communists and Fascists. As Bob Murphy reported, Vichy leaders demonstrated both a weakness for Fascist ideas and a sly
opportunism—a simple desire to be on the winning side. Seeing
a choice in Europe between the Bolsheviks and the Nazis, they
appeared ready to join with Hitler on the ground floor. While
their opinions varied, most Vichyites shared a confidence in
German victory, a hatred for Great Britain and General de
Gaulle, a conviction that America would stay out until the British
were defeated. Had it not been for Anglo-American pressure on

Pétain, the French might have allowed Hitler to use their navy for an invasion of England.

In addition to his fears about fascism at Vichy, President Roosevelt also felt a strategic concern for the rest of the French Empire. He reckoned that the French could do nothing to fight against Hitler in Europe, no matter what their attitudes, but in French Africa they might be encouraged to put up some resistance. At any rate, so the cables indicated. Nominally under the rule of Vichy France, colonial North Africa retained a large local army. The leadership there seemed anxious to prevent any direct intervention by the Nazis. Reassured by these reports, the President called in Under Secretary Welles and chargé d'affaires Murphy to a parley at the White House, where he announced his idea of subverting French Africa, of trying to bring it into the war. A lot more information would be needed first. Murphy should make an inspection tour of the whole area and, "if you learn anything in Africa of special interest, send it to me. Don't bother going through State Department channels."

While this gambit in North Africa became the end purpose of his Vichy policy, Roosevelt's attempt to keep State out of the operation did not succeed. Top officials in the Department— such as Secretary Cordell Hull, Sumner Welles, and Adolf Berle—worked closely on it over the next two years, with Dean Acheson and Bullitt playing a secondary part. Roosevelt's pragmatism held no intrinsic evil for these liberals; most of them had outgrown any notion of a perfect righteousness in diplomacy, if they ever had entertained it. They wished only that the President would bear certain internationalist goals in mind, and that he not forget what the war was all about.

Robert Murphy, our man in North Africa, was Bullitt's most useful gift to the war effort—the embodiment of banality and technical skill. As an opportunist himself, he could get along fine with the officials of France's empire. And his very lack of commitment to political goals made him a serviceable tool for the American President. In the Mediterranean theater, Allied battles were won as much by Murphy's deals as by military tactics or armed force.

In one respect, his political indifference comes as a surprise. Bob Murphy's own hard work and a Roman Catholic schooling had endowed him with a good education, an impoverished childhood notwithstanding. Growing up in Progressive Milwaukee, Wisconsin, had exposed him to German culture and reformist politics. When at age twenty-one he moved to Washington, D.C., he still supported the ideals of domestic progressivism. He was swept up a year later in the tide of World War I, a tide that "produced profound changes in my country. Whatever we Americans might desire as individuals, the United States never could be the same again after 1917 and, I discovered, neither could I." But the only change produced in Murphy was a dim interest in foreign countries. He did his bit for the war gathering data on Central Europe, and then he joined the U.S. Consular Service soon after the peace.

In point of fact, Murphy belonged to that great mass of war patriots for whom the peace program meant little—Wilson's speeches of 1918 passed right over his head. The Versailles Treaty left him only with a vague sense that Central Europe had been mishandled by the Allies, and that they should have been more careful about destroying the Austro-Hungarian Empire. Posted to Munich for several years, he had a chance to see why. The German economy staggered along in a state of turmoil. Hyper-inflation was ruining the liberal bourgeoisie, making them a good deal more receptive to Nazi propaganda. As a part of his job, Murphy became acquainted with some Nazi leaders and witnessed the beer-hall putsch of Adolf Hitler. Later he was assigned to the Paris consulate, so that when he left for North Africa after a decade in France, he had acquired a vast experience with European politics. By then his own politics, insofar as they existed, were settled into a position just to the right of dead center.

Time was on Murphy's side. In late 1940, the stubborn survival of Great Britain was beginning to lure Vichy France away from total collaboration with Hitler. Therefore, he went to Africa with the blessing of Marshal Pétain and Admiral Darlan, both of whom were hoping for American aid. The colonies, Murphy found, were being governed by French officers with a gamut of emotions and prejudices. They worried all the time about German military intervention; they were under constant pressure from Nazi agents. At Casablanca, he got together for drinks with a German who admitted that he "came here for one purpose only, to convince that prize ass in Berlin, our Fuehrer, of the importance of the Mediterranean and of Morocco in particular. Herr Hitler does not seem aware that this area exists." A seizure of French Africa would indeed have strengthened Hitler's position in the Mediterranean, and the Führer did consider such a plan. So after a three-week tour, Murphy decided that his government should give some quiet help to the local authorities—not just to repulse an invasion, but to keep a watchful eye on the African ports and to curry favor for America. Accepting Murphy's advice, President Roosevelt ratified an economic accord with the Vichy regime.

In U.S. diplomacy, nothing touches off a journalistic furor more than the thought that America is appeasing an immoral government. While Murphy's deals were being struck, Cordell Hull and Sumner Welles had to cope with the side effects at home. Welles did not exaggerate when he said America's Vichy policy "provoked recurrent storms of hysterical abuse both here and in Great Britain. It called forth a degree of vituperation rarely equaled in the history of American foreign policy." Of course, it was entirely Roosevelt's idea, but many journalists suspected State of Fascist sympathies and blamed the whole thing on that Department. At times, they seemed to regard Murphy as a kind of Nazi double agent. These criticisms were encouraged by Charles de Gaulle and by elements in the British government, who fussed that American shipments to North Africa might fall into German hands. There was a lot of opposition within the U.S. government as well. With Roosevelt unwilling to give it firm public support, the State Department took a terrible beating in the American news media.

The attack on Pearl Harbor by Japan in December of 1941 finally brought the United States into World War II. Whatever Roosevelt's diplomatic aims, the ultimate decision to fight was made for him. Right away, he decided to direct American power mainly at the defeat of Adolf Hitler, saving Japan until later on; and after a few months, plans for a flat-out assault on Northern Europe were shelved as well. Instead, Winston Churchill and others convinced the President to make an initial effort in North Africa, where the German "Afrika Korps" was threatening England's position in the Middle East. During a visit to British headquarters at Cairo, William Bullitt confirmed that America could hit the Afrika Korps from the rear by invading France's colonies. He sent Roosevelt a plan of attack in which the key factor was Vichyite cooperation: "We think it may be possible to have American forces welcomed in French North African Colonies provided certain French leaders can be approached and informed." The question was, which leaders—and that question had to be answered by someone already on location.

At his post in Algiers, Robert Murphy had achieved at least some of what he set out to do, and in a typically practical fashion. The Nazis continued to put pressure on French Africa for logistical support to the Afrika Korps, while he pulled in the other direction. With the help of Adolf Berle, who had done intelligence work during World War I, he set up a crude system of espionage in all the major cities; he connived at the beginnings of a resistance organization. Unfortunately, there were few local leaders whom Murphy could count on to welcome an American invasion force—a problem made worse because the Germans were decoding his mail. At Vichy, Vice President Darlan warned the United States that, although he had "nothing against Murphy, the Germans are both jealous and suspicious of him." The Germans told the Vichy government to withdraw some colonial officials with whom Murphy was friendly, and the Vichy government felt compelled to obey.

Nevertheless, there appeared a bright spot amid the controversy, for Jean Darlan was jealous himself. He was complaining about the scandal in a jealous manner—while at the same time hinting at his desire to defect and join up with the Americans. Bob Murphy had known him in Paris before the war; he was now in command of all French military forces. He would make an ideal collaborator, if such a defection could be arranged. Darlan's son lived in Algiers where, one evening over dinner with

Murphy, he confided that his father sounded increasingly pro-Ally. Then when final plans were drawn up for an Allied invasion of North Africa, President Roosevelt issued orders to obtain Vichyite cooperation by whatever arrangement could be made. Of course, the agreements must not entail any permanent commitment. "I will not help anyone to impose a Government on the French people," he said to Murphy at Hyde Park. And a short time before the landings, Roosevelt sent word that Jean Darlan might be included in a deal.

It is possible that Darlan had suspected what was afoot—he just happened to be in Algiers, visiting his son, on the day of the Allied invasion. None of Murphy's other contacts in metropolitan France had panned out. No local officers wanted to order a cease-fire, and a long, bloody struggle seemed about to begin. When Murphy met with Darlan and proffered a deal, Darlan agreed—after several hours of fighting—to surrender the city of Algiers. At the secret urging of Marshal Pétain, Darlan went on to arrange cease-fires in the rest of North Africa and, with consummate opportunism, he converted the colonial governors to a pro-Allied stance. The price for his services was hardly excessive. Darlan demanded continued French sovereignty over the empire, French participation in the war against Germany, and a large supply of arms under the Lend-Lease program. Whenever the Allies no longer found him useful, he would be willing to resign as High Commissioner in the colonies.

These demands gave Franklin Roosevelt no trouble whatsoever. Thousands of American lives had been saved and French Africa's weight would be added to the war effort—all for an arrangement that he could alter later on. Roosevelt issued instructions that Darlan should be watched closely. Let him make administrative appointments, without building a political claque. He must be kept in power only so long as it was militarily convenient. Ambassador Bullitt wrote to the President that Darlan might be "eased gradually into a comfortable villa in Africa—or perhaps Palm Beach!—with a good chef and a good cellar and nothing to do—and forgotten. By coming over to our side he has saved his life. That's all he deserves." The suggestion was sensible but, in the event, unnecessary. On Christmas

Eve, 1942, a monarchist fanatic assassinated Darlan in Algiers and his unsavory career was terminated.

A military success, a new ally, and no political commitments—such were the results of Roosevelt's practical diplomacy. No doubt, a modicum of moral righteousness had been lost in the Darlan deal, for Jean Darlan ranked high among the most hated of Vichyites, habitually vilified in the Western press. If the commander in chief had no qualms about embracing him, then other prominent Americans made up for his indifference. The strongest dissent in high places came from Treasury Secretary Morgenthau, who described the Darlan deal to Roosevelt as "something that affects my soul," the kind of bedding down with evil that would cause a third world war. In several U.S. newspapers, the response amounted to a flood of execration of the arch-Vichyite Darlan, of his hirelings in Africa and his allies in the State Department—a flood that flowed on long after the admiral's death.

This wave of dissent, it may be noticed, arose from an old Progressive split. In some respects what occurred was a replay of 1918, when American troops had been ordered into Russia. A whole host of William Bullitts, newly incarnated, were protesting a sellout of liberal idealism. Reluctant as ever to criticize Roosevelt, they instead criticized State. The *New Republic* magazine accepted the Darlan deal as a temporary expedient but demanded the recall of Robert Murphy, "a fanatic admirer of Pétain, a fanatic supporter of the Vichy collaborationist government." Darlan and his subordinates were Fascist criminals who must no longer be tolerated in North Africa—never mind our military weakness, never mind the fight against Germany's Afrika Korps. Even the practical payoffs seemed irrelevant this time.

It was a difficult moment for moderate liberals at the Pentagon and State, who felt pressed on both flanks. An isolationist backlash was a simple threat for them, and one that might be overcome. But to be assailed from the left as a friend of reaction—that was an experience unlike anything since the last war. Moreover, these attacks seemed minor next to the greater problem of America's reluctance to make explicit plans for the peace.

The man at State most intimately involved in the Vichy affair—Under Secretary Welles—happened also to be its most ardent internationalist. On the surface he seemed the model of a cool scholar-diplomat—a power broker who ignored public opinion, dressed impeccably, and carried a cane. Underneath it all was stirring a rekindled youthful idealism. Welles still remembered how, at the close of World War I, he and his generation "had been thrilled to the depths of our emotional and intellectual being by the vision that Woodrow Wilson had held out to us, of a world order founded on justice and on democracy." After quitting the Foreign Service over a quarrel with Republicans, he had come back to diplomacy under the patronage of Franklin Roosevelt; and with the Secretary of State often out of town, he could function as de facto head of the Department. In 1941, when Secretary Hull fell seriously ill, Welles started using his position to push a Wilsonian revival, inside the administration and in the public arena.

Sumner Welles fully understood the importance of propaganda, having suffered badly from its use against Roosevelt's Vichy policy. His own political goal was to persuade his countrymen, right or left, not to repeat a mistake of the past, and to give some precision to Roosevelt's generalities. One of his first speeches on the subject urged an end to imperialism under a new League of Nations—rather strong stuff in an America not yet at war. And two months later, Welles denounced the global barriers to trade which had retarded economic growth, which had helped push democratic Germany to the abyss, which had led to Adolf Hitler: "Forces of aggression now menace us from without. But dangers of another nature here and elsewhere will threaten us even after the war has ended." These dangers included an abandonment of free enterprise, so often related to political liberty; we should spread around our wealth after the war by means of trade and foreign aid, even to the defeated nations. In a firm liberal rejection of pacifists and cynics alike, he declared: "I cannot resign myself to that admission of human incapacity—I cannot concede the inability of man to shape his destiny, under divine guidance, into something better."

One means of shaping that destiny, he felt, would be a new League of Nations. Welles's friends and associates all over the country were becoming more and more vocal on behalf of this idea. Dozens of pro-League groups were being created. Professor Shotwell had founded an ad hoc society to study the postwar settlement, and member John Foster Dulles began proselytizing in churches on the morality of world government. At the start of the war, the Wilsonian Council on Foreign Relations had also prompted State to form a secret committee for planning the peace, of which Sumner Welles became the first head. Though attracted to universal government as a good itself, Under Secretary Welles presented his idea in pragmatic terms. Standing in front of Woodrow Wilson's tomb at the Washington Cathedral, he called it a matter of America's "enlightened self-interest" to join a parliament of liberal states. We cannot again "reject Wilson's plea that the influence, the resources, and the power of the United States be exercised for their own security and for their own advantage, through our participation in an association of the free and self-governed peoples of the world."

When America became an official belligerent in World War II, the internationalist liberals stepped up their own campaign— making a special effort to win over the commander in chief. None of Welles's speeches had Roosevelt's public endorsement, neither were they inspiring any White House initiatives. The President did not mind having Welles launch some trial balloons, just so long as they did not entangle the administration. "The difficulty with the speeches is not that they were bad—in fact they were excellent," Adolf Berle noted in 1942; "but they should have been made either by the Secretary or by the President." As a boyhood friend of the first family, who enjoyed quick access to the Oval Office, Welles had been trying to pressure the President directly. Then, soon after Pearl Harbor, Roosevelt put his foot down. He would not endorse any new League of Nations until the political mood was right; and he wanted no part of State's secret deliberations on the postwar settlement, for his chief goal now was to defeat the enemy. No issue should be raised with the Allies that might damage their solidarity or anger the Russians, who were bearing the brunt of the European struggle.

Perhaps intellectuals, like soldiers, sometimes prepare too carefully for the last fight. Welles and his associates may have been unduly alarmed by Roosevelt's standoffishness—particularly by his resistance to any wartime commitment on European matters. Walter Lippmann shared their mandarin desire to nail everything down. One evening in the spring of 1942, he dropped in at the State Department to inquire about certain aspects of U.S. diplomacy. Still a journalist, Lippmann had undergone a number of intellectual transmutations since 1919 and was currently an admirer of General de Gaulle. After first asking some questions about State's Vichy policy, he proceeded to lecture Sumner Welles on the lessons of World War I: the Fourteen Points had been insufficiently precise; the Europeans had not accepted them before the war was won. Surely we should be extracting guarantees from our Allies right now, especially from Russia. Although he secretly agreed with Lippmann, Under Secretary Welles answered tactfully that the President wished to reserve such details for the postwar conference.

Thus, for the next year or so, an array of internationalist liberal goals remained in abeyance. Roosevelt allowed Welles to go on touting world government on his own, and the other neo-Wilsonians were not silent—certainly not Bill Bullitt, who addressed some "United Nations" rallies during 1943. Speaking with the First Lady to a throng in Philadelphia, Bullitt warned against a postwar retreat from international affairs and a failure once again to win the peace; Wilson had failed because he did not use his power when he still had it. At other public meetings, Bullitt spoke out on behalf of continental Europe, of its need for unity, of his determination that it not be carved up by England and Russia. With respect to the United Nations, "you are eternally right in your conviction that the ultimate hope of mankind lies in a federation of the free peoples of the world"—the notable phrase there being "free peoples." Like Sumner Welles, Bullitt had an updated idea of what constituted a free people and what did not. Yet for all those speeches by Bullitt and Welles and

Europe and the Mediterranean

everyone else, the United Nations still amounted to no more than a name, just a catchy title for the anti-Axis alliance.

A little help came from Congress, where the postponement of these issues was beginning to bother certain politicians. The tribunes of the people were stirring in 1943, while President Roosevelt refused to budge. Delivering a Fireside Chat at the end of July, he almost wallowed in his own evasions and incongruity: "Let us win the war first. We must not relax our pressure on the enemy by taking time out to define every boundary and settle every political controversy in every part of the world. The all-important thing now is to get on with the war—and to win it." Then a month later Sumner Welles suddenly resigned, and in a manner that implied some political tiff with Roosevelt. The main reason in fact was entirely personal: William Bullitt's jealousy, his desire for Welles's job, and his scandalmongering about Welles's homosexual escapades while drunk, had become much too hot for the President to handle. There were more internationalist liberals where they came from. But with these two diplomats destroyed, and with Secretary Hull still feebly running State, no one could be sure where the administration was heading.

Throughout 1943, Roosevelt got on with the war effort according to his improvisational method. At the Casablanca Conference with Churchill in January, he did define one big foreign policy goal, declaring his intention to have Germany's "unconditional surrender" in this war. No matter if that demand led to a tougher resistance by the Germans, he and Churchill wanted no misunderstandings such as occurred in World War I. The President also hoped by his demand to reassure Joseph Stalin, who feared that the Western Allies might be so unscrupulous as to make a separate deal with Hitler. It is true that Churchill had persuaded American officials to postpone, once again, Stalin's request for a direct assault on northwestern Europe. Extremely reluctant to risk an attack across the Channel, Churchill wanted to try some new offensives in Italy or the Balkans.

The second question to be settled at the Casablanca Conference was how to govern French Africa, now that Jean Darlan was

dead. The United States had replaced him as local boss in Algiers with General Henri Giraud, a simple-minded officer with
Fascist attitudes and without any talent for civilian leadership.
So, for the first time, General de Gaulle loomed up as an unavoidable factor in America's plans. He and General Giraud
arrived at Casablanca to talk over French politics, while Bob
Murphy shuttled from villa to villa, trying to arrange a compromise between them. De Gaulle raised endless objections; and at
one point, when Murphy came right out and offered him the
civilian leadership of North Africa, he refused that as well, saying he had too little support among the local population. In the
end, General de Gaulle went back unreconciled to his London
headquarters, and the United States recognized Henri Giraud as
a temporary trustee for France.

General de Gaulle's attitude at Casablanca was one of personal ambition and distrust, a desire to bide his time, a concern
for the postwar standing of his country. Roosevelt's Vichy policy
had inconvenienced him—to put it mildly—and he resented
being left out of the North African invasion. De Gaulle believed
that only a full-blown provisional government, recognized by
the Anglo-Saxon states, could preserve the overseas empire of
France. This worry over his colonies had a real, identifiable
cause. President Roosevelt's one great objection to the Darlan
deal was that it guaranteed the entire French Empire—even
French Indochina, which the President thought should be independent. Moreover, he reciprocated de Gaulle's mistrust. He
saw the general as too aloof from the war effort and too eager
to take power in France before the war was over.[9]

De Gaulle evinced a still deeper distrust of Roosevelt's representative, Bob Murphy, for he believed much of his own propaganda about Murphy's Fascist sympathies. Backing up that
propaganda, several journalists went so far as to label Murphy
an anti-Semite. They wronged him. Murphy still was hamstrung
by military requirements and by White House orders. At one
Casablanca discussion, he mentioned that the Jews in French
North Africa seemed disappointed when their prewar privileges
were not restored after the Allied invasion. To this, President
Roosevelt responded that such privileges should be withheld

awhile longer, so as not to provoke the Arabs. Proposing an affirmative action plan for North Africa, he added that "his plan would further eliminate the specific and understandable complaints which the Germans bore towards the Jews in Germany, namely, that while they represented a small part of the population, over fifty percent of the lawyers, doctors, school teachers, college professors, etc., in Germany, were Jews." This astonishing remark shows some of the high-level ignorance and foolishness that Murphy had to cope with as a subordinate. Compounding the problem, Roosevelt was reluctant at Casablanca to talk about diplomacy at all.

In General Charles de Gaulle, the Anglo-Saxon liberals faced an entity almost pre-World War I in its mode of thought. De Gaulle considered that he embodied French society—from the Reds to the royalists—in the most exalted tradition of Gallic Caesarism. Born into a scholarly, Catholic family from northern France, he had grown up hating the German Second Reich, and he had fought against it courageously in World War I. The Versailles Treaty had been too generous, he thought, and the key to European stability lay in a French alliance with Russia—or else, failing that, in a revival of the Versailles settlement with American guarantees. His dalliance with fascism during the 1930s did not reflect any totalitarian leanings; however, he was not a Social Democrat or liberal either. A fairly staunch imperialist, de Gaulle felt a French lack of enthusiasm for free trade, arms control, or multilateral institutions. Perhaps the British government backed him because it, too, had an empire to protect. Its members could see that he was, at any rate, eager to purify French politics and work with a variety of politicians, just so long as they were French and subordinate to him.

One semi-Frenchman with whom de Gaulle was willing to cooperate was Jean Monnet, who had spent the last two years in Washington as a Lend-Lease agent. Already he was taking rank as one of America's favorite Europeans—he seemed to possess great common sense, with no apparent desire for glory or revenge. Roosevelt's right-hand man, Harry Hopkins, brought him to the President's attention; and the President suggested to

Murphy that he would make an ideal administrator in Algiers. However, upon arriving in Algiers one month later, Monnet discovered such an administrative shambles—in both the French and the American setups—that he secretly regretted de Gaulle's continued absence from the scene. The United States had given him special powers, so he began encouraging and working for the general's return to Africa.

Not until May 1943 did de Gaulle reckon that the time was ripe for an appearance in the city of Algiers. Because of his own propaganda and other people's incompetence, his popularity in North Africa had risen dramatically. He was able to make his entrance to the city with a great burst of fanfare, such as parades and press conferences and lavish banquets. Bob Murphy paid a call on him to discuss once again a compromise with Giraud. Nothing doing, replied de Gaulle, and several names must be dropped from the French governing committee: they were not necessarily Fascists, but old faces associated with France's defeat. Furthermore, Jean Monnet was "a good man, but more of an internationalist than a Frenchman," and should be used mainly for foreign relations. Taking Murphy by the arm he demanded, "Why do you not understand me? Why do you always interfere with me? It is a mistake France will not understand, why your politicians are against me. I represent future France, and it will be better for us all if you support me." Perhaps Murphy was persuaded, for he was nothing if not a realist. When de Gaulle took control of the governing committee a week later, Murphy swallowed the change without much protest. Eventually, he advised Washington to accept the committee as a provisional government of France.

The three people most responsible for de Gaulle's final triumph were not Gaullists themselves. One was Jean Monnet and another Harold Macmillan, the new British representative in Algiers. Responding to a display of impatience in which the general complained about the mood of suspicion toward him, Macmillan delivered a man-to-man appeal. He too had fought on the battlefields of World War I, and had been wounded, and all that. He too saw the need for new and younger leaders, for the spiritual renovation of England and France. So just hang on a bit, and this business would come right. Affected perhaps by Macmillan's speech, de Gaulle decided to remain for a while longer; but one has to keep the de Gaulle question in perspective. These events were intrigues over the rule of a second-class power, whereas there were other problems no less important. The most powerful man in Algiers, General Dwight D. Eisenhower, paid hardly any attention to the Gaullist movement. He understood that Allied military success depended on some political stability in Africa. Therefore, he had accepted the deal with Darlan and did not oppose de Gaulle, letting Murphy work out most of the complex, sordid details.

And his military operations were moving ahead. It took four months of hard fighting to clear the German forces out of Africa, but by July 1943, Eisenhower was ready to move north against the island of Sicily. After a secret deal with the local Mafia—brokered by Lucky Luciano—the Sicilian landings were made and the whole island occupied. The rest of Italian society had been controlled for twenty years by Mussolini's Fascist Party; now suddenly there came a radio announcement from Rome that Mussolini was overthrown and a new government installed. Emissaries arrived in Sicily to arrange an armistice with the Allies, offering a complete and immediate break with Adolf Hitler. Italy's opportunism was equaled by that of America. President Roosevelt ordered Murphy to recognize a provisional government in southern Italy, where a deal should be made for the sake of military convenience. Ex-Fascists in the new government could be replaced later on by less obnoxious players, as soon as the German army had been cleared from the Italian peninsula. Predictably, this latest deal led to tantrums of indignation in the Allied press. By mid-1944, Murphy was one of the most harshly criticized of all American officials, a fall guy for President Roosevelt himself.

Impervious to every attack, Murphy continued in that role until Roosevelt's death and beyond. As the European war drew to a close, the President made him General Eisenhower's adviser for the occupation of Germany—a terrible appointment, as far as the newspapers were concerned, since Murphy was "too Fascist" to punish the Germans harshly. His position was made even more difficult by Roosevelt's usual vagueness on long-term policy. Returning to Washington in September 1944, Murphy found that the President had not endorsed any occupation plan. Roosevelt preferred to play it all by ear, to postpone such trivia until after the war. "I dislike making detailed plans for a country which we do not yet occupy," he wrote in a memo to Hull. And to confuse things even more, three conflicting draft plans were floating around the bureaucracy. One was drawn up by State, another by the Treasury, and another by John McCloy at the War Department. The Allies were hammering at the gates of Nazi Germany, and yet their designated occupation authorities were working entirely at cross purposes.

Like a lot of people, Murphy was beginning to give some thought to the matter of postwar economics. Thought was not his strong point; he traveled light in that regard. But as an old consular agent, he knew something of international finance, and he had learned a few lessons in Munich after the previous world war. Before taking up his new duties on Germany in late 1944, Murphy had a talk with a Communist leader—Yosip Broz "Tito" of Yugoslavia—about how to treat Central Europe during the Allied occupation. He got along fine with Marshal Tito, who seemed the best man to support in ousting the Nazis from Yugoslavia. And Tito offered an opinion similar to that of most liberal economists: Germany "should be used as a unit for the benefit of the European community of nations. That economy has been built up over a long period of generations and represents an element of the greatest importance to the well-being of all of Germany's neighbors. Punishment of German war criminals should not be confused with proper use of German economy."

Already this was being confused in the American bureaucracy. The most drastic plan for the Allied occupation of Germany was sponsored by Secretary of the Treasury Henry Morgenthau—an old hater of Bob Murphy and opponent of Roosevelt's Vichy policy. Morgenthau wanted to strip Germany of its factories and pastoralize the Ruhr area, which was the heartland of West European industry. "This will have a tremendous effect on England and Belgium," he assured the President, "and ought to guarantee their prosperity for the next twenty years because their principal competition for their coal and steel came from the Ruhr." Millions of young Germans left unemployed by this plan could be sent to work somewhere in Africa on a giant water project.[10]

The notion that beggaring one country will guarantee the prosperity of its neighbor dies hard. Sumner Welles had gone overboard when he called Morgenthau a "psychopathic case," but no doubt the Treasury Secretary was governed by some simple instincts and emotions. The year 1944 saw a massacre of Jews in Central Europe worse than anything even in the Middle Ages, and a desire to punish the German people was understandable. On the other hand, Morgenthau's drastic blueprint for Europe reflected exactly the sort of attitude that most economists opposed—a school of thought which John Maynard Keynes had tried to discredit in 1919, and which he now feared might rise again. Remembering the Allied retreat from economic responsibility twenty years before, Keynes felt sure that America would stage some kind of repeat performance.

Now addressed as Lord Keynes, he certainly had made it to the top of the British mandarin classes—conducting important negotiations with the United States, first on Lend-Lease aid for Great Britain and later on economic reforms for the postwar world. Keynes managed to strike up a friendship with the American negotiator, Dean Acheson, with whom he saw eye-to-eye on a number of points: that the international economic system, dominated by Great Britain, had broken down during World War I; that it must be revived with some basic changes, such as an American willingness to take England's place; that the United States also must take the lead in lowering trade barriers, in an expansionary fiscal policy, in making credit available to those countries that could use it. Acheson had spelled all this out clearly enough in a Yale University speech at the start of the war, adding that military force might be needed to back the system up.

However sympathetic the views of Dean Acheson, Lord Keynes had no confidence in the foresight of American politicians. He disliked imperial protectionism; but without American leadership and American help, Great Britain would be able to follow an expansionary fiscal program only within a closed, imperial economy. Free trade and free enterprise alone were not enough, Keynes said in a letter to Acheson, and they "would be a cover behind which all the unconstructive and truly reactionary people of both countries would shelter. We must be free to work out new and better arrangements which will win in substance and not shadow what the President and you and others really want." Multilateral institutions should be established to maintain the free flow of goods and money—and, just as important, to channel loans and direct aid out of the surplus countries. Without that, he told Acheson, the British Empire would do better to remain a self-reliant autarchy.

American politics can be so unpredictable. By the war's end, Keynes actually got what he wanted—or at least substantial reassurance. Most members of Congress were too confused by economics to raise any objection. Others worried about a postwar, global depression, believing that a liberal system in America depended on a liberal world, a world of cooperating, "countercyclical" economies. "We were embracing the Keynesian ideas of an expanding economy," Acheson explained to the British. "If it needed to be managed, let us do it together and not separately." Under Acheson and Adolf Berle, State Department committees had been discussing economic reform for two years with nothing to show for it. At last, in late 1943, there came a White House announcement of a multilateral convention on food relief, at which Acheson and his friend Jean Monnet served as delegates for their governments. Eight months later, President Roosevelt also announced a conference on monetary reform, and the representatives of forty-odd countries gathered to make "proposals of a definite character for an international monetary fund and possibly a bank for reconstruction and development."

That is what was done during the summer of 1944 at Bretton Woods, where Treasury officials ran the conference with surprising astuteness. A monetary fund, with heavy American involvement, was set up to maintain international investment and liquidity; and a world development bank was created, again with

American participation. The dollar, backed by gold, became a fixed global medium of exchange—a system which, for all its rigidity, was justified by two decades of phenomenal success. Although free trade proved to be a stickier issue, the machinery was set in motion for a slow lowering of tariffs.

To Acheson and Keynes, both of whom were present at Bretton Woods, these decisions marked an encouraging advance on the economic orthodoxies of the last twenty years. The Morgenthau Plan to pastoralize Germany would remain influential, and destructive, for a long time to come. Nevertheless, the ground was being prepared for liberal reforms and genuine progress in the international economy.

Financial arrangements were one thing, but the American stand on multilateral politics was more hotly debated, perhaps because so much media attention was devoted to it. While economics might be left to the experts, everyone held an opinion on the subject of world government. Happily the year 1943 ended with an unexpected burst of U.S. governmental initiative on the United Nations issue. Acting on the President's instructions, Sumner Welles earlier had produced a compromise plan for a UN organization. President Roosevelt believed that the League of Nations failed because it tried to be pure and made no concessions to power realities; so Welles's plan called for a general assembly dominated by four Great Powers: China, England, Russia, and the United States. Roosevelt took over the compromise plan, and in November 1943 Secretary Hull delivered a speech about it to an enthusiastic Congress, where isolationism was declining faster than the administration realized.

By 1944, public pressure for a UN organization became so strong that, in one sense, it was getting out of hand. Bewildered citizens sought redemption in a panacea for war, in a rejuvenated League, and the worship of Woodrow Wilson himself underwent a breif revival. Wendell Willkie's universalist sermon, *One World,* had shot up to the top of the best-seller list, even as Vice President Henry Wallace reproached his fellow Americans for having "failed in our job after World War I." Meanwhile William Bullitt wrote: "In this day of hatred, cruelty, battle and death, let no one scoff at Wilson's vision of the future. In his aim he was eternally right." Actually few Americans were scoffing, and cooler heads had to point out some of the UN's practical limitations.

Among the coolest heads was that of Dean Acheson, whose idealism had descended from the heights of the Wilson era. Tempered by two decades of waiting, his old impulses had taken more pragmatic shape in the form of international trade and monetary institutions. Acheson still harbored some naive notions about postwar cooperation with the Soviets, but his optimism did not extend to a global confederation. Rather, the United Nations might serve as a sop for idealistic dreamers, as a way of smothering isolationism, as a convenient umbrella under which the economic agencies might operate.

That essentially was the President's view, and even Sumner Welles shared some of Acheson's doubts: he warned against expecting too much from the UN; power balances between major states would remain basic to global order. These men could not accept the mystical reliance on world government that was inspiriting a significant part of the American electorate. Always they had to cope with the opposition of left-wing, liberal purists, of whom many put their faith in a United Nations Covenant grounded on universal love. Ever anxious to prevent a third world war, officials like Morgenthau and Wallace thought the best way to avoid it was a global New Deal under UN auspices.

The UN project was consummated, for better or for worse. In the spring of 1944, Roosevelt made explicit his plans for a United Nations organization. At a multilateral convention in Washington, general agreements were achieved close to his original proposal; the lawyer-poet Archibald MacLeish launched a propaganda campaign for State; John Foster Dulles and others worked to get Republican politicians on board. By the end of the year, leaders of both political parties agreed to a joint policy on United Nations affairs, and the organization was backed by all but extreme isolationists. Passage through Congress in 1945 appeared a favorable prospect for the UN bill.

It was a long time coming, but the final year of war may have been a good moment for the President to go public on postwar planning. Roosevelt's evasions, his shrewd intermingling of deals and ideals, had served a strategic purpose and had demonstrated his sharp political instinct. Perhaps he sensed all along that this victory would differ from that of 1918, for this time around, the world would be at America's feet. His temporary agreements in the name of the war effort—his agreements with Communists and Fascists—would do little harm in the end. The decision to support Marshal Tito proved a wise one, and relatively stable democracies took root in France and Italy. Without steady pressure from internationalist liberals, President Roosevelt might have waited too long or abandoned much of the program. On the other hand, the United States emerged so powerful from World War II that its leaders could do what they wanted and take their time about it. The USA was rich; Europe was rubble. Americans could afford another two years of delay before some further lessons were learned and applied.

These further lessons in liberal diplomacy would be taught, for the most part, by the example of Russia—especially by Russia's brutal treatment of its neighbors, beginning in 1944. The problem of Soviet tyranny and Russian power had been shoved under the rug for the previous three years. Roosevelt had done little business with Moscow except to extend Lend-Lease aid, which was not the kind of transaction that gave rise to major quarrels. And even if he had wanted a tougher, more hard-headed Soviet-American diplomacy, serious pressure on Russia during the war might have been difficult for him to exert. But during 1944 Roosevelt was hoping to reach a friendly understanding with Stalin, a hope that he transferred to almost the entire American people. President Roosevelt's transferral of optimism about Russia probably was his only important mistake.

III

The Great Wall of Russia

1944–1947

President Roosevelt's uncertain liaison with Joseph Stalin had a lot to do with his refusal to make any long-term commitments during the war. If Stalin would accept a liberal world settlement, then why hurry him into it? And if Stalin would not, better to delay any disagreement until the common foe was beaten. World War II had involved Franklin Roosevelt in a strange and sudden alliance with Russia. While some of his New Deal associates had a naive view of the Bolshevik regime, the President knew it was a tyranny—but perhaps it was a tyranny that was mellowing, that wanted to mind its own business. In the late 1930s, Roosevelt's strategy was to stay on good terms with Stalin, since America might have to work with him in a war against Germany or Japan, both of them equally bad tyrannies that presented a more direct threat.

For several years after 1936, when Bill Bullitt quit Moscow, U.S. relations with Russia had gone into a minor key. Bullitt's successor, Joseph E. Davies, was a political appointee who believed most of what the Kremlin officials told him—and whom the Foreign Service officers detested. "Was a long-suffering, hard-working Embassy to be viewed solely as a repository of political beneficiaries?" lamented Second Secretary George Kennan. On the other hand, President Roosevelt may have had good reasons for sending a fool to Russia. Maybe it took a fool like Ambassador Davies to head that embassy during the late

1930s and yet remain on friendly terms with Joseph Stalin. With its endless purges and executions, the Stalin regime had set a new standard for Russian barbarism. And the Foreign Service staff, no matter how cold-blooded, could not always be trusted to ignore such behavior, not even for broad, strategic reasons.

The President's doubts about the Foreign Service found a measure of justification in the outlook of George Kennan. Here was an expert on Europe who did not think that Nazism was as aggressive as Bolshevism, or that it might have to be confronted first. He wrote in 1936 that Adolf Hitler had no designs on Russia, only on the traditionally German areas of Eastern Europe; more likely, he predicted, the USSR would be the cause of hostilities, on account of its "social fanaticism, militarism, chauvinism, and a cynical policy of driving the wedge between one's neighbors." The Soviets were arming to the teeth in a manner provocative to both Germany and Japan. And there was a serious danger that Russia would reap the profits from a new European war.

Still unformed when he entered the Foreign Service, by now Kennan's world view had flowered into a charming set of prejudices, a few of which had their roots in his early childhood. Like his colleague Bob Murphy, he grew up in Milwaukee among a partly German family; he attended school in North Germany before World War I. His eye caught by the grandeur of the Hohenzollern and Hapsburg empires, Kennan had come to regard that era as a golden age to which the world should somehow return. "It is more important how you do things than what you do," he wrote during Stalin's show trials—therefore, kings and courts sometimes govern more effectively than modern politicians. Good style was of the essence, in statecraft as in the arts; Americanism and Bolshevism alike should be confined to their countries of origin. Kennan wanted a diplomatic system with Europe at the top, a planetary hierarchy in which every nation knew its place.

"Actually, Hitler found his main support in the lower middle class and to some extent in the nouveau riche," he observed in 1936. Without being an outright snob, Kennan had a weakness for old money and venerable names, which seemed to him the guardians of refinement, courtesy, and restraint. At times he would describe himself as an Enlightenment figure, never really at home among the factories and dynamos. He had a close affinity with Henry Adams, that self-styled relic of the eighteenth century, a child of the Enlightenment, a venerable name. But despite his interest in the Enlightenment, at heart Kennan was a North European of the late Victorian era, a little solemn and puritanical, a devout Presbyterian with a bourgeois background.

As he described it to his children, growing up in the Middle West was "the almost unrealistically comfortable and safe life of a prosperous American city before the first World War which you can read about, if you like, in the books of Booth Tarkington. To me, it did not seem provincial. Milwaukee seemed as much the center of the world as any place." Kennan might easily have become a confirmed American liberal. He admired his famous cousin, George Kennan, Sr., a Progressive muckraker who served as adviser to President Wilson on Russian affairs. But George Kennan, Jr., never learned the optimism of the young internationalist liberals, or their zest for America's mission in the world. He digested their ideas only superficially while at Princeton and, after some years in the Foreign Service, whatever Wilsonianism he had learned disappeared.

While he grew spiritually more expatriated, Kennan became culturally and politically more conservative. Returning from various assignments abroad, he noticed on each trip a further moral collapse in his native land. In fact his excursions everywhere confirmed his doubts about any sort of modern movement, whether liberal or otherwise. "Proletarian vacationing was not an inspiring spectacle," he found in southern Russia, and bourgeois vacationing in France was even worse. "Poor Riviera. It had become only one great brothel," reflecting the decay of European society into another world war. And if the Riviera was a brothel, America was a housewife-ridden matriarchy, where the ignorant female dominated purse, family, and cultural life. Her recreation had become "a symbol of futility and inanity. In national politics she has placed her enormous power in the hands of lobbyists, charlatans, and racketeers. Finally, she has not even done well by herself. She has ruined in large part some of the greatest assets of her own sex. She has become, in comparison with the women of other countries, delicate, highstrung, unsatisfied, flat-chested and flat-voiced. The higher she is in the social and economic scale the more true these things are."

George Kennan, it seems obvious, was no friend of Mrs. Roosevelt or the New Deal. He could never stand the give and take of democratic politics, of its pressure groups or its labor unions, and the *poshlust* of American culture made him no less miserable. It was not the countryside that bothered him so much as the cities—the haphazard urbanization, the bland commercialism, and especially the billboards. All through 1938, commuting to Washington from an eighteenth-century house, he had to drive past that scourge. Corporate advertisers seemed as bad as European propagandists, trying to usurp the rightful position of ministers and priests.

By mid-1938, the end of an unhappy year in Washington, Kennan decided that the only political cure for America was a decentralized patriarchy along eighteenth-century lines.[11] Voting rights should be withheld from immigrants, Negroes, and housewives, and a convention should be assembled of the wiser citizens from all classes. At the same time, Kennan left no doubt about which class he liked best. In his belief that only welleducated gentlemen should be running the country, he had a rough similarity to some of the New Liberals of World War I; and absurd as they sometimes sounded, his comments contained a large element of truth. Still, there is no denying that they also showed a certain blindness—what is called that special kind of blindness that pretends to a deeper and clearer sight.

Kennan almost quit the Foreign Service in 1938, disgusted over its lack of influence and low pay, but he decided finally to go back to Europe. Until America's entry into the war he remained an obscure diplomat, composing long memoranda on Nazi Europe with all the morbid tenacity of an unrecognized artist. While deploring the Nazi seizure of Czechoslovakia, he felt the whole mess had been inevitable since the decline of Austria-Hungary—of its church and its nobility, which had ruled Bohemia so well. And that, in turn, was a result of Wilsonian clumsiness. "I found myself unable to share that enthusiasm for democracy in Czechoslovakia that seemed almost an obsession to so many Anglo-Saxon liberals." Now some Czech leaders were turning to fascism and blaming their troubles on the indiscipline of democracy. Perhaps they had a valid point.

Observing what the Nazis were doing almost everywhere, First Secretary Kennan had the same reaction: "There is hardly a stone on the continent of Europe which does not speak of the superiority of the past. But what has happened has been no setting back of the clock"—the problem was that Hitler was moving forward too drastically. A Great Power cannot dominate weak neighbors unless to do so is, economically and culturally, a natural act. Hitler's rape of Europe was not an elegant, eighteenth-century conquest, so it could not last.

World War II overwhelmed Kennan with America's ineptitude at traditional diplomacy, its deference to military requirements, its ignorance of European history. His own war was a safe but frenetic one. In the course of it he was promoted twice and gained audience with the President on a couple of occasions. However, his first big break came in May 1944, when he met Averell Harriman over dinner in Washington. At that point Harriman, having been ambassador in Moscow for eight months, wanted an experienced counselor who could speak the Russian language. Although Kennan made it clear that he disagreed with the President's Soviet policy, Ambassador Harriman decided to hire him anyway.

What really bothered Kennan was the current love affair between Russia and America, which had started unexpectedly about halfway through the war. After the infamous Hitler-Stalin pact of 1939—a pact in which the two dictators agreed to carve up Poland between them—popular opinion of Russia had achieved a new low in the United States. The Soviet Union, Roosevelt declared, "is run by a dictatorship as absolute as any other dictatorship in the world." But all along, diplomats like Sumner Welles never lost hope that the Russians might be brought into the war against fascism. Welles allowed the export of machine tools to the USSR in 1940; and in 1941, he had the satisfaction of warning the Soviet ambassador that Adolf Hitler was hatching plans for a surprise attack on Russia. When the German attack came a month later and the Soviets suddenly found themselves on the side of Western democracy, Roosevelt decided to include them in the Lend-Lease program. By late 1941, American military equipment was arriving at the Russian front.

President Roosevelt now considered it essential to stay on good terms with Stalin. An early German-Soviet armistice would have been disastrous for the West. Even when America itself entered the war, the Red Army continued to do most of the fighting against Germany, and the President wanted it to stay that way. To ensure that Marshal Stalin would keep up the good work—and maybe fight Japan as well—he committed himself in public to an unconditional surrender of Germany. He also avoided negotiations on the future of Eastern Europe. While this evasion was confusing to Sumner Welles and his friends, and probably to Joseph Stalin, Roosevelt did not care. A little confusion seemed preferable to stirring up ultraliberals and isolationists at home, who already were angry over his temporary deals in the Mediterranean. They might become even more angry about a sellout to the Soviets, with disastrous consequences for American postwar policy. That unholy coalition of liberal purists and conservatives had ruined Woodrow Wilson twenty years before.

As a result, Americans were being lulled into a dreamlike ignorance of what Stalin wanted and probably would get. Indeed, many reporters and politicians were becoming strangely pro-Soviet. Some of them thought that good relations with Russia would discourage a return to isolationism—though one should note that isolationism ultimately was destroyed, or transformed, by *bad* relations with Russia. Others thought a pro-Soviet stance was suitable because the Russians were suffering and fighting against Hitler. And still others shared Roosevelt's belief that Soviet-American cooperation was the key to long-lasting peace, more important than the United Nations or any other Wilsonian principle. Some Americans even came to feel that, in the course of fighting fascism, Russian communism had changed: no longer was it a monolithic movement and, in any case, it had a lot in common with Christianity. Averell Harriman remembers that Franklin Roosevelt "was a very religious man. He knew that the Russians were religious. He didn't think that a philosophy that denied God would last forever." The President never said this sort of thing in public, but he confided a hope to Welles and Harriman that the Soviet and American systems might some day converge.

Perhaps the most visible and vocal of pro-Russian politicians was Vice President Henry Wallace. Against his attitude came objections from almost every official with experience in Soviet affairs—such as ex-Ambassador Bullitt, who was growing deeply agitated about the prospect of a Russian victory. In early 1943, Bullitt warned the Vice President that unless we were careful, Soviet communism would "dominate the whole world." The response must be economic—not just military and political—and should offer an expansionary, full-employment program in order to stiffen Europe against the Communist threat.

A day later, Bullitt gave President Roosevelt a memo to the same effect. In it, he explained that Stalin's cynical view of Marxism made him no less dangerous to the liberal cause. Stalin intended to annex more territory in Europe, and "areas annexed by the Soviet Union, will be withdrawn, as heretofore, from the area of normal trade between nations, which it is our policy to extend." Using a blend of threats and offers of postwar aid, we should try to get a commitment out of Russia right away. "Wilson could have written his own ticket before the Armistice of 1918. You may be able to write yours—now." Better still, we should invade the Balkans directly, so as to capture Eastern Europe before the Red Army flowed in. Then, over the long run, opposition to Russia would develop in local strength, because "an integrated democratic Europe, pacific but armed, is a vital element for the creation of world peace."

Bullitt sounded as impractical now as he had during World War I, for there was no effective way the United States could have invaded Eastern Europe. Nor could Roosevelt have kept Stalin out by offering him gifts or making threats. The Soviet dictator was never one to make needless concessions: usually he would hang onto what he had unless physically attacked, so a quarrel over Eastern Europe was almost unavoidable. When Bullitt issued further demands in 1943 for a Western attack on the Balkans—because a divided Europe "would produce at best an uneasy armistice but no peace"—he was mistaken again. Despite a multitude of frustrations, a Europe divided between East and West did produce a stable and long-lasting peace.

Worried about Bullitt's intrigues around Washington, the American Communist Party denounced him as pro-Hitler, but it need not have bothered. President Roosevelt paid little attention to Bullitt. The evidence suggests that by 1943 he had written off Eastern Europe, and he continued to concentrate on keeping Russia in the war. When Stalin, for his own part, went on pressuring the Western Allies to invade northwestern Europe—issuing vague threats about making a separate peace with Germany—Roosevelt really became frightened. Anxious to mollify Stalin, he sent Bob Murphy and Joseph Davies on a goodwill mission to Moscow in May 1943; and four months later, he persuaded Harriman to go to Russia as ambassador, just to coordinate military planning and patch up other differences.

Harriman made a perfect envoy for the commander in chief, better even than Murphy in the Mediterranean. Having known Roosevelt through a family tie for several decades, he was a friend so close that "you can't compare my relationship to Roosevelt to anybody else's." In 1941, he had taken Bullitt's place as the President's chief representative in Europe and, under his management, America's Lend-Lease arrangements with England went smoothly. He was on intimate terms with Harry Hopkins and Winston Churchill;[12] twice he visited Moscow to organize arms shipments there. One aspect of Harriman that especially pleased the Soviets was his business background. "I like to do business with American businessmen," as Stalin remarked in 1944. "You fellows know what you want. Your word is good and, best of all, you stay in office a long time—just like we do over here." Harriman's record of investing in Russia during the 1920s had not been forgotten by the Soviet dictator.

Furthermore, in 1943 Ambassador Harriman did know what he wanted: to help Russia stay in the war by giving as much aid as possible. By now he had experience in dealing with the Kremlin, and he worried sometimes about Roosevelt's apparent vagueness, about the postponement of really hard bargaining with Stalin. That, he told the President, was only storing up trouble for the future. Remembering Versailles, he shared the opinion of Bullitt and Sumner Welles that America should reach political and territorial understandings right away. This was but a minor source of friction, for Harriman believed that a long-term arrangement with Stalin always would be possible. The best method of achieving it was personal diplomacy, building carefully on wartime intimacies. "As you know," he wrote to Roosevelt, "I am a confirmed optimist in our relations with Russia because of my conviction that Stalin wants, if obtainable, a firm understanding with you and America more than anything else—after the destruction of Hitler." Stalin might respond well to reasonable treatment. Anyway, it would not hurt to try.

At the Teheran Conference of late 1943—the first meeting of Roosevelt, Churchill, and Stalin—all the Soviets got from Roosevelt was an unspecific hint. The President told Harriman that he would try some personal pressure on Stalin; but since the Russians could take what they wanted in Eastern Europe, the best plan was to yield quietly. He wanted no public concessions on Poland until after the 1944 election and the acceptance by Congress of a United Nations. During the summit conference, Roosevelt intimated that he did not care too much about the nations bordering on Russia. Marshal Stalin ought to keep up appearances and allow at least some independence in those countries, but the U.S. President could not afford to make an explicit deal on the matter. So Stalin probably received an impression, largely correct, that for all Roosevelt cared the Soviets could do what they wanted in Eastern Europe.

Looking at all this dimly from afar, George Kennan still worried that America was pursuing a foolish policy. He knew Russia so well, and these amateurs knew so little. Kennan had great affection for the childlike mannerisms of ordinary Russians—a

Gogolian affection, really—but the Russian body politic was a more mysterious animal. Always he interpreted it in deeply historical terms, finding patterns and causes as far back as the Middle Ages. During Stalin's Great Purge in the 1930s, bedridden from an attack of ulcers, Kennan had grown stronger in the belief that "Russia had to be looked at from a long range point of view, that Bolshevism, with all its hullabaloo about revolution, was not a turning point in history, but only another name, another milepost along the road of Russia's wasteful, painful progress from an obscure origin to an obscure destiny."

At Ambassador Bullitt's urging, Kennan had come up with a prognosis for Soviet-American relations—*viz.* that the two countries were unlikely ever to have good political commerce, or even much trade. He agreed with Bullitt that Russia's driving force was autarchical imperialism, not Marxist dogma. Disliking balance-of-power diplomacy, Russian governments sought either to dominate other countries or else to hold them at a distance. Basically hostile in their foreign relations, they inherited from Byzantine Christianity a conviction that they would someday rule the world. Tartar invasions encouraged these hostilities and intensified their xenophobia. "The theory of the parallel between the childhood psychology of peoples and of individuals, incidentally, is one which has been extensively developed by Freud," Kennan argued during a series of lectures in 1942. Thus, the methods of Stalinism were an old Russian psychosis: only the upper crust of Russia ever had been Westernized; perhaps the only civilized era of czarist rule was the late eighteenth century. After the trauma of World War I, the country's baser instincts had taken over, and it regressed into czarist barbarism. Communist and Fascist dictators belonged to the same primitive tribe or, to put it another way, Nazism was the offspring of Joseph Stalin.

Arriving back at the embassy in mid-1944, Minister-Counselor Kennan saw that his prognosis had been verified by the war, that "until the Chinese wall of the spirit has been broken down" in Russia, poor relations with foreign powers would probably be the norm. Not that any of this condemned the Soviet Union within Kennan's own soul. Simple and straightforward people might regard such a system as intolerable, but he felt a special insight beyond the horrors of totalitarianism. For most Americans, the truth is whatever works and seems just; for the Bolsheviks, the truth is whatever an infallible Kremlin says it is. And who are we to say that the closed, hierarchical, and theocratic state—i.e., the Soviet state—is not preferable? Is reality any more valid than appearances? "The apprehension of what is valid in the Russian world is unsettling and displeasing to the American mind," he wrote in a memo. "He who would undertake this apprehension will not find his satisfaction in the achievement of anything practical for his people, still less in any official or public appreciation for his efforts. The best he can look forward to is the lonely pleasure of one who stands at long last on a chilly and inhospitable mountain top where few have been before, where few can follow, and where few will consent to believe that he has been."

At this point the author might as well admit that he feels squeamish about discussing Kennan's visit to the mountaintop. He thinks he knows what Kennan divined there, but he cannot be sure, and it is anyway a hard thing to set down in writing. Some matters are too delicate for detailed scrutiny. But the broad facts are that George Kennan, like many a sensitive and timid nature, like Henry Adams, could never feel at ease in a pragmatic, pluralist democracy—with its disregard for scriptures and for the interpreters of those scriptures. Underneath, perhaps, he had a midwestern sense of decency—after all, he remained hesitant to spell out his dirty secret in public—but he could never repress a certain foul temptation. He was a Europeanized intellectual, and an artist, and he could not repress it.

Kennan found that his vision of Soviet affairs held no more interest for his new boss than it did for most Americans. He handed over his mountaintop memorandum to Ambassador Harriman. Harriman sent a copy on to the White House and then, with perfect tact, returned it to the author without comment. That reaction heartily vexed Kennan, for he felt proud of this memo. "I did think he might have observed, if he thought so, that it was well written. I personally felt, as I finished it, that

I was making progress, technically and stylistically, in the curious art of writing for one's self alone." Kennan was determined this time to leave government service, as soon as the war was over, to take some sort of college teaching position.

Meanwhile, all the ambassador was trying to do was what worked and seemed just, which he did for more than sixteen hours a day. As a man of affairs, he wanted advice that was practical. "My business in Moscow was not to look at Stalin with the curiosity of an historian or the questioning eye of a political philosopher. I was sent there by the President to keep Russia in the War and save American lives." Oh, sure, the Red Army was brutal—but it fought well against the *Wehrmacht* and, besides, Harriman had no time for theories or speculations or diplomatic socializing.[13] Even some of his Wilsonian ideas he repressed during the war. He ignored the Foreign Service at first, focusing his attention on week-to-week military matters and on private talks with Joseph Stalin.

Perhaps Harriman's philistine ignorance of the historical big picture led him astray for a while. However, he did appreciate the importance of expertise in Soviet affairs; and he at least was reading Kennan's memos, attempting to filter out whatever was useful. One subject on which Kennan had something to teach the ambassador was that of Soviet-American commerce. Harriman had come to Russia with a feeling that international trade and a growing economy would soften the Bolsheviks. He said in January 1945 that America should offer them commercial credits because "the sooner the Soviet Union can develop a decent life for its people the more tolerant they will become." Several New Deal enthusiasts in the administration went farther than Harriman, urging that a huge loan be extended with no bargaining at all. "I think that the carrot should be put before their nose when you first get there," suggested Treasury Secretary Morgenthau. That would help reduce unemployment in America and show the Russians that we trust them. Harriman, Dean Acheson, and the President himself had their doubts about a loan, but they did give it careful consideration.

So Harriman entertained an old liberal notion that commercial credits could be linked to political disputes, and thereby used to influence the Kremlin. George Kennan demurred. The Soviet Union was not an open, trading country like the United States, he told Harriman; and the Bolshevik regime had little interest in raising the living standard of ordinary Russians. There was nothing wrong with Soviet-American trade *per se*— but Western imports would be used by the Kremlin only to expand its own power, as they had been used by the Nazis and Japanese militarists. The Kremlin might even use foreign trade to manipulate the West: "Actually, the Soviet Government views foreign trade in general as a political-economic weapon designed to increase the power of the USSR relative to that of other countries. It will view imports from our country only as a necessary means of hastening the achievement of complete military-economic autarchy of the Soviet Union." Moreover, the proposed loan did not make much business sense. We were not logical trading partners, and it would be difficult for the Russians to repay what America lent out.

Another subject on which Kennan could instruct Averell Harriman was Eastern Europe. At the time of Kennan's arrival, the ambassador was undergoing a slow disillusionment because of Soviet actions in Poland. To Kennan he looked "shattered by the experience," and it certainly was something that hit Harriman hard, for he had come to Moscow with scant appreciation of what was in store for Russia's neighbors. Several months earlier, he had declared to a group of journalists that the Soviets did not intend to create puppet regimes in other countries. He urged State to come up with an American plan for Eastern Europe, thereby encouraging democracy and economic growth.

On the other hand, George Kennan's sense of history made him immune to disappointment. He remembered that several years before, when they and the Nazis had carved up Poland, the Russians treated the Poles with extreme brutality—not to mention their treatment of Poland over the previous several centuries. Kennan reckoned that this treatment would soon be repeated, and likely followed by a Communist-dominated dictatorship. All the Russians were after was power, he explained to Harriman, and they viewed America's United Nations idealism as a sign of weakness. Kennan cabled similar advice to

Washington; and privately he judged that Russia might cause a division of Europe, an outcome in which "the solidarity of the Atlantic community will undoubtedly play a tremendous role." It was a repugnant prospect. A separate peace with Hitler would have been better for the West. But, as he told Averell Harriman, the result probably was unavoidable, and he could see no point in public hypocrisy. We should state openly what the Russians were up to, make a deal with Stalin on European spheres-of-influence, and not indulge in joint declarations of good intent. There was no need to incite an overreaction among Americans, but there was no reason not to level with Americans either.

"I know you do not see these things as blackly as I do," he said to the ambassador, "and that you will probably not share these views." That was true in a way. Harriman kept blowing hot and cold on Russia, issuing dire warnings and then expressions of optimism. He had become annoyed by Soviet refusals to cooperate even on military matters, by their huge demands for aid, by their all-round chilliness. At the same time, he went on thinking that some progress was possible if America quietly pressured the Soviets. Withal, Harriman proved a diligent learner in the face of hard evidence.

None of Kennan's advice would have had much influence on a President of the United States, for in America "spheres-of-influence" was regarded almost as an obscenity. Roosevelt had waged enough unpopular deals already, and he had no intention of coming clean on Eastern Europe in public. Privately, he did have a few second thoughts in 1944, when the Red Army entered Poland on its way to Germany and Stalin created a puppet regime. Polish-Americans, isolationists, liberal purists all were raising a sudden ruckus about the future of Eastern Europe, saying that Roosevelt ought to help those countries out. With the UN still unratified by Congress, and with an election coming up in the autumn, the President hesitated. Then, refusing to change his original stance, he gave Harriman a somewhat ambiguous order: Tell Marshal Stalin please to give the Poles "a break"—and, incidentally, to keep Poland out of the news. The Polish issue must be dampened to preserve Allied and American unity—and, incidentally, to ensure a Democratic victory. Just before the November elections, Harriman went back to America to do some campaigning for his boss. "Never in the history of the world has one man—Roosevelt—had the confidence of the peoples of so many nations," said Harriman in a radio advertisement, though privately Roosevelt expressed to him "very little interest in Eastern European matters except as they affect sentiment in America."[14] This attitude did the Democratic Party no harm. While feeling powerless to affect Poland, Roosevelt won quite comfortably in the American elections.

His little domestic victory having been secured, the commander in chief hoped to accomplish something constructive with Stalin in a second summit conference. That conference was duly convened three months later at Yalta, a Russian resort town on the northern Black Sea. The phrase "Yalta Conference" still evokes strong emotions in many different people. After the war, Bill Bullitt would help to propagate a myth about the Yalta Conference, that it represented a depressing replay of 1919 in which "Roosevelt had not gambled. He had been gulled." Once again, a sick and simple-minded President had handed people over to imperialist domination, banishing Eastern Europe and portions of China from the brave new world of liberalism. This time, of course, it was not French and English imperialism that won the day, but Soviet imperialism, the most baneful imperialism of all.

Bullitt's version of Yalta should not be taken seriously. Far less important than Paris in 1919, the Yalta Conference gave almost nothing to the Soviets that they did not already possess. Stalin was offered some concessions in the Far East, to ensure that he would enter the war against Japan. But on Eastern Europe, the only surprising thing is that Roosevelt started pushing hard for Poland—insisting that non-Communists be included in its government, that elections be held there with non-Communist candidates. On this and other issues, a joint Allied declaration was released to the public, asserting their "determination to build in cooperation with other peace-loving nations a world order under law, dedicated to peace, security, freedom and the general well-being of all mankind."

President Woodrow Wilson throwing out the first ball of 1916. John Maynard Keynes later remarked that Wilson, like Odysseus, looked more impressive seated than he did standing. (Library of Congress)

EUROPE, 1916

A newspaper cartoon by Boardman Robinson in October 1916 depicts the American view of Europe and its endless fratricidal war. During the war, Robinson left his job at the New York Tribune *to go to Russia with John Reed.* (Library of Congress)

William Bullitt with his younger brother. (Courtesy John Bullitt)

(Below) *Grazing flocks added a rustic note to the White House after America entered World War I—releasing farmers for active duty as part of the government's war effort.* (Library of Congress)

Walter Lippmann with Franklin Roosevelt, Assistant Secretary of the Navy, at a labor relations board session in December 1917. (Library of Congress)

An American guard ladles out rations of rice to Bolshevik prisoners of war in Archangel during October 1918. (National Archives)

The negative side of U.S. war propaganda depicted the Germans as bloodthirsty Huns. Democracy, Christianity, and motherhood were under attack. (Library of Congress)

This was done to Canadians by the Huns. Will America wait to see it done to her soldiers before aking up to the entire earnestness of the war?

"The Dawn of Democracy": The positive side showed clean and decent American soldiers bringing American-style democracy to Europe. (Library of Congress)

William Bullitt (front row, center) poses at the Hotel Crillon with members of the American peace delegation. Also in the front row are Christian Herter (second from left) and Allen Dulles (far right). (National Archives)

Middle Eastern delegates to the Paris Peace Conference: In the front is Prince Faisal of Arabia, in the rear is his Sudanese freedman. In the center row are Brigadier General Nuri Pasha Said (second from left) and Colonel T. E. Lawrence (second from right). (National Archives)

Raising a "No More War" banner at the National League of Women Voters building during 1922. Most of the pennants in this picture describe agricultural and professional women's associations. (Library of Congress)

President Calvin Coolidge receives the graduating class of the school for Republican women campaigners in 1928. This class includes Mrs. Edward H. Harriman, Averell Harriman's mother, on the left end of the front row—but young Averell voted a few months later for the other party. (Library of Congress)

(Above) *President Franklin D. Roosevelt congratulates William Bullitt on his departure for Moscow as the first U.S. Ambassador to the Soviet Union.* (National Archives)

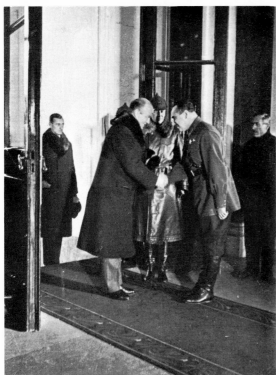

Ambassador Bullitt in Moscow, in December 1933, is greeted by the commander of the Kremlin guard. George Kennan, the ambassador's aide, stands in the doorway. (National Archives)

William Bullitt (seated fourth from right) at a Paris banquet with the Duke of Windsor (seated far right). (National Archives)

Ambassador Bullitt meets with the Premier of France, Edouard Daladier. (National Archives)

A Good Time for Reflection

A cartoon during the Munich crisis of 1938 reveals America's moral disdain for Europe's war scare and its determination not to get involved this time around. (Library of Congress)

PATH OF APPEASEMENT

Another cartoon, after the German invasion of France and bombing of Great Britain, suggests a new American view on the fascist threat—but U.S. isolationism would remain strong even after Pearl Harbor. (Library of Congress)

President Roosevelt, his secretary "Missy" Le Hand, and William Bullitt drive to Roosevelt's Hyde Park house in July 1940 after Bullitt's return from France. Bullitt had had a love affair with Missy Le Hand but later broke off their marriage engagement—to Roosevelt's great annoyance. (AP/Wide World)

Marshal Henri Philippe Pétain, the collaborationist leader of Vichy France, meets with Adolf Hitler in October 1940. (National Archives)

After church services on the HMS Prince of Wales *during the Atlantic Charter meeting of August 1941. Standing directly behind Roosevelt and Churchill are (left to right) Harry Hopkins, Averell Harriman, Admiral Ernest King, and General George C. Marshall. Sumner Welles failed to get any reference to a postwar international organization included in the Atlantic Charter, which consisted mostly of platitudes.* (National Archives)

General Dwight D. Eisenhower, Admiral Jean Darlan, General Mark Clark, and Robert Murphy in Algiers after the North Africa landings of 1942. (National Archives/Signal Corps)

(Above) *William Bullitt and Sumner Welles.* (National Archives)

General Henri Giraud and General Charles de Gaulle shake hands at the Casablanca Conference. They were put under considerable pressure to do so by Roosevelt and Churchill, who are sitting behind them. (National Archives)

Felix Frankfurter and his protégé, Dean Acheson, during hearings on Capitol Hill before World War II. (Courtesy Alice Acheson)

One element of the Wilson revival at the end of World War II was a Broadway play, later the Hollywood movie Wilson. *This promotional photograph shows Georges Clemenceau, premier of France (played by Marcel Dalio), berating the righteous President Wilson (played by Alexander Knox) at the Paris Peace Conference. On Clemenceau's left sits Lloyd George, the British prime minister (played by Clifford Brooke).* (The Museum of Modern Art/Film Stills Archive)

German Foreign Minister Joachim von Ribbentrop, Stalin, and Soviet Foreign Minister Viacheslav Molotov stand in the foreground after the signing of the Nazi-Soviet pact in August 1940. This led directly to the Nazi-Soviet invasion of Poland and the beginning of World War II. (National Archives)

AND NOW LET ME HAVE YOUR VIEWS ON RELIGIOUS FREEDOM.

STALIN

W. AVERILL HARRIMAN U.S.A.

ISN'T IT A RATHER ODD TIME TO BRING THAT UP?

This cartoon shows a new feeling among American journalists that U.S. officials should not be too concerned about human rights in Russia, now that it is under attack by Hitler's Germany. (Library of Congress)

Churchill, Harriman, Stalin, and Molotov meet at the Kremlin in August 1941 to discuss war strategy and Western aid to Russia, which had just been invaded by Germany. (Library of Congress)

Several pro-Communist films were made in Hollywood during World War II, including Mission to Moscow. *This promotional photograph shows Ambassador Joseph E. Davies (played by Walter Huston) meeting with a kindly Joseph Stalin and President Mikhail Kalinin to discuss American aid to the beleaguered Soviet government.* (Turner Entertainment)

A poster in Washington's Union Station suggests that World War II and the War of Independence had much in common—perhaps encouraging a belief that America's allies were democratic, or soon would be. (Library of Congress)

1778   1943

AMERICANS
will _always_ fight for liberty

(Below) *Ambassador Joseph E. Davies, Soviet Ambassador Maxim Litvinov, and Vice President Henry Wallace at a Madison Square Garden rally in 1942 felicitating the Soviet Union on its 25th anniversary.* (National Archives/Acme)

Unfortunately, that summation of the conference distorted the truth as much as Bullitt's did. President Roosevelt came home and delivered a speech before Congress, describing the Yalta declaration as "a turning point—I hope in our history and therefore in the history of the world." It was a triumph of cooperation that meant the end of alliances, of spheres-of-influence, of all those nasty, prewar, illiberal deals. Several points should be noted in Roosevelt's defense: he had to create a positive atmosphere among senators, who still had not ratified the United Nations; a feeling persisted that isolationism would be ended only by international harmony. There also was great pressure to demobilize right after the war, which would require some attempt at friendship with the Soviets. It could be that the President almost meant what he said to Congress; but in his more lucid moments he must have known it was a sham.

And privately he began to hesitate again. When the Soviets neglected to broaden the Polish government in accordance with the Yalta declaration, Harriman and Winston Churchill urged the President to intervene personally, to make a threat. The failure of Yalta must be openly admitted. So after enormous pressure and long weeks of delay, President Roosevelt caused a letter to be sent to Stalin—a letter full of guarded complaints like "I am frankly puzzled" and "I do not fully understand," and drawing the marshal's attention to a "discouraging lack of progress" in Poland. But the long and short of it was that Roosevelt had no great concern about Poland; and not much, in any case, could be done about it. Then a few days later Roosevelt died. He went to the grave refusing to admit in public that Yalta only papered over differences in the Grand Alliance, that he could not stop Russia from controlling Eastern Europe. Death was his final evasive tactic.

Roosevelt's death in April 1945 did accomplish something positive. It made American acceptance of the United Nations, his memorial, almost certain. Even so, the great anti-Fascist coalition was already falling apart. At the inaugural session of the United Nations Assembly in San Francisco, Averell Harriman made a pessimistic comment about Soviet-American relations before a closed meeting of journalists. Several people at the meeting appeared taken aback by his comment—Walter Lippmann, for some reason, walked out of the room in a huff—but a lot of UN delegates were even more annoyed than Harriman was by Russia's stonewalling tactics. And most of the American media were heading in the same direction.

The new President, Harry Truman, was going in this direction too, paying close attention to Harriman's cables. While Harriman may have egged on Truman a little too much, his advice generally was balanced, urging restraint as well as firmness—don't rush into any agreements with Russia, demand something in return for economic concessions, insist clearly that Stalin stick by his engagements. The evidence suggests that both he and Harry Truman wanted to continue Roosevelt's policies as they understood them, seeing Poland as their government's most pressing problem. But perhaps they, like most Americans, never quite understood how little Roosevelt had cared about the fate of Eastern Europe.

After the surrender of the Nazi government in May 1945, Truman long remained puzzled how to make an honorable arrangement on this issue—or on the control of Germany, now occupied by the Allies. One thing, however, was clear from the sudden start of his presidency. Unlike Roosevelt, President Truman felt no personal attachment to several New Deal figures who favored an open hand attitude with Russia. Before going to his first and only meeting with Stalin—the Potsdam Conference of July 1945—he dismissed Treasury Secretary Morgenthau. And at the conference itself, he resisted pressure to send more German reparations to Russia from the Western zones of occupation. Truman reckoned, quite rightly, that all Europeans would be needing whatever industry they had left for their own survival. America should not foot the bill for German reparations, as U.S. banks had done in the 1920s. When he returned from Potsdam, the President still felt ambivalent about the Soviet Union, hoping that somehow a new estrangement might be avoided.

Over the next few months, Ambassador Harriman in Moscow came to realize that the Kremlin would yield nothing in ex-

change for German reparations or American loans. The successful use of an atomic bomb made America's victory over Japan an
easier one than most Americans expected, yet Russia seemed
unimpressed and no less rigid in negotiation. In the course of
a talk at Stalin's vacation retreat, Harriman was told by the
marshal that he had "never favored a policy of isolation, but
perhaps now the Soviet Union should adopt such a policy. Perhaps, in fact, there was nothing wrong with it." While it is untrue
that Stalin had never favored isolation, Harriman considered
this as honest an outburst as he had heard from that source. And
at the theater soon afterward he also ran into Maxim Litvinov,
former Commissar of Foreign Affairs, who indicated that a decision to isolate the Soviet bloc already had been made.

Ambassador Harriman did discover that there was one thing
the Kremlin found it painful to give up. He resigned as ambassador at the beginning of 1946 and, in a farewell chat, Stalin put
a question: Was there any chance of U.S. trade credits without
political strings attached? Harriman replied that he would take
this question up with Truman, but American public opinion on
Eastern Europe might make a loan compromise difficult. And
there the question rested for twenty-five years.

Harriman's reply to Stalin was apt, for among the numerous
East-West issues of 1945 Eastern Europe was the crux. Americans and their Congress could not accept Soviet control of that
area. The Soviets could not accept less than total control. The
decision to retreat into total self-reliance, giving up any attempt
at collective security, fit in with standard Russian practice. It
might mean a clash with the West and a lot of economic sacri-
fices, but by Bolshevik reasoning that was entirely worth it. For
them a wall—or "iron curtain," as Winston Churchill already
was calling it—was a way of keeping foreign infections out as
well as their own people in. The political and spiritual control
of Russia came first.

In early 1946, Truman and his advisers still had no clear idea of
what their Soviet policy should be. But with a souring of U.S.
opinion on Russia, the President was being pushed toward a
somewhat firmer stance. Prominent Republicans, especially

John Foster Dulles, encouraged this change, and most of the Democrats also were chiming in. A public speech by Joseph Stalin in February had the effect of focusing things more sharply in the American bureaucracy—the message of his speech being that, in the fullness of time, a Soviet-capitalist showdown must inevitably occur. For the final achievement of their Marxian destiny, the Russian people must rely upon their own hard work.

Stalin's speech expounded a policy that had been brewing for several months. It elicited a strong reaction from the American media and some blustery comments from Western politicians. The most significant response, however, was a telegraphic memo from the Moscow chargé George Kennan which, quite unexpectedly, created a sensation at the State Department. Since the end of the war, Kennan had continued to feel irritated by State's unending indifference. After the surrender of Japan he had considered leaving the Foreign Service, citing frustrations over "our failure to follow up our victories politically and over the obvious helplessness of our career diplomacy to exert any appreciable constructive influence on American policy at this juncture."

Even at this juncture, though, maybe Kennan suspected that his moment was at hand. If what he was saying about Russia was true, then Washington had to realize it sooner or later. His dispatches were sounding more self-confident in tone. State wanted to know if Russia would take part in the world trade discussions being arranged by Dean Acheson; irritated as usual by the naivete of the request, Kennan explained that the Soviets were unlikely to join such discussions except to manipulate them. The question of lowering Russian tariffs was irrelevant, since the Bolshevik state monopsony would always impose hidden tariffs. Kennan long had urged that instead of wasting their money on Russia, Americans should be forming a West European federation and getting on with the business of helping their friends.

Soon after Stalin's speech, Kennan was asked by State for his analysis of it. At the same time, he received a bewildered query from the Treasury Department. Why had Russia missed the deadline for joining the World Bank and International Monetary Fund? The Treasury Department's bewilderment was typical. "Nowhere in Washington had the hopes entertained for postwar collaboration with Russia been more elaborate, more naive, or more tenaciously (one might almost say ferociously) pursued than in the Treasury Department," Kennan remembers. "Now, at long last, with the incomprehensible unwillingness of Moscow to adhere to the Bank and the Fund, the dream seemed to be shattered." As early as 1944, Averell Harriman had informed Secretary Morgenthau that the Soviets were not much interested in the International Monetary Fund or World Bank—or in anything that required payments to a general fund. Soviet acceptance of the United Nations had come with considerable ease, probably because Stalin wanted a veto on its activities so it could never be ranged against him. But the economic agencies, which might lend support to capitalism and impinge on his internal control—these were an entirely different matter.

Kennan's response to the Treasury's request was a dispatch which later became known as the "Long Telegram" and which, lacking any literary or philosophical pretension, may have been the best thing he ever wrote. The Long Telegram comprised another general summary of Soviet affairs—in Kennan's own description, "all neatly divided, like an eighteenth-century Protestant sermon, into five separate parts." Stalin's speech had led Kennan to conclude that Marxist ideology remained more important to the Bolsheviks than he had supposed. However, Marxism still was primarily a "fig leaf of their moral and intellectual respectability," a way of covering up their lust for domestic and external power. "At bottom of Kremlin's neurotic view of world affairs is traditional and instinctive Russian sense of insecurity." Their economy would remain closed, unless they saw the prospect of a big loan; they would try to achieve their aims abroad by means of intrigue and subversion; they would seek to demoralize the democracies, and to turn them against each other; they would seek to destroy Western influence in underdeveloped countries and then move into the vacuum; strong governments that opposed them they would try to have overthrown.

The best answer to this challenge was to plan as if for war, although our plans need not involve any violent clashes. We must promote Western unity and firmness; we must educate our public, without igniting an overreaction; we must offer a more positive program, especially to Europe. The Europeans "are seeking guidance rather than responsibilities. We should be better able than Russians to give them this. And unless we do, Russians certainly will."

Most of the points in his Long Telegram Kennan had been making for a year—indeed, for ten years. But this version of them suddenly made a tremendous hit in Washington. Wonder of wonders, Harriman sent Kennan a note of "congratulations on your long analytical message." The President himself was given a copy; and Harriman also passed it along to his friend at the Pentagon—Secretary of the Navy James Forrestal—who was so delighted with what he saw that he sent it to several cabinet members and made it required reading, as the phrase goes, for hundreds of top officers. Curious to meet this eloquent, learned student of communism, Forrestal asked that Kennan be recalled to a new job in Washington.

Forrestal's patronage proved a great breakthrough for George Kennan's career. If not exactly an intellectual himself, Forrestal did have a weakness for such people and his own background struck a responsive chord in Kennan. An old Princetonian who admired Woodrow Wilson and Al Smith, he had combined his liberalism with a career in Wall Street finance—a meteoric career in his case, since he had started out with nothing. He had supported most of Roosevelt's banking reforms and left for Washington in 1940 to help organize the rearmament effort, working closely with Harriman on the Lend-Lease program. While resenting the anti-business attitude taken by some New Dealers, Forrestal believed in the kind of government planning used in World War I, and he tried to profit from its lessons. A mix of private enterprise and public coordination seemed to produce the best results, at least in a crisis situation.

Along with those of many Washington officials, Forrestal's politics lately had taken on a more international coloring, moving away from the issues of domestic reform. In one sense this turning outward was predictable, a repetition of what had happened to liberals during the Wilson presidency. However, the fact that so many New Deal reformers appeared so strangely ignorant of Soviet reality may also have encouraged Forrestal's alienation from them. It struck him as ominous that hardly anyone in the Roosevelt administration seemed to care about Bullitt's or Harriman's warnings. To Harriman he issued his own warning in 1944 that, "as you and I found in the 20's, it is easy for success to pry the best of friends apart. There is a great admiration here for the Russians and I think an honest desire, even on the part of the so-called 'capitalistic quarters,' to find an accommodation with them. Some of their enthusiastic friends, however, hinder rather than help the result we are after." By "enthusiastic friends," Forrestal meant the New Deal radicals who had such ferocious expectations of Soviet-American friendship. Forrestal wanted an understanding with Russia to help preserve peace. Still, he doubted if it was possible.

Good manager that he was, Forrestal gave his new protégé exactly the right kind of work. Instead of depositing Kennan in some bureaucratic hole, he asked him to go on a speaking tour, to do some more writing on the Soviet Union, to become a lecturer at the new National War College. For years Kennan had been advocating a Foreign Service academy somewhat along these lines. He had a vocation as a teacher. If not precisely what he had in mind, being "deputy for foreign affairs" at the War College came as a more-than-welcome substitute.

Kennan and Forrestal served each other's immediate purposes, even if their cross-fertilization tended to bring out the worst in each of them. Under Forrestal's patronage, Kennan's statements on Soviet conduct often exceeded the limit of scholarly caution. And under Kennan's influence, Forrestal's fear of Russia was becoming an obsessive dread. Having encountered Marxism-Leninism late in life, he allowed his fears to take him over, heart and soul. Obviously poor Forrestal had other problems to cope with. A few years later he would go, quite literally, over the edge—committing suicide by jumping out a window— but the Russian threat was getting all bound up in the nexus of his emotional difficulties. What especially troubled him was the old question of Soviet aims and motives. Did the Russian government stand for a traditional, closed empire, or did it stand for a new religion? The Long Telegram seemed to provide the desired answer—that it stood for both, that Stalin needed Marxism to maintain his power and respectability, and that he was to some extent a prisoner of it. Given Stalin's dependence on ideology, we could exert little influence on Soviet ambitions except by economic and military force.

The United States changes its direction but slowly. During 1946 there emerged, if not a positive program for Western Europe, at least an American moratorium on concessions to Russia. Having spent a long year formulating the problem of Soviet Russia, the administration would spend another year deciding how to solve it. By a series of gentle threats, Russia actually was induced to withdraw its troops from Iran; and in response to Stalin's demand for military bases in Turkey, an American naval force was dispatched to the eastern Mediterranean. At the same time, the new "toughness" with Russia implied a degree of global involvement, both military and economic, that Americans were still unwilling to accept. When Winston Churchill delivered his famous rejoinder to Stalin's speech—accusing the Soviets of lowering an iron curtain across Europe, and proposing some sort of Anglo-American alliance—the popular reception in America was chilly. The public reacted against any suggestion of new military commitments, and they disliked the idea of making loans even to England. Soviet communism might indeed be a sinister new religion, but it seemed possible to resist it while returning to a prewar non-involvement with the world.

Furthermore, this hardening of official policy toward Russia encountered another kind of resistance from the Democratic left. Henry Wallace, now Secretary of Commerce, was perhaps the chief spokesman for ultraliberal purists, and he spoke out frequently on Russia's behalf. No amount of persuasion would quiet him down. Beside himself with exasperation, Bill Bullitt met Wallace for lunch one day to set the Commerce Secretary straight, once and for all, on a number of vital points. Bullitt declared himself a good Democrat who thought Wallace's domestic reforms were marvelous; likewise, the Russians were a wonderful people whom Bullitt loved. However, Stalin was an unscrupulous tyrant who had murdered even some of Bullitt's friends. In fact, the Soviet dictator was so unscrupulous that, when it suited his purposes, he could be lovable himself.

"Stalin at one time was very affectionate toward me," confided Bullitt in his agitation. "At one time when he had had a little too much to drink he kissed me full on the mouth—what a horrible experience *that* was!"

He was tremendously upset about the way Stalin had acted. The man had hypnotized poor Bullitt. He had made certain engagements and broken them.

Unsympathetic, Wallace replied that Stalin felt threatened by Western aggression and the atomic bomb. Unless we composed our differences through the United Nations, we would end up in a war with him. The Soviets did not want to communize the Balkans or Western Europe—as a matter of fact, they would prefer not to.

"In the long run they do," persisted Bullitt.

Henry Wallace's position was a hard one to argue with: that ordinary Russians liked the system they lived under, that anti-communism was a silly old dogma, that America bore the blame for East-West tensions. As Wallace saw it, his first duty was to ignore people like Bullitt, who "never in his life has done enough work with his hands or lived enough with the rank and file of the people to understand the world as it is." For years Wallace had worried about the growing influence of others besides Bullitt—especially of Averell Harriman, whose business background gave him a "concealed hatred" for Russia. Wallace sent letters to the President complaining about an arms buildup and asking that a loan be extended to the Soviet Union. Never to be outshouted by any politician, he castigated Winston Churchill in public for his "iron curtain" speech: an Anglo-American alliance would destroy the UN and all it stood for. And Churchill's remarks were in especially bad taste considering that Churchill had backed an invasion of Bolshevik Russia in 1918–20.

For that matter, the best way of explaining Henry Wallace is by reference to that earlier era. Wallace, though a rich agribusinessman and ex-isolationist, had emerged during the 1930s like a pure-bred Wilsonian out of World War I—and many of his supporters had changed hardly at all since the Versailles settlement. As in 1919, they preferred even another bout of isolationism to this emerging tension with former allies, otherwise Americans would be facing a dictatorship at home and a third world war. Good relations with *all* foreign powers—without military alliances—were a prerequisite for membership in the UN and one-world internationalism. Universal trade was important, but what would best resolve differences was a universal honesty and exchange of ideas, for we all in the end were fellow human beings.

These were strange lessons to draw from 1919; after all, American isolation had made the Fascist successes possible. Moreover, there is little evidence from 1946, a time of massive demobilization, that America was being more warlike than Russia. Ultraliberals did show some confusion over Russia's refusal to join the International Monetary Fund and World Bank; and Wallace admitted later on that he had been utterly wrong about Stalin. But in the years right after World War II, this vocal minority stood firm in its belief that the Soviets would reciprocate a Western show of goodwill.

James Forrestal, whose obsession it was to educate Americans on the Soviet menace, developed an impatient contempt for New Deal radicals like Secretary Wallace. There was no obvious, causal reason why the Democratic left should have been unconcerned about Bolshevik power, but that old correlation still existed. Forrestal complained about the Commerce Secretary in public, at cabinet meetings, and behind his back—and others in the administration felt discomfited by Wallace's remarks. The whole conflict came to a head in September 1946, when Wallace let fly a speech at Madison Square Garden: our get-tough-with-Russia policy would accomplish nothing, and Russian imperialism was no worse than Western imperialism. Forrestal and the Secretary of State responded angrily and, after Wallace declared that he would go on speaking his mind, the President was persuaded to fire him. Averell Harriman became Commerce Secretary in his place.

* * *

The widespread feeling of satisfaction over this change was fully shared by George Kennan. "One of the most preposterous and fantastic distortions of contemporary history that has ever seriously been put forward by thinking and responsible people" was that put forward by Wallace, according to Kennan in a history lecture. And his feelings of satisfaction must have been doubly acute because, even as Wallace was being edged out, Kennan was moving up in the government. The Foreign Service in general was enjoying more support by late 1946, which lifted his spirits mightily. Moreover, his own students—coming from important positions throughout the government—sometimes included generals, senators, and cabinet members. "Soviet authorities evidently don't rate highly the capacity of foreign diplomats for influencing people in their own countries," he said to a class at the War College—which may have been true, but Soviet authorities surely had underrated George Kennan himself, who in a short time was to become the most influential Foreign Service officer of the century.

In addition to his classes, Kennan held meetings with citizens' groups all over the country, wherein he discovered that one thing had not changed. The women of America were as inane as ever, with a hankering after Russia that resembled a form of sexual escapism. Kennan's message had not changed much, either: the Soviets, while cautious, would always try to expand their power; we must rearm to deter a war and yet not overreact; we should offer a program of our own to Europe, something beyond just democracy and human rights. This message he transmitted personally to foreigners as well as Americans. At the end of 1946 he met with officials in Canada to offer suggestions on the problem of continental defense: "A firm and patient policy of 'containment' pursued by us over a period of 10 or 15 years might well result in a frustration which would in itself lead to a period of peaceful policy on the part of Moscow." And his appeals for a positive U.S. program were being heard, for in early 1947 Dean Acheson informed him that the new Secretary of State, George Marshall, wanted to set up an overall planning unit for American policy. Kennan soon might be appointed as its first chairman.

Unexpected developments over the next two months speeded up the process of Kennan's promotion. Ever since the spring of 1946, the Greek government had been under heavy attack by leftist and Communist guerrillas; in late February 1947, the British informed Washington that their economic plight made it impossible for them to continue giving aid to Greece or Turkey; therefore, if the United States wanted to stop another totalitarian advance in that part of the world, it would have to take England's place. This was the latest in a series of British withdrawals from their overseas holdings. Most of the State Department and cabinet were agreed that America should do what England was asking and take up the burden of Anglo-Saxon liberalism—presumably without the extra baggage of an imperialist past. Right away, Under Secretary Acheson summoned George Kennan back to join an ad hoc committee on the Greece-Turkey question, which met the same night in a crisis-panic atmosphere. The committee settled on a recommendation for American aid, and Kennan "returned to my home late that evening with the stimulating impression of having participated prominently in a historic decision of American foreign policy."

A major hurdle, the committee knew, would be the U.S. Congress. Such a policy of anti-Communist aid meant a new kind of commitment that the legislators might not accept. One person suggested that a universal program be "presented to Congress in such a fashion as to electrify the American people"—which over George Kennan's objections is exactly what was done. A group of congressmen came to the White House and went away electrified by Acheson's harangue on the coming struggle with communism: Soviet control of Greece and Turkey would put the Kremlin in a position to corrupt Western Europe and, not long after, three quarters of humankind. It was a question of stopping the rot before it infected its environment. Congressional leaders indicated that if the President made a personal appeal in these apocalyptic terms, then Congress would provide him with the necessary funds.

Forthwith, Acheson, Harriman, and Forrestal helped to prepare a grandiose speech for the President, advising him to deliver it before a joint session of the House and Senate. At a

Senate hearing soon after Truman's speech, Acheson cautioned that the President was not requesting an open-ended commitment to stop communism everywhere. Financial and military aid to foreign countries always would be considered on a case-by-case basis. Nevertheless, on the same day at a House hearing, Bill Bullitt frightened some of his listeners with the opinion that "if Russia had the atomic bomb it would already have been dropped on the United States." That double note of caution and alarm was the right mixture to win the support of American politicians.

It was no exaggeration to call this sequence of decisions a great transformation of U.S. foreign policy. The so-called Truman Doctrine now would defend American interests by preventive action outside the western hemisphere. At the same time, it is well to remember that Wilsonian goals were not abandoned in the process; rather, they were being pursued in a more dynamic way. For two years the United Nations had worked somewhat according to Wilson's original intent. Stalin had not managed to manipulate it and, on the contrary, the UN was lending some legitimacy to liberal ideals. But an international parliament alone, even with its aid programs financed by the U.S. Treasury, could never make the world safe for Anglo-Saxon liberalism. Smaller countries always tended to gravitate toward power, which meant that both unilateral action and alliances would be needed. That kind of unpleasant compromise had been quite familiar to Woodrow Wilson himself, although it took most of his followers a long time to accept it. In fact, some of them never would accept it.

George Kennan objected in private to several aspects of the Truman Doctrine, particularly to its suggestion of a global fight against communism. Truman's sweeping declarations might involve our prestige all over the world, causing both Americans and Russians to overreact. These private objections are surprising, inasmuch as Kennan's more public statements in 1947 often sounded more alarmist than those of President Truman. He told his students in March that if Greece fell to communism, then so might Western Europe—part of a bandwagon effect that might pull in the entire Mediterranean area. Communist advances in some countries were inevitable and unimportant, and a barbarian takeover of Western Europe would not last forever. But the United States would be so isolated, meanwhile, that it too might collapse. "There are openly totalitarian forces already working in our society," Kennan warned. Moreover, "it is not even with these small existing groups of extremists that the real danger lies. The fact of the matter is that there is a little bit of the totalitarian buried somewhere, way down deep, in each and every one of us." Whether observed from the mountaintop or way down deep, it was a disturbing prospect that Kennan painted.

Another statement of Kennan's—in the form of an article published the following summer—made much bigger waves than any of his lectures. Written at the behest of James Forrestal, the article had originated as a classified memorandum on "Russian expansive tendencies," a memorandum published with Forrestal's consent by the Council on Foreign Relations. Although the published version appeared over the pseudonym "X," its authorship soon became an open secret and it was taken to represent official U.S. policy. Kennan's refusal to confirm or deny his responsibility only fascinated the media even more. Portions of the "X Article" were reproduced in popular magazines. Biographical sketches portrayed Kennan as the mastermind behind America's new Russia policy—the great brain who had seen through Stalin all along, once scorned and now elevated to a rightful position of power. A photograph of "Mr. X" was printed next to the Mona Lisa, along with a caption comparing their inscrutable smiles: "What does this smile express? Does this man laugh at us, about us, in spite of us, with us, against us?" Thus, George Kennan woke up one morning to find himself a celebrity, in the emptiest American sense of that word.

What the journalists were celebrating was not so much the X Article's analysis of "Russian expansive tendencies" as its strategy for stopping them, which readers saw summarized in the single word "containment." The militaristic and universal way in which many people interpreted containment horrified George Kennan, and with good reason. But if the X Article and

Soviet expansion did give rise to a simplistic sort of myth, it was a useful myth, for such myths are the groundwork of constructive effort. Moreover, the constructive side of Kennan's plan did not go unadvertised, having been presented clearly at the end of his article. "To avoid destruction the United States need only measure up to its own best traditions," Kennan exhorted his readers. In a biblical peroration, he expressed his "gratitude to a Providence which, by providing the American people with this implacable challenge, has made their entire security as a nation dependent on their pulling themselves together and accepting the responsibilities of moral and political leadership that history plainly intended them to bear."

One man does not a movement make, and a single statement can have unintended results. While Kennan himself was no internationalist liberal, perhaps the doctrine of Russian containment was a natural corollary of the liberals' sense of duty. Because the Soviet bloc would not play by the liberal rules, all they could do was to contain it and get on with more positive undertakings elsewhere.

As for America at large, perhaps the lesson is that ideals are never enough for sustained national action. There has to exist a sense of practical urgency as well. The fear that internationalist liberalism, which most Americans now passively accepted, might be overwhelmed by something else certainly did the trick. The liberal revulsion against Soviet communism caught on with most of the public—and it dovetailed perfectly with the old program of free trade and investment, economic aid, democracy, national self-determination, and multilateral institutions. The Bolshevik Revolution, having swept up some liberals in 1919, now seemed to stand for almost everything that their program was against—protectionist autarchy, atheist despotism, imperialist selfishness—and in such a menacing way. If the Great Wall of Russia, and a lot of grandiose rhetoric about it, was what was needed to inspire Americans, then it may well have been worth it.

A morbid preoccupation with the enemy was not generally an American liberal trait. Over the next two decades, Soviet-American relations were essentially extraneous to the liberal opera-

tion—and, in the perspective of history, less important than
what happened in the "Free World." However, before bidding
goodbye to the Soviet-American confrontation as a central focus
of our attention, a point on its later development should be
made. The twenty-year period after 1947 has become known
under the title "Cold War," a title proposed by Walter Lippmann and intended by him to connote something bad. It was,
on the other hand, a period when per capita standards of living
and income equity progressed at a healthier rate in the developed countries than ever before or since; and even in the underdeveloped world, the spread of local independence never was
more rapid. Had Soviet-American relations been less hostile,
things might have been even better, but let us not be too appre-
hensive about the era known as the Cold War.

IV

At the Zenith

1947–1950

Any reader of books about American diplomacy, when he comes to the winter of 1946–47, has to plow through an overwritten passage on Europe. This is a literary ritual that cannot be avoided. The hard, icy clamp of January always must be mentioned, and followed by the arctic blizzards that blanketed Great Britain under an adamantine mantle of snow. Europe's economic recovery was grinding to a calamitous and catastrophic halt. Too few dollars were available to pay for vital imports, too little investment capital for economic growth. The worst privations of World War II had been suffered in Eastern Europe; but now a drought and pestilence, flooding and famine, spread out across the desolation of the continent, bringing Bolshevism and despair in its wake like an Oriental plague. At the eleventh hour, American liberalism arrived with a stupendous program of financial aid and, for the third time since 1918, rescued Western Europe from an onslaught of predatory and destructive conquest.

So it usually goes. Unqualified, it collapses over one enormous detail. Then and long afterward, public funding from America was a minor element in Western Europe's recovery. The direct economic impact of U.S. aid has been exaggerated—perhaps because the dollars came at a moment of intense diplomatic and political anxiety. Communist takeovers appeared imminent in both Italy and France; President Truman needed a sense of crisis to get the Congress involved. In the great event,

Congress did vote more than $13 billion for a program called the Marshall Plan, which probably made a psychological difference at a critical time.

Ideas like the one for a Marshall Plan had been floating around for decades in liberal circles, as we have seen. John Maynard Keynes had wanted something like it after World War I. During the twenties and thirties, internationalist liberals had talked about a program of U.S. aid to Europe, an end to monetary and trade barriers, a continental plan of economic action. And ever since 1944, when the World Bank and International Monetary Fund were conceived, Dean Acheson had been pushing for an economic *démarche* in Europe, such as a new multilateral conference on trade. He found it very tough sledding in 1946, but the arrival of General George Marshall as head of the State Department seemed to brighten up the prospect for Acheson's plans. One wintry evening at his Georgetown house, where George Kennan was a dinner guest, Dean Acheson was observed "bubbling over with enthusiasm, rapture almost, about General Marshall." Acheson later compared those trying times to a low point of the American Revolution, the winter encampment at Valley Forge, with Marshall playing the role of General Washington. In short, Acheson waited for spring with an almost primitive feeling of anticipation.

And maybe George Kennan was feeling the same way. "The unity and prosperity of the venerable continent of Europe is not something which will grow by itself from the planting of a single seed," Kennan had prophesied at the end of the war. "It will require careful attention and cultivation on the part of extra-European Powers for at least two generations." One of the first seeds was sown in April 1947, when Secretary Marshall called in Kennan for some urgent instructions: he must put aside his work at the National War College and set up a staff to plan long-range foreign policy. As Marshall reported elsewhere, Western Europe seemed at the point of economic collapse and Joseph Stalin appeared almost gleeful at the prospect. If State did not come up with a solution soon, then Congress might barge in with its usual clumsiness.

George Kennan proved a perfect choice to head the planning staff. He had pondered deeply the shape of postwar Europe. He had urged an economic plan as part of his "containment" policy. Alerted months before that he might be chosen to form a planning committee, Kennan now put together a group that made fast and frantic progress—"So earnest and intense were the debates of our little body in those harried days and nights that I can recall one occasion, in late evening, when I, to recover my composure, left the room and walked, weeping, around the entire building."

Not that Kennan and his little body did it all alone. They got help from other branches of the bureaucracy, including other branches of the State Department itself. The financial experts at State all agreed on the need for more American aid to foreign countries. During 1948, they predicted, the means to pay for vital imports would disappear in most of Europe—in France and Italy much sooner—because Europe's dollar and gold reserves were quickly running dry. America's charitable relief through the United Nations, and its various direct and indirect loans, had proven inadequate and were scheduled to end in a matter of months.

During March and April, at Dean Acheson's request, a survey had been made of U.S. foreign aid expenditures—detailing what had been given since the war (nearly $10 billion that went mainly to Eastern Europe) and what America should continue to send out in food, raw materials, and foreign exchange. This survey concluded that America's goal should be to revive production and trade in key areas of the world, particularly the environs of Germany and Japan. With respect to Europe, the revival should include as much of the continent as possible, but aid to West European democracies should always take priority. Without being explicitly anti-Communist, the survey's political message was clear. The United States must help the European political center—that beleaguered group of liberals and Social Democrats in France, Germany, and Italy—by presenting a positive and realistic program, a program more attractive than what the European left and right were offering.[15]

Thus, when George Kennan's council came together, much of

the initial spadework had been completed by others. Under Secretary Dean Acheson had outlined it all in a public speech. Washington's bureaucratic *Zeitgeist* was entirely behind them. The only questions left were exactly how to approach the European governments and how to win support from the American people.

Poverty and misgovernment are the norm in human events, while prosperity remains only an interesting exception. Therefore, the dreadful plight of Europe was a fact less noteworthy than the fact of America's tremendous affluence. Perhaps the greatest legacy of Roosevelt's war was that it turned the United States into an economic colossus, and so soon after the prewar Great Depression. It is no coincidence that human obesity first became a problem for U.S. medicine during World War II—fed by deficit spending on rearmament, the economy had been growing for a good six years. The business boom was still going strong. By 1947, this made foreign aid and trade look less threatening to Americans, so long as it stopped communism and provided an outlet for U.S. exports.

American journalists, moreover, had been pushing such a policy in the media all spring. And now, for some reason, Walter Lippmann went along with the popular trend. He called for a program in the tradition of Lend-Lease—except that this time we should request an economic plan from the Europeans themselves, working on it with them as a single group. That idea was nothing new, but it impressed George Kennan because he so admired Walter Lippmann. Meeting for luncheon in early May, he and Lippmann agreed that their problem was to sell an aid program to both the Congress and the Europeans. "I have never doubted that in the end the paths of Mr. Lippmann and myself would meet. History will tell which was the more tortuous." For Kennan this lunch was the fruition of a higher destiny, a historic as well as a social occasion.

One morning at the end of the month, after Kennan had submitted a preliminary proposal, Secretary Marshall called a meeting at State to discuss it. Sure enough, Kennan wanted to request a plan from the European governments—let them take the initiative and do the job themselves. And he added another idea that he had mulled over with Lippmann: the United States should not seem to be reacting to a Bolshevik threat—let us make our offer to the entire continent, including the Germans and East European Communists. Such a proposal did give rise to serious questions from others present. If the offer was extended to Eastern Europe, then how could it be presented to Congress as an anti-Communist measure? And was it wise, in any case, to offer money to the Soviets?

Answering for Kennan, Dean Acheson said America must never incur the blame for any future division of Europe. While there was a slight chance that the Russians would accept our aid, probably they would not if it gave us open access to their sphere of control. Acheson's point was well taken by Secretary Marshall, who made his famous announcement two weeks later at Harvard University: America would help all Europeans in a program of economic recovery, as soon as they produced a single plan of their own. "Our policy is directed not against any country or doctrine, but against hunger, poverty, despotism, and chaos," asserted Marshall to the graduating class. "Its purpose shall be the revival of a working economy in the world so as to permit the emergence of political and social conditions in which free institutions can exist."

Over the next few weeks, the plot moved on according to Dean Acheson's scenario. He gave warning to the British about Secretary Marshall's announcement at Harvard; and the British responded to it, calling for a pan-European conference in Paris. At a preliminary talk with the Russians, they also proposed a committee to examine the state of each European economy. Taken by surprise, the Soviet delegation protested—this would be a violation of sovereignty, an economic form of outside meddling—but with backing from America, the British and the French stood firm. Then suddenly the Russians, a delegation of eighty-five economists, abandoned Paris in the middle of the night without even saying goodbye and retreated to Moscow, where Stalin issued denunciations of American imperialism and forced Eastern Europe to do the same.[16] George Kennan, for one, was delighted by their behavior. The Soviets had excluded themselves from the Marshall Plan, bringing his diplomatic finesse to an elegant conclusion.

The game, from then on, could be played fairly straight. Fifteen European governments, minus the Communists and Fascist Spain, sent representatives to Paris. They had enough in common to embrace a single program. Equally helpful, they had some big differences too, for each economy needed what the other economies could provide. America, it is true, had to push them in the direction of mutual assistance, of setting up a permanent, supranational council. Europe hesitated on this point so long that U.S. diplomats, including Kennan, came to Paris during the summer to make their disapproval known—insisting also that there be fiscal reform in certain countries, that the request for American money be cut down, and that the European proposal be phrased in terms more appealing to American politicians.

It was a heady moment for George Kennan, telling the Europeans how to get their act together—and for this reason he might not have known that his high point lay behind him. But it did. A useful fellow traveler at first, good for seminal ideas and new departures, he soon became a serious inconvenience to the State Department. Perhaps it was his organic-gardening theory of diplomacy that made him so hesitant about every practical action. He was endlessly pessimistic about how fast the United States ought to go, how hard it ought to push. After Secretary Marshall's announcement in June 1947, Kennan gradually was excluded from the central issues of State Department concern.

Meanwhile, even as Kennan was edged over to nuclear arms control, the Far East, and UN affairs, three new committees were being formed to deal with Europe. The most powerful among them, under the chairmanship of Averell Harriman, was charged with examining Europe's recovery plan, with assessing America's ability to contribute to it, and with making the whole thing palatable to Congress. One year later, the Harriman Committee served as a model for the Marshall Plan administration, in which Harriman again would be the chief Democratic figure—the President's Ambassador at Large to Europe and a traveling salesman of American liberalism.

* * *

Philistine prince, however vulgar it might sound, was a title that fit Averell Harriman beautifully. In 1947, he thought what Europe really needed was a "spark which can fire the engine," and engines were still what lay closest to his heart. Heir to a far-flung railroad empire, one of the largest fortunes ever amassed in America, he had stood at the zenith of an industrial aristocracy. On the other hand, it does seem rather strange that President Truman, even more than President Roosevelt, was listening to Harriman's advice. How could a man with that much money, and with such an awkward air of formality and aloofness, have risen to a place of influence in the Democratic Party?

Public attention had been focused on Harriman from an early age, in much the way Europeans used to focus their attention on royal families. When he fainted in a church pew at the age of fifteen, the *New York Times* turned it into a front-page story, and not every newspaper was as sympathetic as the *Times.* Harriman's father had amassed his millions by devouring other empire builders, which made him a perfect target for journalistic attack—the kind of robber baron every good Progressive loved to hate. The Republican Progressive, President Teddy Roosevelt, once called the elder Harriman "an undesirable citizen and an enemy of the Republic" and a lowdown liar, to boot. Under government investigation for railroad monopoly and stock market fraud, E. H. Harriman died from the strain in 1909. What a mark this made on a loyal son, what a jaundiced view it gave him of progressivism, is not hard to guess.

The year his father died, young Harriman moved from the Groton School to Yale University, a move noted in the national press and crucial, he insists, for the correct molding of his character. Only the "broad environment" of Yale had prevented him from turning into a fearful snob—"I shudder to think what I might have become, had I followed most of the other Grotties to Harvard." Disgusted by Yale's string of losses in the annual boat race with That Other University, he tried to coach the Yale crews in a better rowing technique, what he called "the wonderful machine-like precision" of British oarsmen. And Yale did begin to row a little better, there is no denying it. Perhaps young

Harriman's preference for coaching at college, over direct participation, had something to do with his success after commencement. For this was the golden age of Harvard-Yale athletics, and of the young F. Scott Fitzgerald sports heroes who always amounted to such dismal failures in real life.

As a matter of interest, Harriman's personal recreation included croquet, dog breeding, and polo. Soon after graduating from Yale, he saved a woman's life by subduing her horse when she fell from the saddle—a gallant feat of knight errantry that led to their marriage a few months later. But in an old philistine tradition, his first love remained the business of doing business. Their marriage ended in a divorce and, during the twenty years that elapsed between Yale and the New Deal, his working energies went into industrial growth.

While others were expanding their political horizons in World War I, for Harriman it was a new chance for business expansion. His younger friend, Bob Lovett, took leave from Yale to join the Naval Air Service, but romance and melodrama left Harriman cold. Even as an undergraduate, he had detested humbug. He saw a bottleneck in shipping, so he started a shipping company, installed himself as chairman, and made a tidy profit from government contracts—all while his former classmates were fighting on the Western Front. At war's end, he had not delivered any ships but the coast looked clear for an expansion of North Atlantic trade. Accordingly, Harriman put more money into shipping and transportation; he made loans to Germany right after peace was declared; he set up an international bank, with offices in Berlin. A few years later, barred from financing German trade with the Communists, he coolly went ahead and made a direct investment in the Soviet Union.

Unfortunately for Harriman, that investment turned sour and his shipping ventures did not pay well either. When his politics started changing in the late 1920s, it was for the usual business reasons. The European economies and North Atlantic commerce were somehow not expanding to the full extent previously anticipated—due in part, Harriman decided, to the economic protectionism of Republicans, to their insistence that Europe should repay all war debts to America. If in no great hurry to abandon isolation, Al Smith and the Democrats held out more hope than the Republican Party: "What a thing it was to pull down the Democratic lever, to throw away the past! That was the wrench, that was the break!" The stock market crash of 1929 confirmed Harriman's doubts about Republican economics; and his friendship with the Franklin Roosevelts drew him back three years later to Democratic liberalism. Roosevelt was a Groton graduate who had gone to Harvard College, but still Harriman wanted to help him out. He would work for the new President as a favorite tame businessman, a link between big capital and the New Deal.

A born diplomat, Harriman tried to lower the volume of business-government-labor shouting, to soothe his colleagues, and to keep Roosevelt in touch with whatever business groups would talk to him. Aware of the hot-air aspect of New Deal politics, Harriman never went public in his objections to it. Unlike Forrestal, he did not take personally the New Deal criticisms of private enterprise. He seldom took any kind of criticism personally. Instead, he supported such reforms as government regulation of the stock market—causing Wall Street cronies to cut him dead, literally crossing the Street to avoid shaking his hand. He worked part-time on New Deal planning for industry, and he lectured fellow businessmen on the nature of progress, calling it the "merging of conservative and radical ideas." Business, he urged, ought to try improving its image with the American public.

As it happened, World War II did more for the image of American businessmen than they ever could have done by a deliberate effort. Unlike the Great Depression, the war was an event in which industrialists were seen as important leaders instead of as a part of the overall problem. There is truth in the claim that fascism was defeated partly by American managerial brilliance. While defense adviser to the Commerce Department, Harriman announced in 1940 that "the defense program is in the hands of industrial and business men of wide experience, who are attempting to do in a few months what other nations have taken years to accomplish." Among Harriman's friends who pitched in and joined the War Department were Jim Forrestal and a banking partner, Bob Lovett. They reacted like feudal magnates who, when called to arms by their overlord, served from a sense of duty as well as private ambition—doing well, so to speak, by doing good.

Harriman did not begin to serve full time until early 1941, when he moved to London and took charge of Lend-Lease aid to Great Britain—America's effort to sustain the only power then at war with the Nazi Empire. In this war, as in the last, the great Allied bottleneck was transatlantic shipping, which came under heavy attack from German submarines. Luckily, Harriman had some experience in ship construction and ship repair, having profited from it two decades before; and he also knew the ropes of large-scale bureaucratic management. The "Harriman Mission" was run like a private business in which he owned a controlling interest. Recruited from all over the United States, the mission was negotiating for a hodge-podge of U.S. government agencies. Nevertheless, Harriman could use his private contacts at home—such as Forrestal and Lovett at the Pentagon, Acheson and Welles at State—to cut through red tape and make the whole enterprise run more smoothly.

One can see from this, at any rate, a link between the Marshall Plan and America's experience in both world wars—embodied as it was in the solid, businesslike frame of Averell Harriman. A pioneer in the new world that combined public policy and private capital, he showed how one could manage huge transfers of money and goods from one continent to another. He foresaw a need for postwar aid, and the clear success of Lend-Lease made an ideal precedent for the Marshall Plan. Harriman had arrived at this point through a worship of utility, an endless compulsion to do whatever worked, along with a recent, tentative, experimental interest in liberal solutions.

As World War II dragged on, Harriman was supplying several other theaters of war besides England. Asked to come home and replace Sumner Welles as Under Secretary of State, he chose instead to go to Russia and to remain overseas until 1946. That same year, he accepted a presidential request that he take up the duties of Commerce Secretary in Washington, where his political star was steadily on the rise.

Perhaps the most heartfelt comment on Harriman's elevation

to Secretary of Commerce came from the man he was replacing, Henry Wallace. "I am sure that this appointment will be received with the greatest enthusiasm by the business community"—which was meant as an insult, a New Deal swipe at the anti-Communist rich. The swipe was misdirected because, for all his great wealth, Harriman's thoughts were not on communism so much as on the need for a more positive foreign policy—that is, a more liberal one. He hung up a portrait of Roosevelt in his new office, said nice things about Henry Wallace, and started talking about the misery of Europe and Asia. His rhetoric grew a bit overinflated. At a dinner in honor of Al Smith, he and Dean Acheson backed each other up in their pleas for a more activist U.S. diplomacy. Al Smith, the Happy Warrior, had shown Averell Harriman that "nothing can stop us except our own doubts as to our own ability to accomplish the unlimited. The major part of the human race is looking to us for leadership."

Elsewhere, sounding a little like Sumner Welles, he said America must pull down tariff walls all over the world—reminding fellow citizens of those "abortive attempts after the last world war to expand our foreign trade and finance which ended in the collapse of 1929. We are all familiar with the disaster that followed for ourselves and for the world, contributing to the conditions that led to the Second World War. We must not and will not make these same mistakes again." International commerce was an antidote for war, and free trade would discourage the kind of economic quackery from which dictators profited.

Free trade was one thing, but Harriman said nothing in public about direct aid to Europe until May 1947, just before Secretary Marshall made his announcement at Harvard and the President's Committee on Foreign Aid was formed. Because the Republicans had a majority in Congress, Dean Acheson drew up a bipartisan list of committee members and put Commerce Secretary Harriman at the head of it. The Harriman Committee reported to a special session of Congress in November, after four months of research and meetings with Europeans. Aiming at what it called "the prevention of World War III"—then as later a popular cause—the report made a series of costly recommendations: between $12 and $17 billion in American grants and loans to Europe, plus $6 billion from the World Bank and other sources. While in broad agreement with the Europeans' proposal, the Harriman report laid more emphasis on the lowering of intra-European barriers—which meant not only tariffs, but currency controls that prevented international investment, and all the regulatory restraints on labor, trade, and business enterprise.

Another key American report—key at least on Capitol Hill— came out of a select committee run by Christian Herter, who was a relatively liberal Republican in Congress. Since that humiliating night at the Hotel Crillon when young Bill Bullitt had thrown a yellow flower at him, Christian Herter's career had gone in several directions—from European food relief under Hoover in 1920 to lecturing at Harvard on foreign affairs. By mid-1947, Herter was a congressman of four years' standing and able to exert influence on some of his colleagues. Taking a group of U.S. politicians around Europe, he showed them that a fresh infusion of dollars there might help—although the Herter Committee insisted that America retain a veto on how the dollars were to be spent. Meeting with Harriman and officials from the State Department, Herter said a European customs union would not be enough: if Congress was to approve the Marshall Plan, Europeans would have to establish an agency for economic coordination.

The support of like-minded politicians was essential to the administration. Harriman, Acheson, and other liberal diplomatists were lucky to have strong enclaves of sympathy in Congress, even among the Republicans, and they were all the more effective for having known each other since early youth. At the same time, they enjoyed a strong rapport with President Harry Truman. They controlled the high ground of foreign policymaking—for one reason because they had a common, practical goal, for another because Truman was inclined to listen to them. Where Roosevelt had operated through summit meetings and informal contacts, Truman used his ambassadors and the regular chain of command. For the first time in years, a U.S. President put his foreign policy in the hands of officials with direct experience in the field: international bankers and lawyers and, lower down the pyramid, an increasingly dynamic Foreign Service. Truman's chosen advisers shared a similar background—rich, Ivy League, internationalist liberal—because it was they who had working knowledge of international commerce and diplomacy. They understood what they wanted, so the initiative had fallen to them almost by default.

By and large, non-Communist opposition to the Marshall Plan came from citizens who had little experience with foreign governments. By late 1947, most Americans wanted to give more aid to Western Europe, but opponents to it are worth at least a cursory glance. Important before, they would be important again, for they reflected an elemental American emotion. Resentments were created in the 1940s that sooner or later would take their revenge.

Right-wing opposition to the Marshall Plan arose from a residual isolationism, a fear of deficit spending, a reluctance to help foreigners who had wasted so much aid money in the past. In addition, conservatives were reluctant to help the Democrats—Marshall Plan hearings were used to haul Democratic officials over the coals, and to air a lot of smoldering partisan grievances. To Bob Lovett, who had replaced Dean Acheson as Under Secretary of State, fell the task of defending State on Capitol Hill. At a hearing in December 1947, Under Secretary Lovett sat through a hellfire sermon that included "attacks on lend-lease shipments to Russia, Communism, grain shortage, past relief abuses, German plant dismantling and reparations deliveries, and German currency system. While no direct attack was made on sin, I judge the Committee omitted that feeling that the Department of State was an adequate substitute."

In all fairness, the chief right-wing substitute for sin was Soviet communism, which is why most right-wingers finally backed the Marshall Plan. Some of them, however, agreed with the political left on one thing. American aid, they said, should be dispensed by the United Nations, instead of by a U.S. government agency—a lingering echo of 1918, when left and right were ranged against alliances or unilateral initiatives toward Europe. Isolationism—and populist xenophobia—found an outlet in left-wing as much as right-wing rhetoric. This rhetoric stemmed from an old American similarity to Russia, which was another continental country that saw the world as a vast extension of itself.

Still the foremost advocate for ultraliberals was ex-Commerce Secretary Henry Wallace, who denounced the Marshall Plan on grounds of a purist, one-world internationalism. Interjecting quotations from the Bible into his speeches, he could drive some of his listeners to a revivalist frenzy and did so all over the United States. Our dollars should go to Eastern as much as to Western Europe, Wallace declared; and more should be done to allay Soviet suspicions, which arose from our 1918 attack on Russia. Only goodwill, trade, and economic assistance would prevent Joseph Stalin from going to extremes.

Wallace's preposterous pair of demands—that the USA should not give help to repressive governments, that it should give more help to Stalinist Russia—were ignored by most Americans. Nonetheless, they continued to exasperate officials like James Forrestal, who sniped at Wallace in public and in private. "The practical people are going to have a hell of a time getting the world out of receivership," Forrestal warned, "and when the miracles are not produced the crackpots may demand another chance in which to really finish the job. At that time, it will be of greatest importance that the Democratic Party speak for the liberals, but not for the revolutionaries." While that was an amazingly prophetic warning, Forrestal was in the sad process of going insane—and of alienating the President by flirting with Republicans. Soon after winning the presidential election of 1948, Harry S Truman got rid of James Forrestal, resisting his requests for a vastly higher Pentagon budget. In the same year, most liberals rejected Henry Wallace's bid for the White House. President Truman's re-election was a narrow victory for the Democrats, but for the time being liberal policy would remain in his hands.

Whatever the Marshall Plan's reception in America, the European Communists refused to take it lying down. They reacted in Western Europe with strikes and demonstrations, in Eastern

Europe with a rival economic plan. Russia stepped up its propaganda attacks, launching a new Communist International and denouncing the Marshall Plan as "an embodiment of the American design to enslave" the Europeans. When Harriman called this a sour grapes exercise—Joseph Stalin's anger against a policy that would frustrate his "aggressive program for taking over Europe"—the reply was a counterblast at Harriman himself. But Soviet actions spoke louder than their words. All over Eastern Europe they had installed a series of People's Democratic Republics, using the Red Army and their own secret police. Then Stalin's first action against the Marshall Plan came in early 1948, when he decided to tighten his hold on Czechoslovakia.

Something there is in Czechoslovakia that rather likes a wall. A recent election in that country had given political control to the Communists, enabling them to clamp down without Soviet help. Acting probably on Stalin's orders, they proceeded in February to stage a takeover and get rid of their rivals—such as the non-Communist Foreign Minister, who was pushed or jumped out of a window to his death.[17] Other non-Communists were done away with more quietly. These actions, while they met with considerable support in Czechoslovakia, did frighten a lot of westerners and put new life into the Marshall Plan hearings.

The public hearings on Capitol Hill had dragged on for three months, mainly to give Republicans a chance to let off steam. Although the State Department had been warning of new Communist takeovers, it was the events in Czechoslovakia that finally concentrated the mind of Congress. Russia was "a greater menace than Hitler," asserted Harriman in secret testimony after the takeover; if we turn our backs on Europe again, then "the balance of power, which is now preponderantly in our favor, will be against us." That kind of talk brought all hesitation to an end, and in April the Marshall Plan was signed into law.

First, a few safeguards were attached to the bill. Marshall aid bore a close resemblance to Lend-Lease, but this time the Congress meant to keep a watchful eye on what went on. Inasmuch as the State Department was considered a little soft on foreigners, Congress called for an Economic Cooperation Administration (ECA) to oversee the expenditure of Marshall funds. The ECA was to be oriented toward private enterprise, with top positions set aside for people with business experience. Under Lend-Lease, all foreign purchases had gone through the U.S. government; Marshall aid, on the other hand, would be used by Europe for direct purchases from U.S. companies. In exchange for American money, the Europeans had to make an effort toward continental unity, at expanding their overseas trade, and at other forms of global economic cooperation.

Finally, Congress demanded that the ECA chief be a sound and trustworthy man, which meant above all that he should be a Republican. Somehow Truman found a compatible Republican, Paul Hoffman, who, in turn, wanted Harriman as his second-in-command and head of the ECA office in Paris. Before long, Harriman's Paris office took over many of the ECA's functions, which was a method of forcing Europeans to work through their own economic council in Paris, instead of acting separately through their Washington embassies. Harriman tried from the start to get Europeans to do most of the economic work. Nevertheless, he faced two big political problems which only an American diplomat could solve.

One problem was communism. For reasons that very few Americans understood, Europeans did not want the Marshall Plan advertised as anti-Communist. Harriman therefore had to speak in two voices, depending on where he was. In Washington, right after his appointment to the ECA, he reiterated a belief that "the forces of our recovery program will roll back communism behind the iron curtain"—which sounded just fine for an American audience, but not so fine in France. At a Paris press conference, Harriman commented that Russia had a "distorted conception" of the Marshall Plan—but with a change of attitude, Russia might be entitled to Marshall aid. That comment was noticed and made the rounds in Washington, creating a minor scandal among U.S. politicians, and Harriman quickly backtracked at a Senate hearing. No, absolutely not, never had he advocated aid for Eastern Europe, and the *New York Times* had reported it all wrong. Yes, of course the awful Communists should not have our money, and Harriman would do his darndest to stop them from getting it. All the same, East-West trade might be helpful to Western Europe's recovery.

Americans make life so very hard for their diplomats. And yet, American anti-communism did have its uses. Ambassador Harriman could use it as a stick to prod Congress into voting more money. And congressional disapproval he could use as a stick to prod Europeans toward continental unity—Harriman's second big political problem. The British, after taking a helpful lead in launching the Marshall Plan, were raising tremendous obstacles to unity in Europe. The new Labour government of England worried about losing control of its own economic policy; and most British subjects had a hard time digesting such a foreign idea, when for centuries their aim had been to keep Europe divided. With a vast overseas empire, they still thought of themselves as a special case in Europe, enjoying a separate destiny and a "special relationship" with Anglo-Saxon America.

The trouble was Americans, no matter what their ethnic background, did not fully share that magic feeling. The United States had much higher priorities on the European mainland. Averell Harriman had to tell the British off like a pack of boarding school children—that England was not at the head of any line, that America was not playing favorites with Marshall money— but they refused to listen. When in April 1948 Europe's economic council was overhauled and relaunched, the British tried hard to weaken its authority. There were not, they protested, enough British civil servants to staff a high-powered organization in Paris. And two months later, when Harriman told the European council to allocate Marshall aid on its own, Great Britain again protested: such a task would strain the council beyond endurance; America should divide up the pie. Over endless British objections, a European tribunal retreated to Chantilly and did produce a workable division of Marshall funds, but this proved an isolated triumph for Harriman. He found the British continually "negative in their approach" and their delegate in Paris quite unsympathetic. What with England's negative attitude about European unity, no real progress would be made until a new European group was formed without it.

*   *   *

Over the next year or so, until late 1949, the great achievement of Averell Harriman and his staff was that of economic growth in each separate country of Europe. European output soon broke through its prewar level, and then went on rising by 20 percent. The overall increase was due, for the most part, to a doubling of production in Germany—or more precisely, in the western zones of Germany that were occupied by England and the United States. This area, small as it was, would remain the powerhouse of West European industry.

The expansion of German industry was sudden and something of a surprise. Most German factory equipment was intact in 1945, but for the next three years starvation in Germany was worse than at any time since the seventeenth century. More German civilians died in that period than during all of World War II, a disaster to which Allied confusion had contributed. In the course of an evening with President Roosevelt, Robert Murphy had not been able to extract any coherent instructions for Germany; all he could gather in 1945 was that Roosevelt and Truman wanted to avoid a clash with Russia on this issue and to make it the acid test of Allied goodwill. As an occupation official, Bob Murphy had to give effect to orders that were vague, contradictory, and sometimes absurd. Vestiges of the Morgenthau Plan to pastoralize Germany remained in force for years; whole factories were to be shipped out of western Germany as reparations to other countries, including Russia; severe restrictions were imposed on the level of German industrial output. Whenever Murphy or the U.S. Army began to evade some of these restrictions, they promptly were denounced as Fascist sympathizers.

Of course, the State Department was trying to get the orders changed, but President Harry Truman reacted slowly. As in many other aspects of U.S. diplomacy, a constructive German policy did not take shape until trouble developed with Russia. At first, Bob Murphy had foreseen no great problem with the Soviet Union. He assumed that U.S. occupation forces soon would be brought home. Then, in early 1946, he reported that the Soviets appeared to be clamping down on their zone of occupation in the east and preparing to put pressure on the western zones as well. Chiming in from Moscow, George Kennan suggested that a new, reunited Germany might well come under Soviet control; therefore, we might consider bringing western Germany into "constructive programs looking toward integration of these zones into general economic and political pattern of western Europe rather than into a new Germany and establishment of a barrier to further advance of Communism from East to West."

By mid-1947, when the Marshall Plan was announced, most Americans had come to agree that the Western Allies should concentrate on rebuilding the western sectors: Soviet terms for Germany's unification seemed unacceptable. Averell Harriman paid a visit to the western region that summer, writing to President Truman that "we cannot revive a self-supporting western European economy without a healthy Germany playing its part." Some of the restrictions on German production were lifted. And quietly the State Department, then more noisily the U.S. Army and Congress, started pushing for a German share of Marshall aid.

Ambassador Harriman believed in generous aid to German industry. At the same time, he had to mollify certain countries like France, who did not care to treat this late-hated enemy as an agent of European salvation. Harriman managed to settle a modest amount of money on the Germans in 1948, almost entirely in the form of loans. In truth, the German boom of 1948–49 was due largely to other factors: a well-planned currency reform, a sudden demand for German goods elsewhere in Europe, the prospect of more U.S. aid later on. Soviet actions in the eastern zone also were creating a sense almost of allied solidarity between West Germans and the United States, heightening German morale and hope for the future.

Political life in Germany had revived as well, or been allowed to revive. Gradually, out of a series of meetings and local elections, the conservative Christian Democrats were emerging as the strongest political party. And at the head of the Christian Democrats was emerging one Dr. Konrad Adenauer—though perhaps "emerging" is the wrong word to describe the political rise of Konrad Adenauer, who helped found the Christian Democratic Party and took it over by a sequence of clever tricks and maneuvers. One reason for his rise to power was that none of his opponents thought him capable of it, at more than seventy years of age. An important politician before Hitler's takeover in 1933, Konrad Adenauer had defied the Nazis and been arrested by them several times. But most of his life under the Third Reich was passed quietly at home, cultivating a rose garden and a taste for German wines. His hatred for Adolf Hitler stemmed, as much as anything, from the Nazi handling of Roman Catholic education, and his religious views tended to shape his Westernist outlook. Along with Adenauer's firm anti-communism, his lack of interest in Protestant eastern Germany, went his feeling that a rapprochement with Catholic France would be a natural and useful step for West Germans.

Winning over his countrymen to that was not so easy, for there were strong neutralist sentiments in Germany: a desire for trade with Eastern Europe, and a wish to compromise with Russia to prevent the division of their country. Many Germans opposed Adenauer, but he was helped by Soviet provocations in the east, and—what really settled the matter—his world view blended well with American liberal diplomacy. When Dean Acheson returned to public life as Secretary of State in early 1949, he made Germany one of his top priorities, in particular, the founding of a West German state closely linked to its western neighbors. The Western Allies retained an extensive control over German foreign relations and German industry, but a new Basic Law was accepted in May 1949, and elections held three months later. To everyone's surprise, the Christian Democrats came out of them still the biggest party. By another sequence of shrewd power plays, Dr. Adenauer formed a center-right coalition and made himself the new Federal Chancellor. Then, in September, he convened the government of West Germany at the new capital, Bonn, which was a Rhineland town close to where he lived.

One reason for Adenauer's victory at the polls, and another thing that went over well with U.S. diplomats, was his economic platform—essentially a free trade, free market, welfare capitalism. For two years the Economic Council of Germany had been run by the Christian Democrats, who were lifting economic controls much faster than other governments. They also encouraged exports and held down prices by a program of fiscal and monetary restraint. At the time of the 1949 elections, West German production had risen above prewar levels and the voters were inclined to judge by these results, giving most of the credit to Adenauer's policies.

All very well for European recovery, Germany's revival led to a diplomatic impasse inasmuch as the French hated it. Germany's Ruhr Valley remained the heartland of European industry and, with its coal mines, just as vital to Western Europe as the Persian Gulf would be later on. Terrified that once again it would be dominated by its neighbor, France insisted on having a say in how the German economy was run and demanded international supervision of the Ruhr. Americans and the ECA agreed that an International Ruhr Authority ought to be maintained, if only to reassure France that Germany's coal and steel was being allocated fairly; but this was something that the Germans resented. Invited to control a seat on the Ruhr Authority, Konrad Adenauer accepted the offer and was denounced at home—in a parliamentary uproar—as a puppet of the Western Allies.

Clever old codger, Dr. Adenauer knew what he was doing. The Ruhr Authority was composed of West Europeans and would link German commerce more closely to the West—which Adenauer saw as an opportunity, a chance to form a continental partnership with France. "A lasting peace between France and Germany can only be attained through the establishment of a community of economic interests between the two countries," he had said twenty years before, after drawing up a European economic plan. In September 1949, he suggested that the Ruhr Authority should develop into a high authority for the industries of all Western Europe. The new Basic Law had pledged Germany "to serve the peace of the world as an equal partner in a united Europe"; and Secretary of State Acheson, visiting Bonn that autumn, responded favorably to his call for a Carolingian partnership between the western Teutons, Franks, and Gauls. With America behind him, Adenauer's toughest problem would be to win over the French government.

*   *   *

If Germany was the economic keystone of Europe, then France was the political one. A rapprochement was one solution, that was clear. But to any observer of France in the late 1940s, a Franco-German partnership must have seemed a crazy idea. The French came out of World War II physically plundered and with their scorn for everyone, including each other, at an unusually high pitch. Every new occurrence across the Rhine seemed to cause them enormous distress. They objected to lower German reparations, they objected to higher German production, they objected to pan-German unity, they objected to West German zonal unity and to the founding of a West German government. At the time of France's liberation in 1944, its provisional president was General Charles de Gaulle, whose views were fully shared by most French citizens: that Russia was their natural ally and that their worst enemies were the Germans, who might rise again and reconquer the homeland.

On the other hand, Charles de Gaulle did possess a strain of realism. He had no objection to West European unity, so long as Germany was divided and France retained the upper hand. Better still, other members of the provisional government sounded downright practical. Bill Bullitt, after talking with some of them during 1944, reported in *Life* magazine that they would accept a united Germany. Their chief worry was German industry—the Ruhr basin, in particular—and they intended to push "a proposal to curb German industrial might by putting this area under international control." While the western part of Germany and "all the Ruhr industrial complex should remain politically a part of the German state, the whole region should be attached economically to the economic systems of Belgium, the Netherlands and France, with the participation of England to such an extent as the British government may desire. In this area they would as rapidly as possible eliminate customs barriers and make currencies interchangeable and permit free immigration." Many French businesses, Bullitt knew, had moved in that direction just before and during the war. But he spoke especially for his friend Jean Monnet, whose opinions would carry considerable weight three years later, after de Gaulle had resigned and the French Communists had been excluded from power.

In spirit almost half American, Monnet had got his start as a salesman of Cognac in western Canada. And Ambassador Harriman remembered him from the 1920s as a business colleague, a young banker on Wall Street who dealt in foreign currencies and international loans. He acquired a small fortune on the New York Stock Exchange and lost it all in the crash of '29—a record that did not make for political respect in France, any more than it did in the United States. Monnet's method was to give advice to the more popular politicians. President de Gaulle, for example, put him in charge of obtaining money and supplies from Washington because he seemed to understand Americans so well. In 1945, Monnet also polished off a plan for the modernization of France's basic industries and, for another two years, was content to function as a technocrat in charge of the "Monnet Plan." French politics were in such turmoil that he could best exert his influence by remaining behind the scenes.

In retrospect, the Monnet Plan for France served mainly as a public relations scheme. Monnet tended, like all good PR men, to believe most of what he was saying. In the best New Deal style, his recovery plan bucked up national morale, gave France a sense of economic direction, and he found it effective for persuading U.S. politicians. Even some Americans who abhorred the idea of economic planning at home seemed to go for it in Europe—somehow it reassured them that their money would not be wasted through foreign incompetence or corruption. By talking in Washington about free trade and the Monnet Plan— and by throwing in some warnings about French communism— Monnet managed to extract over a billion dollars in grants and loans before the Marshall Plan was announced. Moreover, his ideas became an example to American diplomats. Secretary of State Marshall, when considering how his own plan should be drafted, wrote to the Paris embassy that "it might be possible for program to be somewhat along lines Monnet Plan but on a much larger scale involving several countries."

While Americans may have loved Jean Monnet for himself, they had a practical need of his services because they had such a wretched time dealing directly with the French. So did every-one. A difficult patient for any statesman, postwar France was behaving like a paranoid, Balzacian miser—and nothing pro-vokes a miser like the generosity of others. First he is amazed, then he takes his benefactor for a fool, then he attributes devi-ous, selfish motives to him. The first two billion or so in Ameri-can loans had been kept fairly quiet, but the Marshall Plan could not be hushed up and it struck many French people as sinister, inexplicable, almost infuriating.

As for the problem of basic anti-Americanism, France was one of the few countries that felt this affliction on the political right as much as on the left. On the left side, Russia was perceived as good, the United States as evil and ready to use France for waging an imperialist war against communism. Among the French right, there existed an intense resentment of American incursions on French sovereignty and national culture. "Ameri-cans are naive, ignorant, and understand nothing!" blurted the first president of the Fourth Republic, who was somewhat pa-tronizing anyway. To French officials, American manners and bad taste seemed a serious political issue—for what was Ameri-can liberalism except philistine pragmatism in its most overpow-ering political form?

What perhaps enraged the French most of all was the soften-ing American treatment of Germany and hints that the Germans should be rearmed. They had resented deeply the American loans to Germany in the 1920s, some of which were made by Averell Harriman and which Harriman was about to make again. When he met with Foreign Minister Georges Bidault in 1947, Harriman found the latter "in a hysterical condition." M. Bi-dault complained about proposals to centralize western Ger-many, to raise German steel production, to send Germans back into the coal mines of the Ruhr. "I am not in a position to overcome the simultaneous opposition of General de Gaulle, the Communist Party, and a not negligible fraction of my own friends," he protested. "Besides, I don't want to!"

Harriman's argument that the Allies could maintain control of the Ruhr, that low levels of production there put a strain on U.S. industry, made no impact on Bidault. He answered that his government was "in danger of being placed in a tragic situation."

Bidault was wrong. By late 1947, some degree of economic revival in Germany became so obviously essential that the French started giving way—albeit hysterically, and complaining bitterly about Harriman's allotment of aid to the Germans. Outside the government, both de Gaulle and the Communist Party still were forces to be reckoned with; they went on hurling insults from the sidelines, seeing no need even for Marshall aid to France. But if Harriman felt little sympathy for hysteria, other U.S. envoys like David K. E. Bruce were able to hold France's hand and reassure it about Germany.

Of course, the French economy needed something more than reassurances. When David Bruce—described by Harriman as his "oldest friend and banking associate"—took charge of the Marshall Plan for France, he was faced with widespread poverty and an archaic system of production. The Monnet Plan helped out a little, but new social programs at home and a colonial war in Indochina caused enormous public deficits and shortages of investment capital. To turn things around, Bruce applied a mild form of carrot-and-stick therapy. At times he used Marshall aid for leverage on issues like European unity; at other times he allowed it to be used for plugging the French deficit and thus dampening inflation. Under his discreet influence, the year 1948 saw the beginning of a series of monetary and fiscal adjustments which, however painful, turned the French economy upward.[18] Inflation started unevenly to subside and production unevenly to gain speed—not so much speed as in Germany, but soon breaking through the prewar levels. In France as elsewhere hope was dawning amid despair. And for the first time since 1871, a large portion of the country was looking ahead economically, rather than sideways or behind.

When year two of Marshall aid began in July 1949, Averell Harriman was able to point with pride to his record. "The plan is going ahead very well," he proclaimed. "Now, with the world changing from a seller's to a buyer's market, the next year will be more a question of trade and international payments." This, he kept saying, meant there must be more progress toward trade and monetary unity in Europe—if economic growth was to continue, and if Congress was to vote more aid money in 1950.

Intra-European trade did pick up in 1949–50, but most of what Harriman got were just promises. The Europeans wrongly considered their overseas exports more important then intracontinental trade. And they put up strong resistance to ending import quotas and economic controls. For Harriman, the chief problem still was Great Britain, which he tried endlessly to pressure and cajole. When he explained that what America wanted was a customs union—a free movement around Europe of money, goods, and people—the English called it insufficiently precise. A British cabinet minister complained about the "schoolboy lecture" style in which certain transatlantic officials spoke to the Europeans. Somehow Harriman managed never to lose his patience, wishing to "be tender with the British people and be sure not to arouse their resentment." Nevertheless, in the autumn of 1949 one can sense a growing acceptance among U.S. diplomats that Great Britain would have to be cut adrift.

Secretary Acheson—it was his great diplomatic weakness— had an abiding love for England. Still, he saw which way the wind was blowing and in October 1949 sent a cable to his European embassies saying, "France and France alone can take decisive leadership in integrating Western Germany in Western Europe." American diplomats should encourage France to act. Ambassador Harriman responded by talking publicly about "regional arrangements" on the continent; in Germany, Chancellor Adenauer announced that he would welcome a marriage of convenience with France; and the current French Foreign Minister, Robert Schuman, had no personal objection. An Alsatian-German himself, Schuman happened to be a devout Roman Catholic like Adenauer and went through the war under similar circumstances: house arrest, arrest, escape, and refuge in monasteries. The time was ripe for a rapprochement. The Congress soon would be debating a third year of Marshall aid and during May a big conference was to take place in London. Acheson said he wanted to see a breakthrough before this conference—something to keep Western countries on the offensive and capture the public's imagination. Meanwhile, Robert Schuman and the French government went on wringing their hands and doing nothing.

Not so Jean Monnet. At his cottage outside Paris, Monnet was working on an economic proposal to Germany, having reluctantly decided that England could be left out. What he wanted was a pooling arrangement for German and French production—an arrangement that would replace the current system of foreign control in the Ruhr. Other countries could join if they accepted the ground rules. Badly in need of a bright idea, Robert Schuman met with Jean Monnet, who said that M. Schuman was welcome to announce the proposal and could call it the "Schuman Plan." Schuman for a moment barely restrained himself from embracing Monnet, so grateful was he for this suggestion. After retreating to his own cottage for a last session of hand-wringing, he approached Adenauer about the proposal; he presented it to the French cabinet; and at a U.S. Embassy reception given by David Bruce, he mentioned it to Secretary Acheson. Everyone seemed agreeable, so on May 9, 1950, Schuman summoned a press conference to make the new proposal public.

Though Schuman read it awkwardly in a thick German accent, Monnet's prose was relatively clear, having already gone through thirty drafts: "The French government proposes that the entire French-German production of coal and steel be placed under a joint high authority, within an organization open to the participation of other European nations." If accepted by France's neighbors, this would "create the first concrete foundation for a European federation which is so indispensable for the preservation of peace." Amazingly, that said no more than the truth. The Schuman Plan took the world by surprise, and yet the Western press liked it, the U.S. Congress loved it, and the smaller countries of Western Europe sounded interested. Most important, Chancellor Adenauer declared to the German parliament that he was in complete accord with "Schuman's" proposal. The only significant objections came from the British government, which "bristled with hostility to Schuman's whole idea," as Acheson and Harriman observed in London. While England refused to join, six other West European countries convened in June 1950 to hammer out a formal agreement.

President Truman announced his support for the plan one

week later, but American participation had to be quiet and tact-
ful. After discussing it with European officials, Harriman and
Bruce reported that the "proposal may well prove the most
important step towards economic progress and peace of Europe
since original Marshall speech." America should reject England's continuing requests for a bilateral "special relationship"—and to help maintain the momentum toward unity, U.S.
diplomats should encourage the French plan without appearing
to be involved.[19]

Delighted though he was to see France taking the initiative,
Ambassador Harriman had just done something equally important for European commerce. For years he had been trying to
arrange a new monetary system in Europe, with the dollar as the
chief international currency; and as usual it was the British who
had resisted him. They feared that free conversion to any currency would cause a flight into dollars, ending the pound ster-
ling's importance and weakening their economic bargaining position. Harriman kept pressing them until, by June 1950, the
English assented to a system of partial convertibility into dollars,
a lowering of import quotas, and a multicurrency pool to finance
European trade. The European Payments Union would allow
each country to use any currency for settling its accounts—
easing the intercourse of money, and therefore goods, throughout Europe on a multilateral basis. Sporting a sixgun and a
ten-gallon hat, Secretary Acheson in Texas hailed Harriman's
achievement as the second of two steps which "hold the promise
of a great new era in Europe."

The European Payments Union and the Schuman Plan did
resolve a century-old economic impasse. No longer were France
and Germany too hostile to allow West European cooperation,
and no longer was England strong enough to get in the way.
Certainly, the English caused an immense deal of trouble. The
autarchical leanings of John Maynard Keynes, late in his life,
reflected a pessimism in England, where politicians feared that
an open economy would harm their full-employment program.
Economic efficiency seemed not worth the bother of economic
change. But they made a serious mistake. With strong American
support on the continent, the Schuman Plan became the Euro-

pean Coal and Steel Community in 1951—an organization that laid the groundwork for a continental boom lasting over two decades.

Dean Acheson's sixgun made a perfect prop for his Texas speech, most of which was aimed at the Soviet military threat. What the United States needed, he declared, was neither isolation nor a preventive war but a much stronger deterrent to Communist attack. The need for a better-planned and better-financed defense was of increasing, and probably excessive, concern to Acheson and the State Department. In any event, the spring of 1950 saw the establishment of a North Atlantic Treaty Organization—the fruition of two years' effort in response to Soviet military pressure.

You have to hand it to Joseph Stalin. Doing anything really provocative to America must have taken a lot of nerve during the late 1940s. Western conventional forces were quite weak, but the United States did monopolize the A-Bomb and it controlled most of the world's productive capacity. Sooner or later a war would have ended in defeat for the Russians. And yet, despite everything, Stalin had gone ahead and imposed the so-called Berlin Blockade. The western half of Berlin, where the Western Allies had occupation rights, lay entirely within the Russian zone of Germany; in mid-1948 Stalin sealed off eastern Germany and stopped all ground traffic into West Berlin, forcing U.S. authorities to provision the city by air. Until ground access was restored one year later, the Berlin Blockade generated something close to a wartime atmosphere in Central Europe.

As it turned out, Americans did not respond violently at any geographical point. Instead, they started moving toward a military alliance with Europe. The first step toward a North Atlantic Treaty had been taken by the British a few months before the Berlin airlift, when they proposed a series of defense pacts with France, Belgium, and the Netherlands. Military unity presented no threat of economic cooperation and the British generally were in favor of it. The Czechoslovak takeover, as well as the blockade of Berlin, added greater momentum and intensity to their initiative; the blockade scared even France into the Western military camp. Great Britain already had asked the United States to join a military grouping which could be broadened to include all of the North Atlantic countries. Entering into a peacetime alliance with anyone went against a sacred American tradition, but once again most politicians were persuaded, and in 1949 the North Atlantic Treaty was signed.

It was clear to U.S. diplomats that the North Atlantic Treaty would require a program of military aid in Europe. The question was exactly how much aid. Averell Harriman warned that the United States must consider both American and European constraints and not push anyone too hard—military aid should be treated as a part of the economic recovery program. Harriman soon came to embody a connection between these programs and—along with Lovett, Acheson, and the generals—became a spokesman in Washington for military assistance. West Europeans regarded the Marshall Plan as more important, he explained; at the same time they believed in a unified military effort which would also require U.S. help: "If we turn aside today or put off action on the proposed assistance, doubts may well arise again. The voices of the subversive elements, the appeasers, those who would trust 'neutrality,' would rise again." Neutralists in Europe equated security not with deterrence but with a friendly dialogue between the two superpowers.

Nor did Harriman neglect to talk up the alliance among European leaders during 1949. In Lisbon, he expressed pleasure that Portugal had joined not just the Marshall Plan, but also its corollary, the North Atlantic Treaty—which was "probably the most important single international step taken in modern times."

"We shall see," remarked the Portuguese premier with a smile.

"You seem to be somewhat skeptical," Harriman put in. "May I ask why?"

"I am not really skeptical, but you Americans are apt to entertain an optimism about your sincere intentions and altruistic plans which has at times gone unjustified by results."

Harriman retorted that while the United States set its sights high, its objectives by and large had been met or exceeded.

Given America's record since 1940, Harriman had scored a

point, and events over the next six months continued to validate his optimism. As usual the Congress wanted, if it were to vote more aid, a new organization in Europe, a pooling of military resources to prevent excessive duplication or waste. Harriman and Acheson as usual wanted it too. At the London Conference of May 1950, they insisted on an integrated defense structure and concurred with Great Britain—over French objections—that Germany should somehow be brought into the arrangement. All agreed to a coordinating body and a charter for the North Atlantic Alliance, making it the North Atlantic Treaty Organization under a unified command. As Harriman described it some years later, the London Conference made possible an effective defense of Western Europe by putting the "O" in NATO.

Another thing that the conference did was to reveal a basic source of tension in NATO. When Dean Acheson submitted his request for higher military budgets, the Europeans balked. American diplomats until then had been careful not to put that sort of pressure on Europe. Trade between Western Europe and Russia, for example, continued with little interference from the United States. Both Acheson and Harriman well understood that economic warfare seldom was effective and that Europeans would resent a large-scale embargo.[20] Put in charge of East-West trade, Harriman pressed for an increase of European exports to the Soviet bloc while creating an Allied committee to embargo strategic items.

Unfortunately, such American restraint was being abandoned in the matter of military budgets. Politicians of both parties earlier had opposed sending more U.S. troops and military aid overseas; the President also had resisted higher defense spending. Then a Communist takeover of mainland China—followed by the first explosion of a Soviet nuclear device in August 1949—suddenly frightened Congress into voting over a billion dollars for military assistance. The new Communist successes, and an unexpected upsurge of political pressure at home, started to unnerve some of the diplomatic professionals. "We are confronted with total cold war," Averell Harriman worried in March 1950. "We must somehow reach and inspire people's

minds. The flames which we have put out are still smoldering."
Harriman asked for a stepped-up campaign of propaganda
against Russia, plus another billion dollars in military aid; and
Secretary Acheson made a secret request for the quadrupling of
U.S. defense expenditures to $50 billion a year. That sort of
request, and the rhetoric that went with it, may have foreshadowed some important errors yet to come.

By June 1950, Ambassador Harriman was ready to come back
home again. Much touted as a possible presidential candidate,
he chose instead to accept Truman's offer of a White House
job—that of adviser to the President on foreign affairs and, in
1951, head of the new "Mutual Security Agency." The creation
of this agency was a significant bureaucratic event, for no longer
would economic development be the chief object of U.S. diplomacy. As Harriman put it the previous autumn, "security, and
not economic integration or political integration, should be the
point of departure of our policy." Civilian aid was diminishing
even as military aid increased. Economic progress was but one
aspect of a policy based more and more on security against
Soviet military blackmail or attack.

Still, what Harriman and his associates had wrought economically was phenomenal by any historical standard. Using 100 as
each country's prewar high, Western Europe's index of industrial production had gone up from 87 to nearly 120 in the past
three years. Food production, too, had risen at an impressive
rate. While the causes differed from country to country, probably the most important was the effect of Marshall aid—both
material and psychological. The Marshall Plan provided essential commodities from North America and opened important
bottlenecks; the United States also sent over some capital equipment. But the psychological aspect of the Plan surely counted
for more. The morale boost meant greater political stability,
harder work, and the release of assets being hoarded or withheld
in Europe. Moreover, the move toward regional unity would
force a more rational allocation of human and material resources. A continental market, for example, would make possible a revolution in management and mass production; European

output could increase without the addition of a single man or machine.[21]

All of this required the kind of philistine adjustments that Europeans sometimes found hard to accept. Which is why the move toward unity called for a supreme diplomatic effort by Americans. The task of working with Europeans occasionally proved similar to that of working with underdeveloped countries later on: childishness, hysteria, ignorance, vanity, the appeals to local prophets and traditions—many of the usual elements were there. To cope with them, Harriman found himself running all over the continent and working a fourteen-hour day. While West European unity and American fears of Russia dovetailed pretty well, still Harriman and Acheson were facing a complex task abroad. England would accept a West German revival and not European economic unity; France would accept, increasingly, European economic unity but not a German revival. By using their presumed economic leverage and their real control of Germany, and by playing each country off against the other in proper sequence, American diplomats secured both economic unity *and* a German revival. Not everything had been thought out ahead of time—often it was done intuitively and step-by-step—but still it amounted to a brilliant series of finesses.

Another card that U.S. diplomats always tried to remember was political opinion at home. Congress could be galvanized by the threat of Soviet communism and the need for military security; on the other hand, Europeans were interested primarily in economic aid. So economic and military concerns had to be addressed at a different pace on the different continents. NATO probably never would have been accepted by Europe without the Marshall Plan; nor would the Plan have been accepted by Americans without their deep fear of Soviet power.

For all their anti-Soviet fears, it could not have been easy for Americans to get behind the Marshall Plan. The program after all cost more than $13 billion, and it sometimes is forgotten that the United States had a hard time just producing the goods required, let alone raising the money to buy them. American sacrifices were made from a sense of generosity, as well as from the perception by American leaders that the Marshall Plan was in America's long-term interest. John Maynard Keynes was correct when he said that only a second world war would jolt America into running the public deficits required to end the Great Depression. He might have added that it would take another crisis, after the war, to jolt Americans into reducing their foreign payments surplus. The Marshall Plan was a very mild form of Keynesian economic pump-priming—government spending on an international scale to revive trade and commerce. Its advocates generally realized this, but they relied upon a generous impulse among their fellow citizens. In that sense, perhaps, they were no more than the worthy representatives of a great people.

On a somewhat limited scale, the old "New Liberal" ideals had been implemented through the Marshall Plan and would continue to proliferate around the globe. A strong precedent was set for reciprocal aid during peacetime, and the cooperative spirit of Marshall aid was more than just a matter of economic growth.[22] It buttressed a democratic revival in Western Europe, and European developments had their counterparts elsewhere. The United Nations was weak, but part of its original purpose was being served by other multilateral institutions. The World Bank and International Monetary Fund would help more and more to channel foreign aid and maintain international liquidity. Established in 1947, the General Agreement on Tariffs and Trade would have an impact on worldwide commerce. None of this was possible without a superpower always ready to back it up, always ready to step in during any major crisis. Having first conquered fascism and American public opinion, internationalist liberalism was winning the passive support of most countries outside the Soviet bloc and China. The liberals had conquered most of the world.

Whereas internationalist liberal successes had been spectacular since 1940, a spectacular success creates new problems and pitfalls. One problem is the resentment of those who are beaten. Two groups in America were defeated utterly by liberal achievements during the past decade—and not just defeated but shown to be obviously wrong, which is the worst humiliation of all. One group was the isolationist right, and the other the ultraliberal or socialist left. Each in their turn would try to take revenge and destroy at least part of what had been accomplished.

One method of staging a comeback was to make political hay out of a frustrating and unwinnable war, and the right wing would take its turn first with the military conflict in Korea. There were of course many reasons for a right-wing upsurge besides the resentment of isolationists or the Korean War. And right-wing attacks on the Truman administration had been going on for years. At the urging of Congressman Richard Nixon in 1948, the House Un-American Activities Committee accused Averell Harriman of coddling a treasonous subordinate who had permitted U.S. exports to Russia. Harriman refused to honor a congressional subpoena and President Truman backed him up, but the issue would not go away. Adolf Berle testified that the Communist "apparatus" in America had recruited some young New Dealers before the war. Republican paranoia was intensified by William Bullitt, who claimed that New Deal Democrats like Roosevelt and Harriman had sold Eastern Europe down the river into communism and "predatory totalitarian tyranny." During 1949, the fall of China to communism made things look even worse, eventually leading many politicians to claim that China had been "lost" because the State Department was full of Communist spies and sympathizers.

Right-wing hysteria mounted as the months went by in 1950, having as its worst effect an influence on the judgment of experienced diplomats. They lost some of the relative sense of balance and restraint which they had shown hitherto. One can see this in Acheson's request for vast increases in military spending and his decision to give France direct aid for the Indochina War. Republican charges of incompetence, or of outright treason in the executive branch, were lent greater immediacy by yet another Communist advance in the Far East. On June 25, 1950, a Communist army suddenly attacked across the border into South Korea, and the Korean War began.

V

Machiavellian Moments

1950–1963

The triumph of communism in China. That event may strike westerners as quite unremarkable, decades after it happened. But in 1950—the moment that concerns us—China remained an object of deep sentimentality to many Americans. Already it had a population of half a billion souls. The Communist Revolution, therefore, would be greeted in the United States as a cataclysmic change—unforeseen, unnecessary, and pregnant with terrifying consequences for Asia.

On more careful reflection, perhaps Americans should not have greeted it as so important or so surprising. The spread of Chinese communism had started during the 1930s, when the Japanese invaded and colonized much of the country. Anarchy throughout China and the misery of foreign conquest had strengthened the local appeal of communism. And the further chaos caused by Japan's defeat only speeded up a Communist victory that may have been inevitable. The Communist Party touted a number of attractive alternatives, such as land to the peasantry, the expulsion of foreigners, and an honest government. Meanwhile, the non-Communist regime of Chiang Kai-shek had grown so corrupt and inefficient that the mass of Chinese felt no loyalty to it; they went over in ever larger numbers to the Communist side. Continued shipments of U.S. aid to Chiang Kai-shek had a negligible effect upon the Chinese civil war. Starting with great inferiority in armaments and troop strength, the Communist Party by 1950 had made itself the master of all mainland China.

The reader may have noticed how little this book has said about the Far East, reflecting a basic judgment of Truman's top officials. A passive attitude toward China seemed the better part of wisdom to U.S. diplomats, most of whom shared a Eurocentric background or training. Rather like the Soviets, they considered the future of Europe far more crucial to their own security. Anyway, the takeover of so large and remote a place as China seemed impossible to stop with the means at America's disposal. Dean Acheson and others at State saw no point in pouring more money into that part of Asia; and by 1947 they had quietly given up on influencing Chinese politics. By 1949, Secretary Acheson was saying publicly that "the ominous result of the civil war in China was beyond the control of the government of the United States." He predicted an eventual Sino-Soviet split and advised a policy of selective containment in Asia, pointing out that most Americans were opposed to stronger action.

Some Americans saw it differently, to say the least—especially the Republicans in Congress, who were feeling restive under the partisan cease-fire on foreign affairs. Although the China Lobby included a number of Democratic politicians, the "loss" of China could be used as a partisan issue. And the Far East, in any case, had long been closer to the Republican Party's heart. Ever since Pearl Harbor, conservative newspapers and magazines had been denouncing the Eurocentric, anti-China bias of Democratic administrations.

Then, in the late 1940s, as Generalissimo Chiang Kai-shek lost more ground to the Communists, the Republican attacks on Truman's passivity grew more violent and hostile. Among the more vehement spokesmen for non-Communist Chinese was Ambassador Bill Bullitt, who helped lead the charge. In 1948, Bullitt told the readers of *Life* magazine that America could put Chiang back on his feet with a rescue package of $1.35 billion— and the right man to head this rescue was General Douglas MacArthur, the U.S. proconsul in occupied Japan. One year later, with the Communists at the point of victory, Bullitt made an impassioned plea before the Texas legislature: the United States should make a last-ditch effort to halt the Red Chinese advance. "China is the key to all Asia. If China goes, Indo-China, Siam, Burma, the Malay States and Indonesia will fall into the hands of the Communists. India will be at Stalin's mercy, and the Japanese who depend on Asia for raw materials and food, and markets for their products, will know that they can become self-supporting only by crawling under Stalin's iron curtain."

Bullitt, along with his friends in Congress, assumed that "Red China" would become a Soviet puppet—which was a mistake, evidently, but an irrelevant mistake in the year 1950. Having taken control of the Chinese mainland, Chairman Mao Tse-tung soon decided voluntarily to ally himself with Russia. And Mao was giving vent to some anti-American tirades unlike anything ever heard from a foreign government. "The newly arrived, upstart and neurotic United States imperialist clique," said Mao in reference to the Truman administration—though if anyone was newly arrived, upstart, and neurotic it was Mao Tse-tung, who proceeded to murder about five million Chinese and subject foreign diplomats to violence and imprisonment. Given the sentimental view of China taken by most Americans, such behavior came as a rude shock, in some ways ruder than the Red victory itself. First Eastern Europe, and now this. Over the next twenty years, Republican attitudes toward China resembled those of a rich man whose daughter has run off with a tramp.

The Truman clique had a somewhat calmer reaction. Political pressure did persuade Harry Truman to delay recognizing the arriviste government of mainland China, to bar it from membership in the United Nations. And of course the Secretary of State did not take kindly to the strident tones of Maoist propaganda. Such "customary ill-mannered and boorish" behavior, thought Dean Acheson, was well described by Bret Harte's observation.

> That for ways that are dark
> And for tricks that are vain
> The heathen Chinee is peculiar.

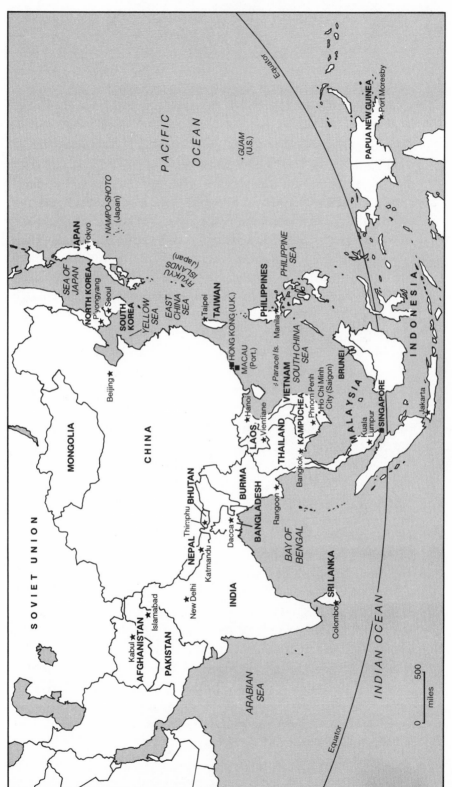

South and East Asia

But on a more prosaic level, the administration decided simply to give firmer support to other nations in the Orient. Instead of trying to liberate half a billion Chinese, as some politicians demanded, it seemed wiser to extend civilian aid to nearby countries like Korea and Japan.

For much the same reasons as in western Germany, the Marshall Planners of 1947 had wanted economic aid for Japan. And the Japanese, in their turn, had proven quite hospitable to democratic capitalism. General MacArthur and his staff were functioning there as conquerors, revolutionaries, and a relief agency all rolled up into one. They had imposed a constitution on Japan that shifted power from the executive to the legislative branch; and by instituting some drastic socioeconomic reforms, they were pushing a feudal system toward American social change and mobility. "When one compares the impact of American ideals on Japan with that of Communist ideals on China," wrote one historian, "there can be no doubt that in an Asian setting ours are the more revolutionary." Perhaps MacArthur's one great error lay in stressing social change more than economic growth; not until 1949, when a modest amount of aid was given and legal impediments removed, did Japan's industrial output start to revive.

What really did wonders for the Japanese economy, though, was an outbreak of war in Korea, less than two hundred miles to the east. A recently liberated colony of Japan, the Korean Peninsula was torn between communism and American power— torn both politically and geographically. During 1945, the Soviets had set up a Communist government in northern Korea, providing it with tanks and heavy artillery. The United States backed a different government in the south. All Koreans resented the prolonged division of their country; and there was no lack of threatening rhetoric from both regimes, each of which wanted to unite the peninsula by force. In the event, civilian aid to South Korea was not enough to deter a Communist attack. Launched probably with Joseph Stalin's approval, the Red invasion of 1950 overwhelmed a poorly equipped South Korean Army—which, indeed, might have been pushed into the sea had not Truman committed U.S. forces.

Besides providing an export market for Japan, the Korean invasion gave some new opportunities to General MacArthur. He organized a brilliant counterattack that turned into a total rout of the Communists. American troops marched north, unopposed, up the peninsula. And everything went well for the general until November 1950, when the Red Chinese Army intervened and the conflict became, in MacArthur's words, "an entirely new war."

The strongest repercussions of the Korean War, new or old, were felt outside the Far East, in the war's effect upon Western policy. The shockwave of Korea proved almost as shattering as the surprise attack on Pearl Harbor, back in 1941. Secretary Acheson feared that the Korean invasion might just be a diversionary tactic, that Stalin was planning a more drastic move somewhere else. And, typically, his prime concern was what that meant for the North Atlantic Alliance—Western strength and morale must be enhanced as soon as possible. The end result of such concerns was a much higher budget for the Pentagon, great pressure on Europe to strengthen its military posture, and a broadening of U.S. commitments worldwide.

If Acheson was the architect of Western rearmament, then the chief engineer was to be Averell Harriman—helping to manage a military buildup for the third time in his life. Right after the President announced that U.S. forces would defend South Korea, Harriman telephoned from Europe to say how glad he was. In fact, he could not bear to stay in Paris one moment longer. Counting on Dean Acheson to "square it with the boss," he said he would start his new job sooner than planned and catch the next airplane back to Washington.

The return of Averell Harriman put a strain on his partnership with Dean Acheson, who was now one of the most vilified Americans in public life. The Congress considered him a prime culprit in the recent loss of China—and perhaps even a closet Communist sympathizer.[23] While politicians called for Dean Acheson's impeachment and columnists gossiped that Harriman wanted to take his place, the Secretary of State seemed unperturbed. Had he not known Harriman since the two of them were schoolboys at Groton and Yalemen together, when Averell had coached him on the freshman crew? He "warmly welcomed" Harriman's presence in Washington, as he told a group of journalists. Some of them might not remember, but since 1905, "we have been close friends and worked together on all sorts of things."

In such public remarks did Acheson and Harriman respond with a comradely firmness to the Korean invasion. Meanwhile, the reaction in Europe proved a lot less simple and affectionate. As Harriman reported, European leaders greeted the American stand in Korea "with great relief and confidence." They welcomed a proposal to send more U.S. troops to Central Europe, and they agreed to increase their military budgets. What with Russia now ready to back an armed invasion, more must be done to deter such an attack on the West. Then, during the autumn of 1950, Red China's entry into the Korean War gave rise to a new kind of fear among Europeans: all of the hysteria in Congress, and wild statements from General MacArthur about using atomic bombs, made it seem that America might start a global war. The British prime minister came scurrying over to have a talk with President Truman. And France said the United States ought to tone down its rhetoric, rely more on diplomacy, and be more responsive to Soviet proposals for a disarmed and neutral Germany.

As the Soviets well knew, Germany was a complicating element in the North Atlantic Alliance. West German participation in NATO seemed essential, and yet the term "German rearmament" still sent shivers of fear and loathing down European spines. Even the Germans and Americans did not relish this idea, but to a country like France the suggestion was anathema. The French president—the same politician who thought Americans were "naive, ignorant, and understand nothing"—told Harriman in 1951 that the Germans were revengeful, nationalistic, and could not be trusted. Distracted by a colonial war in Indochina, the French had no money and little stomach for an arms buildup at home. On the other hand, they did not want a new German Army to take up the slack for NATO. So with Soviet encouragement, they kept waiting for an East-West détente that might make the rearmament of Europe unnecessary.

One way or another, French objections had to be met. But what was to be done, and who would do it? The man put in charge of resolving that impasse was Ambassador to France David Bruce, one of Harriman's oldest cronies and Acheson's favorite envoy in Europe. Those three gentlemen thought as one on most issues of the day—except that, while his friends in Washington wanted European integration, David Bruce was obsessed with it. Military integration would strengthen European morale, he believed, and thus "weaken and perhaps sublimate the intense nationalism which has twice in a generation sucked us into its tragic vortex." However, it might also be possible to use rearmament as a tool for strengthening political and economic unity in Europe.

What Bruce had in mind to reassure France was a single army of six nationalities—a continental army that would serve "as a collective enterprise and not an agglomeration of national efforts." Proposals for a European Army had been in the air for months. Winston Churchill had given it an oratorical boost; David Bruce had been pressing France to launch another initiative. Certainly it proved convenient that the current French premier was an old associate of Monnet who had helped prepare the Schuman Plan.[24] Under his and Monnet's guidance, there took shape a new plan for a pool of European soldiers and weaponry—rather like the coal and steel pool—that would comprise an integrated European force under a single European authority. Removing as it did the danger of a separate German Army, this plan was deemed acceptable by the French parliament.

Ambassador David Bruce embraced the plan too, but most officials on either side of the Atlantic did not like it—including the first Supreme Commander of NATO, General Dwight D. Eisenhower. Economies of scale did not always apply to military matters; and a big, integrated force might not work as well as allied national armies. Similarly, the State Department was polite but pessimistic about the plan. Dean Acheson suspected that it was just a French delaying tactic—to fend off a national German rearmament—and no one at State really understood its details. Nor did Bruce try to explain, telling State not to worry and leave everything to him. So lacking any alternative that France would accept, Secretary Acheson was sucked into the vortex: "We proposed, therefore, that the United States go all out for it as I had deduced it to be, without stirring up trouble by asking for clarification from Paris."

Six months later, the European Army treaty was agreed upon provisionally by six European governments. And Ambassador Bruce was promoted to Under Secretary of State, an appointment that delighted the social doyennes of Washington almost as much as it did his colleagues at the Department. In fact, David Bruce's charm and social background were captivating not just Washington but an entire generation of Western officials.

What it was about Bruce that so pleased other diplomats, that so inspired their instinctive trust, cannot be explained by hard facts or measurements. Secretary Acheson had grown quite attached to his ambassador, frequently staying with the Bruces in Paris. "It is no exaggeration to say," says Acheson, "that not since Benjamin Franklin had anyone been closer or more understanding of the French situation than David Bruce"—and yet that was a vast exaggeration. Perhaps what Acheson and others saw in Bruce was a Platonic archetype of themselves, the sort of person that they at their best wanted to be. For its new diplomatic role, the United States apparently needed a very old diplomatic model.

Bruce displayed all the right prefigurations. Having roots in rural, Episcopalian Virginia, he spoke with a slight Tidewater accent and walked with a limp that was explained, variously, as a war wound or the gout. He had a proud, vacuous face, intelligent eyes, and a clear complexion. To give them credit, his admirers were after something more than just snob appeal and perfect form. For them Bruce seemed to possess a substance now almost forgotten, but then still taken quite seriously by certain U.S. diplomats—what might be called the social and civic virtues of an eighteenth-century landed gentleman.

David Bruce sprang from that most absurd and incongruous of American backgrounds, the proud old family that has fallen on hard times. It almost goes without saying that his first Virginia forebear arrived in the seventeenth century—attendant upon a royal governor—and that another Bruce served in General Washington's army. During the War of 1812, David's great-grandfather had cornered the tobacco market and made a pre-industrial fortune. Considered one of the richest men in the United States, he lived on a huge tobacco plantation that was tended by several hundred slaves. Almost all of this fortune was lost in the Civil War, reducing Bruce's family to a state of genteel poverty—real *Gone With the Wind* figures, who had even more family pride than most old plantation owners. Always on the verge of losing their homestead, Bruce's father and grandfather nevertheless hung onto it, flouting every rule of Yankee prudence and common sense.

Much of David Bruce's charm must have come from his father, who was elected a Democratic senator from Maryland during the Republican 1920s. While certainly no liberal reformer on economic matters, Senator Bruce spoke out against Prohibition, the Ku Klux Klan, and "the savage and abominable practice of lynching." And in 1928 he lent strong support to the candidacy of Al Smith—in part, perhaps, because he hoped that the Democrats might revive a Wilsonian foreign policy better than Herbert Hoover. The United States is a "land which, after attaining a degree of material strength and prosperity unexampled perhaps in human history, holds out to itself no ideal less lofty than that of the moral leadership of human civilization," said Bruce in the Senate chamber, prompting most Republicans to walk out.

While his plantation served as a rural retreat, Senator Bruce earned a living from his law practice in Baltimore, and it was there that his children were born and bred. In 1915, young David went from a local prep school to Princeton, where he took part in an undergraduate campaign to close down the campus "eating clubs." This campaign actually stood for something important. Ridiculous as it appears today, the social snobbery issue tended to define a student's politics during World War I. The New Liberals affected a hatred of snobbery. They seemed eager to abolish it. And there is no question that in Bruce's day social success went with political apathy or conservatism. On the other hand, one should not forget that young liberals had an arrogance of their own, even then—an intellectual snobbery that became social, after the triumph of liberalism in the academic world and American diplomacy.

Dropping out of college to go to war, Bruce signed up as a buck private and saw Europe for the first time from the deck of a troopship. He got into an artillery regiment that did not reach the Western Front in time to see any action. During the peace conference, Bruce took courses at the University of Paris—eventually joining President Wilson's staff as a diplomatic courier, then returning to practice law in Maryland. The law and public service were cast aside soon after his marriage to Ailsa Mellon, daughter of the Honorable Andrew Mellon and perhaps the richest heiress in the world.

One of the few men in America with more money than Harriman's father was Bruce's new father-in-law. An American *Schlotbaron* if ever there was one, Andrew Mellon had put together a fortune in coal, oil, steel, and aluminum—for which effort Republicans awarded him the job of Treasury Secretary. And his daughter's marriage, in 1926, was very much a Republican event. President Calvin Coolidge, members of his cabinet, the entire Supreme Court, and ambassadors from several first-class powers all came to the reception, a glittering spectacle by any standard. Each of the two thousand guests took home a box of cake embossed in silver; each of the bridesmaids wore a circular brooch of diamonds; and Ailsa herself had on a pearl necklace that had been donated by her father. To top it all off, Secretary Mellon had made a present of one million dollars to Bruce and ten times that amount to the bride. Literally overnight, Bruce had recouped the family fortune and entered an industrial aristocracy, defeating even Prince Otto von Bismarck in the contest for Ailsa's hand.

A logical next step for Bruce was to go into Wall Street high finance. He became involved in running the Mellon empire and serving on various corporate boards—nor was it long before he ran into Averell Harriman. The two of them traveled in Europe together on banking business; and in 1933 Bruce joined Bob Lovett as a director of Harriman's Union Pacific Railroad. At the same time, he was growing richer in his own right, investing his wedding present in business ventures that somehow prospered even during the Depression. Obviously Bruce was no fool when it came to money—which was important, for a big independent income would prove crucial to his diplomatic career.

Bruce's career in diplomacy would be helped along by another personal trait, already clear from his very Republican marriage: an indifference to political passions at home. "The cardinal rule for an ambassador in a foreign country," Bruce would say, "is to cherish no antipathies or attachments for particular domestic political parties or programs." The only country where he himself followed that rule was America. When his father-in-law came under attack from New Deal enthusiasts, who regarded Andrew Mellon as an economic archfiend, David Bruce stood behind him foursquare. And the whole time he remained an official Democrat, campaigning for Al Smith and hoping for a job under President Roosevelt. The New Deal had no place for Bruce and, perhaps a little repelled by Wall Street, he went back with Ailsa to his old Virginia home—where he sat out the Depression in an apotheosis of the family tradition. Striking in appearance, fastidious in dress, courtly in manner, dignified in bearing, wise in counsel, skillful in field sports, and hospitable as Timon of Athens, he was the ideal of a southern cavalier.

If that description sounds overdone, it only quotes what Bruce said about his hero, George Washington, in a book that he was writing on the earliest U.S. presidents. Bruce's book, on the whole, took a classical-republican view of the American Revolution. He told his readers that the United States was founded by men who saw themselves as natural aristocrats, embodying all the special advantages of "real" property, leisure, and learning. President Adams had opposed democracy and was sympathetic to aristocratic rule, believing that popular power leads to military dictatorship. And President Jefferson certainly felt that city dwellers were suspect. The poor must be protected against the rich, Bruce conceded, but there must also be a check on mass action against the rural, landowning classes, where the natural aristocracy flourished.

Some of these ideas, of course, were familiar enough to Wilsonian liberals. Certainly the first stages of progressivism marked the last constructive assertion of rural "virtue" in American politics. The American Revolution was seen as a rejection of European urban and commercial decadence, and progressivism, likewise, as a reaction against the evils of big city life. As Progressives saw it, the Founding Fathers had been superseded by urban, mercenary politicians and their clients, the source of whose money made them unfit to govern. Small businessmen and professionals could be trusted, since they were close to the source of their income and controlled it; however, the classical civic virtues were most likely to be found among the heirs to autonomous agricultural wealth. For many liberals, the gentleman farmer remained a political icon, which is one reason why Ambassador Bruce always had a special cachet with some of his diplomatic brethren.[25]

But something else was going on as well. We have seen how an aversion to city life had become quite inconvenient by the twentieth century, when almost no one could live like a gentleman anywhere else. After all, to make a decent living Bruce's father had left his plantation for Baltimore; and Bruce's life of reason was made possible only by his marriage to a commercial fortune. Aware of this contradiction, the *New Republic* Progressives had suggested a political equilibrium between town and country, between rural values and the new personal freedoms offered by modern industry. By giving supervision of the cities and big business to the right sort of people—exercising their power through a strong central government—America might enjoy the best of both worlds. And David Bruce seemed to embody that new Attic ideal, a balance of civic virtue and economic dynamism, of landed gentry and commercial baron.

All the same, it was his lightness on either side of the scale that makes one a bit suspicious of Bruce. He had married his first million, not made or inherited it; and so much went into his rural form that something had to be missing from the substance. Indeed, for him everything might have ended in the sterile, pointless life of an idle country squire—dabbling in state politics and some literary recreations, savoring his mint juleps and a terminal case of Virginia Gentleman syndrome. Then World

At the Yalta Conference of February 1945, Churchill confers with Roosevelt, who already is looking rather unwell. He died two months later. (National Archives)

President Harry S Truman at the presentation of a proposed United Nations charter in San Francisco during the spring of 1945. (National Archives)

(Above) *An inspection during the Potsdam Conference. In the helmet is General George Patton; to his left in the front row are Assistant Secretary of War John McCloy and Secretary of War Henry Stimson; in the rear between McCloy and Stimson is Assistant Secretary of War Harvey Bundy.* (National Archives)

Secretary of the Navy James Forrestal in Honolulu during World War II. (National Archives)

Winston Churchill and President Truman leave Washington in March 1946 on their way to Fulton, Missouri, where Churchill delivered his "iron curtain" speech on the Soviet Communist threat. (National Archives)

George Kennan at his desk in the State Department during June 1947. (AP/Wide World)

(Above) *Secretary of State George Marshall in procession at the Harvard commencement of June 1947. It was at this ceremony that he delivered his speech inaugurating the Marshall Plan.* (Agency for International Development)

This "Design for Union Station" illustrates E. H. Harriman and his belief in one-man control of the railroads. Averell Harriman was his oldest son. (Library of Congress)

Secretary of State George Marshall administering the "Junior Marshall Plan" in 1948. (National Archives)

At a testimonial dinner honoring Henry Wallace, Paul Robeson sings while Congressman Vito Marcantonio and Wallace listen attentively. (National Archives)

The Marshall Plan in agriculture: a Nebraska Congressman (Karl Stefan), Marshall Plan chief Paul Hoffman, Ambassador Averell Harriman, and a French farmer examine an American tractor during the summer of 1948. David Bruce, not shown in this photograph, also was present. (National Archives)

"The Heart of the Ruhr": Krupp factories at Essen in 1949. (National Archives)

Jean Monnet and Robert Schuman discussing the European Coal and Steel Community. (National Archives)

(Below) An American "Globemaster" during the Berlin airlift delivers sacks of flour in 1948. (National Archives)

Italians stop work in April 1949 to join a demonstration against the signing of the Atlantic Pact. (National Archives)

"Another Stepping Stone." This cartoon depicts an American view of the creation of NATO and—in May 1950—the proposal for a European Coal and Steel Pact. (Library of Congress)

Some American officials predicted that Red China would not become a puppet of Stalin—but others considered that prediction inaccurate or, at best, irrelevant during the early 1950s. (Library of Congress)

"How Good a Golfer." Secretary of State Acheson faced some serious dilemmas even before the right-wing attacks on him began in earnest. (Library of Congress)

(Above) *Secretary of Commerce Averell Harriman swears in his old friend David Bruce as Assistant Secretary in July 1947.* (**AP/** Wide World)

After a hunt organized for the diplomatic corps, President Vincent Auriol of France admires a rare white pheasant shot by U.S. Ambassador David Bruce (wearing knickers). President Auriol was absent during the hunt because of a ministerial crisis but arrived in time for lunch. (National Archives)

Senator Joseph McCarthy at a Senate Foreign Relations subcommittee hearing to investigate his charges of communism in the State Department. McCarthy brandished photocopies of Communist newspapers as "evidence" and accused the committee of being a tool of the State Department. (National Archives)

General Douglas MacArthur receives an offical welcome on the Washington Monument grounds in April 1951 after an absence from the United States of more than fifteen years. (National Archives)

(Above) *John Foster Dulles and Averell Harriman debate U.S. foreign policy on "Pick the Winner" in September 1952, with Walter Cronkite moderating.* (CBS Photography)

McCarthy!

COME NOW, JOE — LETS BE REASONABLE!

DULLES

STATE DEPT.

McNaught Syndicate, Inc.,

REG-MANNING

This cartoon of March 1953 suggests with some exaggeration that McCarthy was a political inconvenience for whom Dulles had no sympathy. (Library of Congress)

East Berlin police struggle with a photographer after dragging him across the line dividing West and East Berlin in 1957. (National Archives)

(Below) *Chancellor Konrad Adenauer of West Germany and President Charles de Gaulle of France emerge from a Paris meeting on Franco-German relations.* (AP/Wide World)

(Above) *This 1944 cartoon shows one of Chester Bowles's difficulties in administering the price control program and wartime rationing.* (Library of Congress)

Chester Bowles speaks on rationing over the radio in 1946. (Marie Hansen, *Life* magazine © 1946 Time, Inc.)

Bowles and his family leave for India in October 1951. (National Archives)

Bowles lends a hand at the start of a road-building project in India. (AP/Wide World)

Secretary of State Dulles and Premier Jawaharlal Nehru, during a visit by the secretary to India. (National Archives)

(Below) In a scene reminiscent of World War II, French troops land at Port Faud during the Suez invasion of 1956. The invasion soon bogged down and was ended under American pressure. (AP/Wide World)

War II intervened and rescued Bruce from his passivity, as it did so many unemployed Americans, rich and poor alike.

Back in 1917, William Bullitt had refused to become a spy, thinking it no fit occupation for a gentleman. Twenty years later, that ethos had changed. American intelligence in World War II recruited through an old-boy network, favoring people whose ancestors had been gentlemen for three generations. After helping to organize the Office of Strategic Services, David Bruce went to London in 1943 as the head of U.S. espionage for Europe. He carried out his duties in a relaxed and fun-loving spirit—working with the British on sabotage operations before the Allied offensives, sharing the direction of anti-Nazi cadres in a dozen different countries. In liberated Paris, one of the first things Bruce did was to join Ernest Hemingway for champagne at the Travellers' Club and, yes, to order martinis at the Ritz Bar.

Besides his share of high jinks, World War II gave two things to Colonel Bruce: a new wife and a new career. England during the war had made fertile ground for romance, and it was there that Bruce began his private life afresh—in the consonant company of one Evangeline Bell, age twenty-eight. He was divorced from Ailsa in 1945 and, after a decent interval, married "Vangie," who bore him three children in steady succession. Meanwhile, he and an old Princeton chum, Allen Dulles, spent two years lobbying for a permanent intelligence agency. State had been too amateurish during the thirties, Bruce wrote. What we needed now was a "total" intelligence network—a system of espionage conducted through international businesses and banks—and an agency to conduct secret operations, because "although the products of clandestine operations do not constitute a complete chaplet of jewels, they are the precious gems of intelligence." With strong backing from the President, he and Dulles helped to ensure that U.S. espionage was not abandoned in peacetime, as it had been after World War I. Amid a good deal of muttering about an "American Gestapo," Congress passed a bill creating the Central Intelligence Agency in 1947.

And it was in that *annus mirabilis* of American foreign policy that David Bruce re-entered public service. Through the patronage of Secretary Harriman, he got a job at the Commerce Department and, next spring, went back to Paris as the Marshall Plan czar for France. This position called for skills that Bruce possessed in abundance: the soothing of political passions and the careful disbursement of other people's money. He never took much interest in public relations. News reports about Bruce, Harriman, and a Nebraska congressman tramping around a French farm one morning to dramatize the need for tractors may have done something good for Franco-American friendship, but Bruce did better at insider's work. During his time in Paris, he saw about ten French cabinets collapse. His endless chore was to buttress the political center, considered relatively pro-American, and work closely with whoever was running it.

We have seen what a good job Bruce made of the Marshall Plan—so good that in 1949 Dean Acheson appointed him Ambassador to France, providing new scope for one of his talents: the giving of, and going to, dinner parties and balls. In the best Bullitt tradition, Ambassador Bruce used such occasions for greasing the diplomatic wheels, for staying in touch with every element of the upper crust. Beautiful, energetic, dependable, fluent in several languages, and possessed of a brilliant sartorial flair, his new wife made a suitable aide-de-camp. At a charity masquerade, the two of them showed up dressed as the Knave and Queen of Spades; and Bruce himself, usually bland in secret talks, had a social panache that sometimes dazzled French officials. Clad in a pair of knickers, he went out on a hunt at the French president's estate and killed a record ninety-nine pheasants.[26] He could discourse learnedly on antique furniture, porcelain, and wine. The French proved as ready as some of Bruce's own countrymen to accept him as something rare and special, one of the semi-precious gems of North American semi-civilization.

With an economic recovery under way in France, Ambassador Bruce turned to a task that had been on his mind since a courier trip from Venice to Constantinople in 1919. "The fragmentation of Europe, instanced after the First World War, for example, by the division of the Austro-Hungarian Empire, makes it as uncoordinated as were the Italian City States before a United Italy came into being," he explained to Harriman in March 1950. One month later, he told Acheson that Americans must press for political-economic unity at the May meeting of the North Atlantic Alliance; on the issue of integration, Europeans still were looking to the New World for leadership.

David Bruce deserves recognition as a midwife of the European Coal and Steel Community, which is what emerged from the Schuman Plan. While America stayed officially neutral, Bruce's influence made a difference in the year of negotiations. The U.S. High Commissioner in Germany, John McCloy, worked on the problem with Konrad Adenauer, but Ambassador Bruce in France was better situated to make things happen. Since Monnet was a delegate to the Schuman Plan discussions in Paris, Bruce could always chat with him, get the lowdown, and report it back to Washington. He presented the American view on price flexibility and tariff reform. And pressure from Bruce helped to strengthen the new "European High Authority," so that it had enough power to make unpopular decisions.

The Korean War did much to concentrate West European minds. In the final analysis, though, it was a French-German-American agreement on fundamental issues that brought about such a satisfactory result. The treaty for a European Coal and Steel Community was initialed in early 1951 and ratified eventually by six European parliaments. Jean Monnet had persuaded Bruce that he should keep the European Army separate from economic matters, not mixing the problem of guns with that of butter. Still, it may have been the success of his economic arrangements that made Bruce keep pushing for military integration. Now anything seemed possible in the long, march toward demi-continental unity.[27]

When Bruce went back to America in 1952, he found himself covered with a limited sort of glory. At any rate, his fame throughout Europe and Georgetown was secure. And if most Americans had never heard of David Bruce, that only made him more acceptable to the right people of Washington.

At the same time, Bruce discovered the "wrong" people of

Washington waging a separate war against communism—entering the last throes of a witch-hunt that surpassed even the Red Scare of 1919. Partly the revenge of defeated isolationists, the latest Red Scare flowed out of several currents, one of them a deep partisan resentment over twenty years of rule by the Democrats. Many Republicans found it easy to believe that foreign countries had been lost to communism because of Democratic treason. Always ahead of his time, Bill Bullitt had warned Congress in 1947 that the Communists were trying to subvert the United States—"I am perfectly certain that a time will come, and it may be close at hand, when it will be essential to our national safety to break up this criminal conspiracy, which is world wide." He jacked things up one year later, saying America's diplomatic troubles were caused by Communist sympathizers at the highest level. The New Deal had brought them into public office, and "the State Department and the Foreign Service are still rancid with those men."

We have noted how the effect of Red China and the Soviet A-Bomb made the Democrats toe a harder line. Well, it was not hard enough. The unmasking of some genuine Communist spies set the stage in 1950 for a political inquisition. Senator Joe McCarthy announced that he knew of eighty-one, or fifty-seven, or over two hundred Communists—the number varied—who were still working at State. William Bullitt felt a bit taken aback by this announcement. "It is not necessary to conclude that our Department of State is filled with Soviet agents," he said to a group of Yale undergraduates. But it was too late. The fat was in the fire, and for another three years State was spattered by a constant barrage of accusations. Strangely inarticulate in its own defense, the Truman administration heard itself described in the U.S. Senate as a "crazy assortment of collectivist cutthroat crackpots and Communist fellow-traveling appeasers." The same senator, warming to his theme, asserted that the U.S. government was "a military dictatorship, run by Communist-appeasing, Communist-protecting betrayer of America, Secretary of State Dean Acheson!"

Why Acheson had taken rank as the right wing's worst enemy is not hard to figure out, for a major theme of McCarthysim was social class resentment. The Groton-Yale network served a useful purpose for the Secretary of State; but so many U.S. diplomats seemed to share his educational background, his Eurocentricity, that other people had come to resent it.[28] And it is true that certain liberals, once the self-styled enemies of snobbery, were showing a trace or two of hauteur themselves. A "cheapskate, and almost unbelievable cad" was David Bruce's private opinion of Joe McCarthy; and in response to the crazy charges from Congress, Acheson allowed his public arrogance to expand—sometimes taunting politicians for their crude opportunism. Once at a meeting on Capitol Hill, he jumped up and told a senator to stop shaking his "dirty finger in my face." Many Americans suspected that Secretary Acheson thought them dirty, and they may have been right.

To the bitterness of class resentment was added a more tangible cause for complaint—namely, a severe setback in the Korean War, which is what gave Joe McCarthy his national appeal and momentum. So long as the war went smoothly, Congress had been unified behind the President's policies in Korea. Then after Red China entered the war in late 1950, forcing General MacArthur into a disastrous retreat, Republican support on Capitol Hill faded away as well. Inevitably, Senator McCarthy said that Democratic treason had caused the military debacle. And MacArthur complained to journalists that it was Truman's refusal to wage an all-out war that made the U.S. Army's mission so difficult. Orders from Washington to stabilize a battle line, to confine all combat operations to Korea, were an insufferable restraint. We must seek total victory by an assault on mainland China.

Such criticism of Truman found a ready audience among conservatives, for whom Douglas MacArthur was a long-standing hero. At the same time, MacArthur's public dissent and his connivance with the congressional opposition could not long have been tolerated by any administration. In April 1951, the President's "War Cabinet" recommended that MacArthur be fired, which was done forthwith. Amidst another outburst of GOP anger and recrimination, MacArthur came home to a Caesar's welcome and President Truman saw his popularity sink to a new low.

The Democratic Party was in bad shape politically and the

Republicans well situated to capture the White House in 1952. When Truman started looking for a way out of his troubles, not for the first time did his eye fall on another general, Dwight D. Eisenhower. He did not exactly know what General Eisenhower's politics were. No one knew. But Eisenhower did support the President's foreign policy, and so immense was his fame coming out of World War II that Truman had been trying for years to persuade him to join the Democrats; after "Ike" was made Supreme Commander of NATO in 1950, his relations with Bruce, Harriman, and the President had grown fairly close. So in the summer of 1951, when non-partisan Eisenhower-for-President clubs started springing up, Truman made one last effort to get him on a Democratic ticket. Still it was no go. Refusing even to say what party he supported, Eisenhower went about his work for NATO. Not until nine months before the 1952 election did Ike announce, from his NATO headquarters in Paris, that he would run for President—out of a sense of soldierly duty, and as a Republican.

Under these circumstances, it is perhaps not surprising that Eisenhower had some trouble winning the Republican nomination. It was a very narrow squeeze for him at the GOP convention. But win it he did, and from then on his political fortunes were not in serious doubt. Eisenhower defeated Governor Adlai Stevenson with 55 percent of the vote, bringing in enough "other" Republicans to take control of the Congress in 1953.

Eisenhower's victory meant an incomplete victory for conservatives. If the Democrats were out, conservatives were not entirely in. While the new President backed them up on domestic issues, nothing much had happened to change his view of foreign affairs, where he differed little from President Truman. The Republican platform of 1952 condemned "containment," demanding a more aggressive effort to "roll back" communism. On the other hand, General Eisenhower was a latecomer to the Cold War. In common with the NATO Allies, he objected to talk of liberating Eastern Europe by force and he wanted military restraint in the Far East. So except for a cut in defense expenditures—due largely to a winding down of the Korean War—little of substance was changed in American policy.

The Republicans on Capitol Hill, of course, demanded some tougher rhetoric and a few symbolic changes. Eisenhower had promised on the hustings to banish "any kind of Communistic, subversive or pinkish influence" from government. Suitable scapegoats had to be found right away. The task of purging left-wing degeneracy from State was given to an FBI agent who, as *Time* magazine reported, "fired 24 homosexuals in his first three weeks on the job"—a source of deep happiness to people like Bullitt, who saw the Foreign Service in general as a pack of pro-Communist snobs and liberal fops.

More important to the historian are those whom Dwight Eisenhower hired. To his top diplomatic posts—Ambassador to the United Nations and Secretary of State—he appointed Senator Henry Cabot Lodge, Jr., and John Foster Dulles. Foster Dulles's brother, Allen, was promoted to head the Central Intelligence Agency. All three of them were foreign policy liberals and Europeanist by inclination.[29] For seven years, off and on, Foster Dulles had worked at the highest levels of State, an informal representative from the GOP and a symbol of bipartisan diplomacy after World War II.

The Dulles brothers had grown up in a mixture of two worlds, one of rural piety, and another of politics and European travel. Their father was a Presbyterian minister, their maternal grandfather a Secretary of State. After graduating at the top of his Princeton class in 1908, Foster Dulles had gone on rising in the world of international finance and law. When his uncle, Robert Lansing, became Woodrow Wilson's Secretary of State, young Foster started doing part-time work for the Department in Central America. And four years later he was made a delegate to the Paris Peace Conference.

While lacking the zeal of a William Bullitt, John Foster Dulles had supported President Wilson's war program. He understood the need for a conciliatory peace with Germany, and he wanted all European debts to America forgiven. Wilson had no objection to giving Dulles a key role at the conference, having known about the young man even at Princeton. A counterpart to Keynes on the British delegation, Dulles became in effect the chief U.S. negotiator on war reparations. Of course, the Anglo-American liberals failed to limit the reparations payments required of Germany, but Dulles remained optimistic about the Versailles Treaty. He thought it should be ratified and published a short rebuttal of Keynes's denunciatory book on the Paris Conference. "Your letter to the 'Times' was the first serious and responsible criticism with which I have had to deal," wrote Keynes to Dulles soon after, "and I entirely appreciated, as I hope I made clear in my reply, the reasonableness of the standpoint from which it was written. I fancy we agree pretty much at heart about what happened in Paris."[30]

What made Dulles more hopeful was his feeling that the treaty terms could be watered down—and that private businesses and banks would recycle enough dollars to keep Germany afloat and North Atlantic commerce moving. The problem of German reparations to Europe, and of European debts to America, could be circumvented by more U.S. loans and by an ever-expanding world economy. Working with his brother at the Wall Street firm of Sullivan & Cromwell, Foster Dulles was deeply involved in arranging those loans to Europe for American financiers. It was a futile, inflationary effort, as he discovered, and foolish from a business standpoint. With the onset of the Great Depression, world trade slowed down, billions of dollars in debt went unpaid, and some of Dulles's clients went under.

So Dulles traveled the same route as his friend Averell Harriman, one of Sullivan & Cromwell's best clients. Both of them had felt unsure of their politics during the 1920s, and they ended up in different parties. But by World War II both wanted a refurbished Wilsonian program—not as political theorists so much as financiers seeking a solution to the problems of their daily work. Already Harriman respected Dulles's grasp of international issues and the two agreed on basic principles, Dulles finding a niche for himself in the "internationalist" wing of the GOP. He was a liberal Republican much like Colonel Henry Stimson, typical of internationalist liberals in almost every sense but party membership.

Dulles lost his bearings briefly during World War II. While taking no direct part in government, he gave firm support to the United Nations before church groups—invoking the example of Wilson and the Founding Fathers as models for mankind. "Our nation was designed to help others," said he; "the founders of our nation dedicated us to show how men might organize a good society." Nation-states could be federated as the United States had been, and Americans should assert their "moral leadership in the world." Leadership and power would be good for U.S. citizens, forcing them to examine their consciences and purify their souls.

Postwar politics proved a lot less high-minded. As early as 1945, Dulles had begun to serve as the GOP's representative at the State Department, and he went on doing so for most of Truman's presidency—until just before the 1952 election, that is, when he jumped like General Eisenhower into the political fray. Suddenly Dulles got all steamed up about treason at State, about Democratic blunders in the Far East, about the need to liberate Communist countries. At one point in the campaign, he had a knock-down, drag-out TV debate with Harriman and became a bit personal, needling his opponent for not inviting Dean Acheson to the Democratic Party Convention.

> DULLES: In 1944 and 1948, you boasted about your Secretary of State! This time you did all you could to forget him. Why—if his policies are so perfect and fine?
>
> HARRIMAN: Well, that is a matter which has nothing to do with policies. I did not—
>
> DULLES: Why, if you were so proud—
>
> HARRIMAN: I *have* been proud of the action of the Secretary of State.
>
> DULLES: Why didn't you bring him to Chicago and show him—
>
> HARRIMAN: *You* showed some people that weren't a very great credit to the Republican Party!

The exchange left each of them panting with indignation—it was all Walter Cronkite could do to compose them—yet what must be remembered is that this was a family squabble. Even in

1952, Harriman recalls, "We were friends, so there wasn't any bitterness. This wasn't like my debating someone that I disliked. I had a personal, warm feeling for Foster." The brothers Dulles had been so long involved professionally with the Harriman-Lovett-Bruce coterie that one cannot take their quarrel very seriously. Foster had worked for them, they had worked for him. They had praised each other's speeches and articles, they found jobs for each other's friends. They belonged to the same clubs—like the Century Club and the Council on Foreign Relations—having helped each other to get in. None of this social network started to unravel until the Korean War, and then only for superficial, partisan reasons.[31]

President Eisenhower took office deeply worried about a resurgence of Republican isolationism and hostility toward the Western Allies. The isolationist impulse of many Republicans—as in the past—was taking the form of a desire to act alone in the Far East, and to ignore Europe. One great task for the new President and Dulles was to teach something new to the GOP: that an activist and collectivist policy in Western Europe did not have to go with liberal activism at home. On the whole, they succeeded in teaching that lesson.

Thus Eisenhower and Dulles found it natural to follow a liberal, bipartisan policy abroad—especially when it came to West Germany and the Atlantic Alliance. Their credentials as Europeanists were impeccable. Dulles had been among the first to urge a revival of West German industry; he had worked closely with the Democrats on the Berlin airlift and NATO; and now he wanted to incorporate German soldiers into a European Army. Somehow Eisenhower, too, had been persuaded that a European Army made good military sense. The President thought that NATO was in need of something flashy, that "there is going to be no real progress toward greater unification of Europe except through the medium of specific programs of this kind."

The European Army program had bogged down badly during 1952. The treaty text had been agreed upon, but not ratified, by six countries of Europe. Few American diplomats really knew much about it. So one of the new Secretary's first actions was to recruit David Bruce to put the project back on track. Republican politicians could find nothing wrong with Ambassador Bruce, and his appointment would show the allies that America still meant business about the European "six-country movement." Dulles and Bruce had first met during the 1920s at a New York wine auction; they had played tennis together and kept in touch through brother Allen. Though Bruce was on vacation when Dulles first contacted him—shooting wild turkeys in South Carolina—he agreed to cut it short, to leave right away for Europe, and to set up a special mission in Paris.

Right after Bruce arrived at his new post, a news flash came in from Moscow. "The heart of the inspired continuer of Lenin's will, the wise leader and teacher of the Communist Party and Soviet people—Joseph Vissarionovich Stalin—has stopped beating." The old tyrant was dead. A collective sigh of relief was emitted from Eastern and Western Europe, and followed a few months later by an armistice in Korea. A series of Soviet and American "peace offensives" were launched—culminating in the mini-détente of 1955, when Eisenhower held a summit meeting with the new Soviet leaders. All of these developments had the effect of making Bruce's assignment harder, of diminishing Western Europe's fear of Soviet power. Perhaps further rearmament would not be necessary. The more Bruce warned against complacency, the more he urged haste, the less Europeans seemed to care about military organization or deterrence.

Even before Bruce had returned to Washington—in early 1952—French resistance to the European Army had been strengthening. Now it was almost unstoppable. Few French citizens wanted military unity for the region, especially when political unity came as part of the package. Plans for a European Army were submitted under duress and did not include the British. They meant a surrender of national sovereignty that was repugnant to General de Gaulle, who spoke for at least one third of his nation. Moreover, France still suffered from material and financial troubles. While the war in Indochina dragged on, a bigger war in Korea also had hurt the European economies— reigniting inflation and dampening economic growth. Lately things had picked up again, but the French people continued to feel pessimistic and resentful.

It was all quite frustrating for David Bruce, and for his *idée fixe* on continental unity as the bulwark of Western civilization. To Washington he wrote that the Anglo-Saxons must "bring this wayward, unreflecting, illogical neighbor to a sense of its responsibilities if it expects to share with them the prestige as well as the burden of leadership in the free world." France was getting on his nerves. He told the State Department to try making some sort of private threat—to warn that we might cut off military aid to France, move closer to England and Germany, or maybe even retreat to Fortress America. That was bad advice, for anti-Americanism was on the rise everywhere. Such warnings were taken as a stupid bluff in France, or else an irritating reminder of accomplished facts.

Indeed, by late 1953 Ambassador Bruce already was getting cosier with Chancellor Konrad Adenauer of West Germany, who generally remained more open to his influence. Meanwhile, in Paris, there was taking place "the greatest ideological and political debate France has known since the Dreyfus affair," as one Left Bank pundit wrote. The French left and right were growing stronger, the "Europeanist" center much weaker. Violent passions were directed against Jean Monnet, considered the chief conduit of Europeanism in France. And David Bruce became a target for the French press and parliament, where he was accused of plotting among politicians to win more votes for the European Army.

Just when things came to a head in 1954, when it seemed that the French parliament might finally vote yes or no, the government fell and a new premier emerged: Pierre Mendès-France. Probably the most able politician of the Fourth Republic era, Mendès-France came to power promising to disentangle France from the Indochina war—an awesome feat of legerdemain that he managed to perform in less than one month.[32] That vexed question having been settled, he promised that within another month he would bring the European Army treaty to a vote. He was coming under pressure to do so in the most exalted quarters, from the West German government to Eisenhower and

Churchill. European statesmen held frantic meetings late into the night, even as David Bruce went into a final frenzy of lobbying and intrigue, making vehement accusations against Mendès-France. At last, in August 1954, the European Army treaty was put before the French parliament and rejected—decisively.

The rejection of the treaty came in a tumultuous session. At the end of it, a group of deputies jumped up to sing the *Marseillaise*. But David Bruce took his defeat with feelings of horror and dismay. As he put it to Secretary Dulles, this "neurotic" decision was "a major tragedy for the true interests of the West, and especially for those of France." Soon thereafter, Bruce resigned his position and an equally disheartened Monnet announced that he was stepping down as head of the High Authority for Coal and Steel. European unity and the Europeanists seemed, once again, to have run aground.

Actually, things looked a great deal worse than they were. All that had happened, really, was that Europe had declared its greater independence from America—and from such proconsuls as David Bruce—making it plain that any further moves toward unity would have to originate in Europe itself. America's behavior had led to some needless confrontations. Under pressure from the congressional right wing, the Eisenhower-Dulles-Bruce policies lacked the balance and subtlety of the Marshall Plan era. Even as their power in Western Europe declined, the more rigid and demanding U.S. diplomats became. It had been hard enough to change Europe in the late 1940s, but by now Europeans had recovered sufficiently to reassert their national prides and a clash with America was bound to occur. Except in West Germany, the heyday of U.S. influence on the continent had drawn to a close.

France had rejected the European Army. But its politicians proved ready to keep on moving toward economic integration. This could be done without much loss of national sovereignty, and the mid-1950s affluence also helped to encourage an attitudinal change. By 1955, the economic boom was again at full tilt in Central Europe and northern Italy, while the ground was being prepared for a similar expansion in France. Growth rates returned close to their 1949–50 levels; Europe was regaining its pre-eminence in world trade. Populations were rising, living standards were improving, and an American-style bourgeoisie was emerging in the Old World. Amid such unexampled prosperity, Europeans found free trade and economic adjustment relatively easy to accept.

One sign of changing attitudes was the formation of a customs union called the "Common Market." No progress had occurred on this front during the European Army furor, but in 1955 a new spurt of activity began. Jean Monnet spent several months traveling around the continent, urging politicians to "relaunch the European idea by extending the attributions of the Coal and Steel Community." Soon a conference was convened to work on a tariff-cutting program. Though it dragged a bit at first, the Soviet invasion of Hungary in 1956 helped give new impetus to Monnet's idea. A treaty was completed and ratified the following year—establishing a European Commission in Brussels, with the power to draft new economic treaties and work toward a closer contract and customs union. In 1958, the convertibility of West European currencies was achieved and the European Economic Community—or Common Market—came into being.

As for military unity, that turned out to have been a phony problem. After all, a multinational force made no sense from the professional soldiers' point of view. The Pentagon never had liked the European Army, always preferring separate armed forces for each country. Ten years after World War II, fears of German militarism were subsiding and France was ready to accept Germany into regular NATO membership. The Germans could have their own army, just so long as a few legal safeguards were provided—such as a British and American agreement not to withdraw soldiers from the continent.[33] Overcoming strong Communist pressure, Mendès-France won approval for this solution in the French parliament and, during 1955, the German Federal Republic obtained its full sovereignty and admission to the North Atlantic Alliance.

Rich and dynamic though they were, the West Germans suffered from an intense diplomatic and political *angst*. The East German regime was conducting a campaign of massive espio-

Delian League that would include the USA and Canada. Perhaps liberal snobbery was maturing into something more serious, something akin to simple arrogance.

The Grand Design for a North Atlantic cosmopolis was unworkable, in any case. What doomed it to immediate failure was the restoration to power of Charles de Gaulle. The French Fourth Republic had fallen from ineptitude and immobilism to outright decadence. The Algerian struggle for independence from France had so split the French polity that by 1958 a civil war seemed imminent, or perhaps a military coup d'état. Just back from a visit to Paris, Bill Bullitt reported to Secretary Dulles that "conditions there were deplorable. The Government was rotten from top to bottom and it would continue to be this way until there is some strong action. He felt that de Gaulle was about the only hope." de Gaulle had resigned the French presidency in 1946 because he wanted a constitution with a stronger chief executive. This time he would get what he wanted. The general gave notice that if he returned to clean up the mess, then he must have sufficient power over parliament. In 1958, he initiated steps toward a Fifth Republic and proceeded to govern France by a kind of plebiscitarian Caesarism.

Charles de Gaulle had mellowed a bit while in retirement—sometimes likening himself to Napoleon, and yet adjusting to certain twentieth-century realities. He came to accept that France's empire must be dissolved and the Communists treated as enemies, at least for a while. Nor did he object to European economic and "cultural" unity, except to insist that it should rotate around a Franco-German axis under his domination.

To some extent this was an arrangement he inherited. The German Federal Republic was making an ideal husband for France—providing most of the money, while treating France as a senior partner. It was a modern, bourgeois marriage in that respect. Then, after de Gaulle's restoration, it took on some old-fashioned characteristics. Konrad Adenauer believed in personal ties to other statesmen, and he had much in common with the new French president: his Roman Catholicism, his autocratic temperament, his patrician disdain for the common herd. De Gaulle once said that when he walked among German crowds, he felt the same sense of mystical communion as among the cattle and peasantry of his own French village—a remark that must have pleased Adenauer no end. He loved it when de Gaulle spoke of a Paris-Bonn alliance that would exclude certain Anglo-American influences from the continent. To the old chancellor, this sense of personal communion with France's chief seemed the fulfillment of a dream for Western Europe and Germany.

Other Germans knew that President de Gaulle was not being so nice out of a sense of Christian charity. He had his own reasons for buttering up this eighty-year-old man, who had grown rather senile and sentimental about France. Adenauer, for example, felt profoundly reassured when de Gaulle did not pull out of the Common Market in 1958. But de Gaulle chose to maintain the European customs union largely because it gave a great advantage to his peasantry—protecting French farmers from overseas competition. More important, the French president wanted to maintain his country's position in Western Europe. Although Germany had a larger industrial base, he meant to keep the upper hand for France in such spheres as agriculture and politico-military power. In his first five years as president, de Gaulle withdrew French naval and air squadrons and many of his troops from the unified NATO command; he also extruded American atomic bombs from France, while pushing his own nuclear weapons program. All of this went against a fundamental policy of Adenauer, who had been one of NATO's most enthusiastic backers.

A bigger disappointment was in store for the backers of political unification. De Gaulle's continental strategy was to prevent any European grouping in which France would have its influence diluted—losing its room for independent maneuver or its sense of national identity. It followed that all new applicants must be kept out of the Common Market. This might not have mattered to France's neighbor across the English Channel. But HM government of Great Britain—after experiencing a further decline of empire and ten years of economic decay—was finding Western Europe's gravitational pull too strong. In an uncharacteristic burst of initiative, Prime Minister Harold Macmillan applied to join the customs union in 1961. The president of France at first seemed to encourage Macmillan's suit. Then, in January 1963, he rejected it, at the same time making it clear that he would allow no further steps toward the political unification of Europe.

De Gaulle's self-assertion did him no harm whatever at home. The French hated the idea of foreign troops or weaponry on their soil; they still had no use for political unity in Western Europe. And attitudes elsewhere on the continent were not so different. The smaller countries of Europe had wanted England in the club—thus to obtain a larger market for their goods and another country to weaken the Franco-German hegemony. However, many Europeans took an adolescent satisfaction from provoking the U.S. powers that be. Great Britain had applied to join the Common Market partly at the urging of the Kennedy administration, transmitted through Under Secretary of State George Ball and Ambassador to England David Bruce. "The inability of nations to compose their differences constitutes a disharmony that would be insufferable to any art-loving audience," complained Ambassador Bruce a few years before—and it is clear that he considered France's conduct, if not insufferable, then damned annoying. He could not forebear to express his feelings about Charles de Gaulle, referring in private to "the General's fulminations," his "parochial comments," his "bad manners," and his "bad style."[34]

Bruce confined such opinions to secret exchanges and correspondence, advising the White House always to deal politely with France. Unfortunately, his annoyance found a public echo in the New York–Washington press, which in those days generally supported U.S. foreign policy. A harsh chorus of objection issued forth from its editorial pages. Columnists demanded to know what this haughty general was trying to do anyway, making so much trouble for England and upsetting the President's best-laid plans.

The ritornello came at a Paris press conference in mid-1963. There stood Charles de Gaulle, all six feet eight of him, with an eighteenth-century elegance and aplomb that no transatlantic diplomat could equal. He opened with a put-down of editorial writers.

"After my personal experience of nearly twenty-five years of public reactions in the United States, I am hardly surprised by the ups and downs of what it is customary there to call opinion. But, all the same, I must confess that recently the tone and the song, as regards France, have seemed rather excessive to me." Such was the song I heard when I formed a provisional government in Algiers during the war, when I denounced the European Army ten years later, and now again when I express my disapproval of political integration.

Nevertheless: "This agitation by the press, political circles, and more or less semi-official bodies—which rages on the other side of the Atlantic, and which naturally finds a ready echo in the various sorts of unconditional opponents—all this agitation, I say, cannot alter in France what is fundamental as regards America. For us, the fundamental factors of Franco-American relations are friendship and alliance."

The friendship of France and the United States has existed for two centuries, observed de Gaulle—"since the days of Washington and Franklin, of Lafayette, of de Grasse, of Rochambeau." And the Atlantic Alliance must be upheld in the face of a continued Soviet threat. On the other hand, France under my leadership is ready to declare its own independence anew, and to reject "the project for a so-called supranational Europe, in which France as such would have disappeared, except to pay and to orate; a Europe governed in appearance by anonymous, technocratic, and stateless committees; in other words, a Europe without political reality, without economic drive, without a capacity for defense, and therefore doomed, in the face of the Soviet bloc, to being nothing more than a dependent of that great Western power which itself had a policy, an economy, and a defense—the United States of America."

President de Gaulle's message to Washington derived from one of his several pet theories—*viz.* that only a sense of nationhood gave people the vital *élan* for economic growth and an effective defense. Therefore, the French could be good allies of America only as the citizens of a sovereign nation-state. In a denationalized union of countries, Europeans would be dominated by the

United States; and under American command, their willpower would desert them. Be it carefully noted that de Gaulle's concept of nationhood was quite narrow, involving distinct races and national cultures and traditions. The United States confused him because, although not really a nation, it somehow acted like one. But his argument had a certain validity in the context of Europe, where cultural and racial antagonism between countries still ran high.

That is the very best that can be said of de Gaulle's diplomacy, which otherwise comprised no more than a blend of hypocrisy and illusion. Some bad diplomatic habits did develop elsewhere in Western Europe—of America always demanding greater effort from its NATO Allies, while its NATO Allies resisted.[35] On the other hand, President de Gaulle tended to make this bad situation even worse. Behind his rhetoric against Anglo-American hegemony lay his own ambition to have France dominate the region. He believed that when nations do come into existence, they often are created by a central "federator" state, and that if a European federator could be found—say, France—then even Western Europe might become a single nation. Of course, France was too small to play such a federating role. De Gaulle's efforts in that direction only muddied the problem, turning Europe's political unification by consensus, already a difficult undertaking, into an impossibility.

France, however small, could not be ignored. By late 1963, President Kennedy had been assassinated, Macmillan and Adenauer had resigned, and France entered a long economic boom. Gaullism seemed to have a veto on the continent. Unable to adjust to their own reduced influence, some Americans went on pushing old ideas to a utopian extreme. Although his shining moment in the Kennedy administration was spent as Ambassador to England, David Bruce took a proprietary interest in continental matters. So when de Gaulle pulled all French forces out of the unified NATO command in 1966, that really came as the final straw. Bruce went so far as to fulminate in public—describing the French pullout as "illogically reckless." Other NATO members must be careful to keep "burnished and sharp the shield and sword that have served us so well."

With or without de Gaulle, one can see how by 1963 American diplomacy toward Europe was falling into a state of slow petrification. Like David Bruce himself—a lifeless adornment on a sterile policy—U.S. diplomats glittered and were worth a lot of money. And they managed to have a pleasant time of it, too. But the reader should remember above all that their stodginess brought no harm to the continent. No matter how rigid and unimaginative, the United States did keep the peace. During the palmy days of Eisenhower and Kennedy, little was needed from America besides its military might: a burnished shield facing east, behind which European prosperity could grow and European democracy could flourish. New ideas and mental effort did not count for so much as good manners and good style. Hardly surprising that Ambassador Bruce subsisted happily in England for eight unproductive years.

Sometimes even a vigorous man will slip into pomposity late in life, but a number of Bruce's friends were trying to avoid that human tendency. Old in years, they felt young at heart. It was an impulse felt most notably by certain Democratic politicians, like Governors Adlai Stevenson, Averell Harriman, and Chester Bowles. These activists had no interest in doing nothing in Europe, where the great liberal enterprise had so little room left for maneuver. Along with some young intellectuals and technocrats in their party, they started moving into a political wasteland called the underdeveloped, or "third," world. In the starving tropics and subtropics, opportunities for yet another New Deal appeared similar to those of Europe in the 1940s. Here was a place where they could distance themselves from the GOP—a place where Republican passivity seemed as foolish as before World War II, and where many Democrats scented new grist for the liberal mill.

VI

Triumphalism

1950–1963

Along the western coast of India are many villages of a kind common to tropical countries—poor, illiterate, and isolated from the modern world. But if the reader had lived in one of them during 1952, he might have seen an uncommon sight one day, the sight of an advertising tycoon from Connecticut helping a turbaned fisherman to haul in his net. It was the American Ambassador to India, Chester Bowles.

This is the story of the great war that Chester Bowles fought single-handed, through the lobbies and offices of the big American Democratic Party. Adlai Stevenson, twice a nominee for President, helped him. And Averell Harriman, a moderate liberal, who never comes all-out for Third World diplomacy but always creeps around by the wall, gave him advice. But Chester Bowles did the real fighting.

Chester's family sprang from a tribe of Republican mugwumps, which is an animal that flourished in New England after the Civil War—progressive, reformist, and disdainful of party loyalty. His eyes were brown but his skin very white. He was a cuddly, pear-shaped creature with a warm, generous smile. And his war cry, as he scuttled through the long grass of three continents, was: *Down with colonialism and exploitation!*

His life began quietly in a Unitarian clapboard house near where hundreds of Bowleses had lived for two centuries. His grandfather, Samuel Bowles, had been a friend of Henry Adams

and editor-in-chief of the Springfield *Republican*—an anti-imperialist, muckraking newspaper that was famous in the post-Civil
War era. Young Chester read old copies of it and decided, then
and there, to be a writer for the paper when he grew up. In 1916,
he felt the same uncertainty about World War I as did the *New
Republic* crowd. But when he heard Woodrow Wilson speak in
New York, he thrilled to the President's liberal oratory. At his
prep school in Connecticut, he became utterly devoted to Wilson's Fourteen Points and "I followed his crusade for the
League with great interest and fascination." From school
Bowles went on to four years at Yale University, then from Yale
to his job at the Springfield *Republican.*

So far, so good. That pattern was a standard one for many
New Liberals coming out of World War I. Bowles's metier as a
journalist was in the best Progressive tradition, his private
school education in perfect taste. Even so, there did exist some
crucial deviations from the norm. His family barely could afford
to send him to boarding school. He had to help pay his way
through Yale by working as a clerk. He did not attend Yale
College but went instead to the Scientific School. These differences counted for a lot in those days. What they tend to suggest
is that Bowles did not belong to any social or intellectual elite.
Where other liberals had repudiated snobbery, he came close to
being a social outsider at Yale—and certainly he left college
feeling quite poorly educated. Worried about the quality of his
unclassical training, he would spend the rest of his life trying to
make up for it.

Bowles quit after a year at the Springfield *Republican,* finding
that the paper had grown almost as stodgy and conservative as
the United States. In his Yale Class of 1924, he had met no
companions in his liberalism: only about thirty classmates
"would admit to being Democrats, and they were largely from
the South." Forced to support his family, he took a job on
Madison Avenue writing ad copy and then, just before the crash
of '29, set up an advertising agency of his own. The corporations
were desperate for any new marketing idea, so while millionaires
went bankrupt around him, Chester Bowles saw his tiny business
expand. He had at least a million dollars himself by the time the

Great Depression bottomed out. College classmates who had gone to work on Wall Street were begging him for a loan.

Along with riches came other new experiences for Bowles. He undertook methodically to improve his mind, devoting one year apiece to every facet of "each major country." He cultivated an enthusiasm for "modern art." He went to "symphonies" three times a week. And in the course of doing door-to-door market research, he encountered hundreds of improverished families— "I can still see vividly the weary husbands returning home from another fruitless day of job hunting with a look of stark fear and hopelessness in their eyes." Bowles accordingly gave his political support to President Franklin D. Roosevelt. However, his writings show a much deeper admiration for President Roosevelt's wife—"a spectacular lady"—whom he felt privileged to meet soon after her husband took office.

Mrs. Franklin D. Roosevelt, First Lady of the New Deal, with whom the reader is acquainted, was becoming a national figure in her own right. A political icon of that kind almost unique to American womanhood, she appealed to certain popular American notions. That men are rough brutes, and it takes a woman's touch to bring out their sensitivity. That men are confused and weak creatures, who must be stiffened by a sure-footed female. That women are superior beings, the guardians of the national conscience. Pandered to in the TV soap operas, these are notions that still run deep in American bourgeois culture.

Perhaps it was his admiration for women that made Bowles so effective at flogging soap. He knew by instinct what women wanted, and he thought it good. He had worshipped his mother and, as a schoolboy, learned about politics from his Aunt Ruth—a pacifist, a socialist, one of the earliest agitators for civil rights. Some of these special qualities were reflected in the character of his second wife. Bowles worked himself into an emotional collapse during the 1930s, until finally a strong woman came in and straightened his life out. Soon he and "Steb" were starting up a new family and reading the great books together. A social worker out of New England, Steb was to become an active partner in all that Bowles did, "while also serving in several difficult situations as my conscience."

Mrs. Roosevelt and Steb of course encouraged Chester Bowles to get involved in public affairs. But by the time of Pearl Harbor, his chief political entanglement was his directorship of America First, an isolationist group that opposed America's drift toward war. Bowles wanted no truck with the Europeans because American intervention would mean American support for their immoral empires. The United States should wait for Adolf Hitler to play himself out and then pick up the pieces. "We have already spent enough on the Second World War (in assistance to Britain, France, and the U.S.S.R.) to clear away all our slums, build millions of homes, new schoolhouses, new parks and new buildings, dramatically to raise our health standards and to send hundreds of thousands of our young people to college." There must be no further military spending—for "we cannot guarantee the future of our civilization behind a barricade of armaments, nor can we establish world democracy with the sword."

A historian has to look at people whole. Chester Bowles's view of world affairs may have been a little naive—yet it went with a managerial flair, a generosity, and a patriotism that one cannot help admiring. Maybe that mix of virtues is what was needed in the chief of America's price control office during World War II. Starting in 1943, Bowles served as head of the wartime anti-inflation program, which set the price of every product in the United States from machine tools to hemorrhoid soothers.

Like the *New Republic* liberals of 1917, Bowles regarded the war as an opportunity for government-imposed reform. His assignment was to stop inflation or any repetition of World War I profiteering. The first of his reforms he imposed on the price control bureaucracy itself. Moving people out of Washington to agencies in "the field," he instilled a higher sense of morale into his troops. He revamped the regulations, attacked the special interest groups, and made a series of radio broadcasts—attempting to put across wage-price controls by persuasion rather than force.[36]

Meanwhile, price controls were not enough to absorb his tremendous energy. Worried that the war might end in an economic slump, Bowles spent many long hours with Mrs. Roosevelt discussing what the Democratic Party platform should be. Both of them urged the President to seek a new mandate in the 1944 election—an economic Bill of Rights, promising everyone a good education, good housing, good medical care, a good job or a good business, and a good pension. Month by month, each right could be made the law of the land, and eventually the entire program could be written into the U.S. Constitution. In the event, President Roosevelt did not propose any new legislation. He did not even want to campaign actively during 1944. The First Lady got him out of his wheelchair, Bowles remembers, and she "persuaded him to put on the leg brace that he had not worn for several years and learn to walk again." But the brace did not work effectively and, to the immense frustration of Mrs. Roosevelt and Bowles, the President steered clear of her economic ideas.

Bowles had no more success with President Truman. Losing all sense of perspective, he threw himself back into the wage-price struggle—calling it "the battle of the century." Price controls just *had* to be continued if America was to avoid another crash after the war. Bowles warned on nightly radio talks about the danger of inflation—persuading thousands of frightened housewives to write to their congressmen—and he got into a fight with Harry Truman himself. When the President pushed him into accepting a steel price hike in 1946, he threatened to quit and suffered a physical collapse, sending febrile protests from his sickbed to the White House. A few months later, Congress forced him to resign and Chester Bowles's war was over.

Had any of it been necessary? Inflation skyrocketed soon after Bowles left his job—but then so did production and spending. Living standards went on rising throughout most of the 1940s, without an economic collapse such as he predicted. The boom continued for another twenty-five years. Like most of us, Bowles derived his economic theories from certain personal beliefs. For him, the boom-and-bust cycle was a result of unethical behavior. It arose largely from business and labor greed, which a moral central government could cure through a tempered program of persuasion and control.

Having failed to win over either the White House or Congress, Bowles went home to Connecticut a hero to the ultraliberals. Much of his hard-core support came from New Deal intellectuals who felt angry about his treatment in Washington. During 1946, Democrats did badly in the mid-term elections. The party's immediate future looked bleak. But Chester Bowles and his backers thought that the root cause of their problem was President Harry Truman. The new President had abandoned Roosevelt's positive liberalism, Bowles wrote, coming "more and more under the influence of the purely negative militarists. Moreover, in spite of the liberal stands which he has frequently taken, Truman is at heart a conservative, or even reactionary. I can remember all too vividly the terms in which I have heard him describe Negroes and labor leaders, for instance." Another helmsman was needed to keep the nation's youth from sinking into apathy, or from drifting over to the left wing.

So in April 1948, Bowles announced on national radio that President Truman ought to step aside in favor of Dwight D. Eisenhower. The party's weakness stemmed mainly from reactionaries at the highest level, such as "the Wall Streeters and the Brass Hats who threaten to plunge us into war." General Eisenhower, on the other hand, might be willing to preside over a liberal administration, and surely he would get along better with the Russians. "Although Mr. Eisenhower is a military leader, he appears to be less of a militarist than some of the Wall Street bankers who now hold high positions in our government." Sending a copy of this speech to Eisenhower, he paid a call upon the general just to find out his opinion of it—and of course he found out nothing. Eisenhower had no plans, no politics, and no apparent knowledge of the political system. When Ike finally asked if he could be nominated by both parties at the same time, Chester Bowles left the meeting badly shaken.

Meanwhile, Bowles harbored his own political ambitions. In 1946, he had decided to run for governor of Connecticut and, if elected, to turn his state into a laboratory for liberal reform. By contrast to most ultraliberals, he believed in state power and local autonomy. During what was seen as a Republican year—1948—he went out and won the State House by putting new fight into his supporters, rousing Connecticut Democrats all up and down the ranks. Using ad techniques over the radio, he spoke of a housewives' union, of aid to needy groups, of programs that would elevate the "little people."

And Governor Bowles's effort to keep his promises to the little people, against a GOP legislature, met with surprising success. He launched a building program of schools, public housing, and hospitals. He pushed tenants' rights and desegregation. In some ways his incumbency resembled the New Deal in its prime, with weekly radio talks by the governor and special meetings of the legislature. The electorate either hated or loved Chester Bowles. Ultraliberal votaries may have seen him as presidential material, but his Republican enemies soon came back on the upswing. They called him a "queer duck" who had imported alien creatures—mostly pinkos and eggheads from New York— to administer a program that was bankrupting the state. The Republicans ousted him in 1950.

Ex-Governor Bowles did not brood long about unfinished business. He rarely brooded. He cut himself loose and turned to new enterprises. Declining several other job offers from President Truman, he asked for the U.S. Embassy in India, then a diplomatic backwater. Here was a country that might welcome America's ultraliberal face. Accompanied by his wife, three children, and a cat, he left for New Delhi, a political outcaste.

Ultraliberal or not, why would an isolationist politician want to run off to the other side of the world? The answer lies partly in Bowles's hatred of Western imperialism and his sympathy for its "victims"—not so much its victims within Europe as in the overseas colonies of Asia and Africa. India was the world's second most populous country. It had been the classic example of British colonialism, recently liberated and struggling under a new democratic raj.

The issue of colonialism had been softpedaled by America all through the 1940s. Almost all colonial territories outside the USSR were owned and run by West Europeans—and keeping Western Europe happy was what mattered most to the United States. During World War II, Chester Bowles had pestered the President to proclaim a sweeping program of liberation—such as Wilson's Fourteen Points—which the President refused to do. In some cases Roosevelt opposed colonial rule, in other cases not, and President Harry Truman felt much the same way.[37] For that matter, colonialism had been softpedaled by President Wilson himself, who took at best a patronizing interest in the colored races. A de facto colonialist in Central America, Wilson had directed his own anti-imperialism mainly at imperial rule within Europe.

American ultraliberals, however, never ceased to treat colonialism as an evil that must be denounced, as a cancer that must be cut out. Bowles's world view arose less from his love of economic growth, less even from his love of democracy, than from his moralistic hatred of Western racism—of white people lording it over brown people. Evil though the Communists were, he asserted, at least they did not commit that sin. As for the United States, "a Negro child cannot go to a white school in the capital of our own country—can't go to a white church—can't go to a white restaurant or a white department store—Washington, D.C., the capital of great, *Free* America!"

It is no coincidence that Bowles's career in diplomacy had begun, in 1947, with part-time work for the United Nations. Many other Americans soon would be feeling disillusioned by the United Nations. But in foreign policy as elsewhere, Bowles's heart would often overwhelm his very great intelligence. He went on defending his liberal virtue, refusing to abandon the goal of universal disarmament under a single world authority. "If the United Nations cannot be made to work, there is no real hope left for any of us," he wrote to the UN Secretary General. The danger came from those Americans "who look on the United Nations as purely an organization through which to build a 'moral' case against nations which they fail to understand and, hence, fear and mistrust." Taking charge of the UN's appeal for needy children, Bowles apologized on behalf of all grown-ups for the scourge of poverty and war. He hoped that the UN appeal would bring nations together in greater harmony, that it would "help create international understanding and encourage greater cooperation among all people regardless of ideology."

Bowles's own ideology was typified by that remark. A small

but important segment of the Democratic Party, ultraliberals viewed the world as an extension of the United States, treated diplomacy as an extension of U.S. politics, saw their mission as one of bringing the New Deal to every country on earth. "Scratch an American isolationist and you will find an American universalist," goes an adage that describes many supporters of Chester Bowles. They wanted to dispense U.S. aid worldwide through the United Nations—which presumably shared the goals of all decent people—and tended to blame the United States for most of what went wrong. In 1947, Henry Wallace went on a speaking tour of Europe to denounce the wickedness of U.S. foreign policy, and Bowles praised him for doing so: "You have accomplished a great deal in proving not only to ourselves but to the world that America has not turned wholly reactionary." After that, Bowles was careful to keep his distance from Henry Wallace. He made no objection to most of President Truman's agenda, such as regional alliances and resistance to communism in Europe. For him, Truman's mistakes were mainly mistakes of emphasis—the Marshall Plan, for example, should be undertaken on a much grander scale. In a letter to the President, he complained that America was driving Eastern Europe into Russia's arms: we should try to get those countries involved, and the rest of humanity needed an aid package, too.

During the war, Bowles had asked President Roosevelt to send him on a trip around the world, to develop a plan for improving the lot of humankind. Nothing came of that idea for several years. It was hard enough getting aid money out of the Congress just for Europe. Therefore, no one was gladder than Chester Bowles when Truman took an unexpected tack in "Point Four" of his 1949 inaugural address. "We must embark on a bold new program," Truman declared, "for making the benefits of our scientific advances and industrial progress available for the improvement and growth of underdeveloped areas." It was America's first general commitment to Third World aid.

And President Truman actually meant it. Behind the swelling rhetoric, he felt a real conviction that U.S. aid could help impoverished people all over the world. As he remarked shortly after his inauguration, the whole course of aid to underdeveloped

countries had been charted two years before. Several of his
advisers had considered it "ever since the Marshall Plan was
inaugurated. It originated with the Greece and Turkey proposi-
tion. Been studying it ever since. I spend most of my time going
over to that globe back there, trying to figure out ways to make
peace in the world." Where he and most Democrats came to
differ from Bowles was in their growing emphasis on anti-communism and military aid. American dollars ought to serve global
security first, not the brotherhood of man.

Civilian aid to underdeveloped areas had been extended in a
piecemeal fashion during 1948, when the Communists were
taking over mainland China. Congress had decided that Marshall funds previously intended for Chiang Kai-shek now should
be given to nearby countries—such as Burma, Thailand, Indochina, and Korea—and for several years thereafter, most U.S.
programs in Asia were run by the Marshall Plan office. The
problems, of course, were found to be quite different from those
of Europe. A lot of money went into graft and inefficiency; even
small sums could be distributed only with elaborate safeguards;
and large amounts never could be absorbed, no matter how
enlightened the recipient governments.[38] Still, there did arise a
feeling among Marshall Planners like Averell Harriman that U.S.
aid could help a backward economy much as it helped Europe,
that eventually it could bring about the same happy result.
Though American voters did not share this illusion, many liberals in Washington would cling to it for twenty years.

After President Truman launched his Point Four program in
1949, it took him a while to guide it through the Congress and
bureaucracy. It was not until 1951 that the package emerged as
a "coordinated" effort of government, non-profit organizations,
private business, and the UN agencies. By March of that year,
hundreds of trainees and technicians were at work in twenty-
seven countries. And a few months later, the first grant of money
was made: $54 million to India. Strange as it might seem, Indi-
ans were just as happy about the new American ambassador,
Chester Bowles, who arrived at about the same time as the grant.
They knew that he really believed in helping the poor countries,
that he had done all he could to get Truman interested and push

the aid package through. Trying to achieve in India what he tried to achieve at home, Bowles would end up with a lot more gratitude for his pains.

Chester Bowles's sojourn in India probably was the most emblematic U.S. ambassadorship of the twentieth century—famous for its impact on American relations with India, but even more for its impact on American policy throughout the Third World. Ambassador Bowles created a standard for liberal behavior in the tropical countries. He set a new precedent for American "can-do-ism" against the "challenge" of poverty and Marxist revolution. Perhaps he did so by going abroad at exactly the right time. "India is the key to Asia," he told Truman in 1951, and the key to Asia was what hundreds of American mandarins were looking for.

Actually, Bowles never had been to Asia in his life. He had precious little experience with India, or any foreign country. His wife spent their voyage out reading a book by Mahatma Gandhi, while his daughter held the cat—brought along as "a kind of familiar link for the children between Connecticut and India." And their first impressions hardly were encouraging. From the airport they drove through "one of the world's worst slums, the sidewalks covered with tens of thousands of sleeping people, some on cots but most of them lying on hard pavement, the ever-present poverty, misery and squalor." None of this could sully Bowles's sense of pristine wonderment, his almost mystical belief that Americans had something to learn from this great country.

When he arrived in New Delhi, Indo-American relations were at an impasse. Congress had approved an emergency food loan to India only after long, rancorous, and very public debates. The politicians were disgusted by India's neutrality in the Korean War, by its moralistic criticisms of the United States. Their disgust, of course, was reported in New Delhi and gave rise to even more self-righteous criticisms of America. Even at State there prevailed a sense of hopelessness about India—Bowles had to tell people in the Department just to stop being so negative or they never would get anywhere.

Such was State's inattention to India that Bowles entered a kind of foreign policy vacuum, which left him free to use whatever diplomatic method suited him. In addition to standard reporting, he decided that he would try to "sell" Western democracy through what he called a "new diplomacy"—meaning propaganda, persuasion, and financial aid. He would try to personify the American way, to embody all the warmth and informality of America, and interpret to Americans all that was good about India. To present his credentials, Chester Bowles borrowed a pair of striped pants from the Italian ambassador. He gave his mansion over to the Foreign Service staff, moving into a three-bedroom bungalow. He sent his children to the local public schools. Of course, the Wilsonian "new diplomacy" of reconciling citizens rather than states was an old story by then; indeed, America's emphasis on a simple diplomatic style had started a hundred and seventy years before. But such behavior came naturally to Ambassador Bowles, and India was one of those rare foreign posts where his down-home, human touch could make a difference.

Moreover, Bowles arrived at a perfect time for ultraliberal optimism and reform. Big, poor, isolated, moralistic, racist, and democratic India actually *did* in some ways resemble America of the New Deal. The most chaotic period of independence was over. Disillusionment had not yet set in. India's first election, two months later, proved an exhilarating success. The propaganda battles against Russia and China were intense, but in those days it looked as though democracy had a good fighting chance all over southern Asia.

Ambassador Bowles took to India as he did every place he had worked: like an administrative whirlwind. Immediately he put new spirit into his subordinates—gave them a series of pep talks, got them traveling around and working harder—and he had an amazing effect on Indian politicians. If he arrived eager to learn from experience, he also shared some basic assumptions with the Indians that did not change: a worship of Mahatma Gandhi, a hatred of colonialism, a belief in central planning. He never doubted for a moment that colonial rule had been harmful to India's economic development. He showed respect for India's neutrality. He was candid about America's faults. Though fiercely patriotic, Bowles could say quite honestly that he had fought American racism all his life. Perhaps the main reason why Indians came to love the new ambassador was their sense that he did not care about the Cold War—just racism, colonialism, and helping the poor.

Bowles soon discovered that all roads in Delhi led to Premier Jawaharlal Nehru, founder of a dynasty that would dominate India for at least forty years. "Jawaharlal Nehru *is* the politics of India," he reported to President Truman, who had other worries. "The first thing you've got to do is find out whether Nehru is a communist," was the President's parting injunction. "He sat right in that chair, and he talked just like a communist." And it is easy to see what got on Truman's nerves. Nehru was a warmed-over, 1930s pacifist and appeaser—a Westernized Brahmin who thought that Indians might profit from "a course of study of Bertrand Russell's books." Educated at Trinity College, Cambridge, he was rude and suspicious with American officials, treating them with a mixture of resentment and condescension. No doubt, he deserves great credit for trying to establish a democratic system in India. At the same time, he held other democracies to an unequal standard, usually ignoring the faults of Russia and China while denouncing those of the United States.

Nehru regarded India as the natural leader of the African and Asian countries. Americans were little more than oafish barbarians who should get their fingers out of Indochina, Korea, and Japan; too often they relied on brute strength, having "no understanding of the mind and heart of Asia." Of course, the new American ambassador agreed with him on that point—and on much else besides. Bowles had been a great friend of Premier Nehru's sister, who was India's Ambassador to Washington, and he hit it off famously with Nehru himself. Eventually, the prime minister of India "almost took me as a partner." The only foreign diplomat with ready access to Nehru, Ambassador Bowles saw him several times a week in visits that might last for hours.

Except for racism and colonialism, what the two of them most liked talking about was India's Five Year Plan. Naturally, Bowles wanted to encourage industrial growth in India. However, most of the initial American grant he channeled toward agriculture, through a program that included fifty-five local projects of three hundred villages each. Traveling the length and breadth of the subcontinent, he tried to keep in close touch with the project directors. No mountain was too high for the ambassador, no swamp was impassable. He covered sixty thousand miles, if necessary by foot, pony, or boat. An avid sailor, Bowles could visit remote inlets where the natives scarcely had heard of America. Nor was he above doing manual labor himself. He worried constantly that the projects were not moving fast enough, that not nearly enough was being done. He pushed hard at Nehru and at others in Delhi—not just on programs funded by America, but on civil service and land reform, and on caste desegregation. Every last one of India's problems was taken as a personal challenge by this human dynamo from the U.S.A.

The idea of American aid obviously was not hard to sell in India. Where Bowles had to hustle to put across his program was back in the United States. He directed an advertising blitz at State and Capitol Hill; he sent letters and memos to powerful friends all over Washington; he went home several times to beg for money in person. Throughout Asia, he warned, people were looking to see whether Red Chinese methods worked better than those of democratic India. If Nehru's Five Year Plan did not succeed, then he would lose the next election and the Reds might take over. It was the battle of the century to save Asian democracy from ultimate collapse. "Failure of Indian democracy would in all probability result in disaster substantially greater than Communist victory in China," he cabled to President Truman, "since Southeast Asia and Middle East would become impossible to hold once India is lost. Communist sweep in Asia would gravely undermine our position in Europe and convince hundreds of millions of our friends all over the world they are betting on wrong horse."

Bowles knew that such language was useful for getting money out of Washington. Still, his cause appeared less urgent than that of Europe in 1947. By now Congress had grown almost hostile to foreign aid. Even the White House felt uncertain how much funding was needed, how important it was to American security. Bowles came home and delivered a direct plea to President Truman, but it made little difference.

"The Congress in these matters has been anything but cooperative," explained Truman to his ambassador. "They have had a wave of hysteria which has caused them to almost strip foreign aid and also the Defense Program."

Very well then, replied Bowles, Averell Harriman must take money away from the other aid programs or the Congress must be reconvened. Attempts to limit funding would be "no less than tragic." And of course the President and Dean Acheson were very sorry to hear it—but they could find no more money.[39]

When President Truman left the White House to make way for Eisenhower, other Republicans said that the Ambassador to India was too left wing and should be fired. This was done quite reluctantly by the new President. He and Dulles knew that Ambassador Bowles had brought about a spectacular change in Indo-American relations. Before coming home, Bowles took a triumphal tour around the country—in Delhi, the villages, universities, everywhere, Indians hated to see him go. Journalists dubbed him one of the Founding Fathers of Indian democracy. All of which was enough to make him think that almost anything was possible in Third World diplomacy. His book about his experiences in India, published a few months later, ended on a rousing and portentous note: "We Americans are a pioneer people, still respectful of the old Puritan concepts of common decency and hard work, still guided by moral principles, still stirred by the call of the frontier. Now a new frontier awaits us, working with peoples of all races and religions in the economic, social and political development of every underdeveloped continent and country, which is this century's main adventure.

"If that becomes the great positive mission of America, then I deeply believe that we will rediscover the creative, courageous spirit of our frontier days, and relearn the truths which once we held self-evident."

It would take a few years of sinking in, but the impact of that statement upon liberal diplomacy was tremendous. Bowles's book was a best-seller in the United States as well as India;

aimed mainly at Democrats, it had a certain appeal even in some Republican circles. The call of the wild frontier always had been powerful in American culture, if for widely divergent reasons. What set apart many liberals was their use of the frontier as a rhetorical symbol in their politics. As Bowles suggested in his book, ultraliberals positively *needed* a frontier, a sense of mission to go out and tame some economic wilderness—whether in Europe, or Asia, or the United States itself. For their movement to survive, it must keep moving. Perhaps a feeling of outward but non-imperial expansion would restore the purity of the American republic, or at any rate the purity of American liberalism.

The new Congress swept into power by Eisenhower's victory was, if anything, even more hostile to Third World aid than the previous Congress. While politicians fulminated against pouring money down a "rathole," the new administration had been evasive on this subject. Ike seldom mentioned foreign aid in the 1952 campaign—though when he did, he supported it—and the Secretary of State was even harder to figure out. For more than thirty years, John Foster Dulles had taken a deep interest in the underdeveloped and colonial areas, which he saw as vitally important to America. At the same time, he did not possess much heart or magnanimity, showing little personal concern for the human disasters of poverty. Rather, he hated colonialism for the trade blocs and inefficiency it created. Foreign-owned territories struck him as an economic problem for the USA: the United States needed export and capital outlets, and European imperialism got in the way.

This reduction of so many problems to the solution of free trade and investment was one thing that made Dulles a classic Wilsonian liberal. Another was his hope that the United Nations might serve as a vehicle for enlightened change. To avert another global depression, Dulles said during World War II, there must be economic reform and a sweeping away of imperialism under UN auspices: "The capitalistic centers, notably the British Empire and the United States, have developed some major defects. One of these is imperialism, with its by-product of racial intolerance. Another is the failure to maintain steady production and employment." Cataclysmic change in the colonial areas might be made more manageable by the United Nations. During 1945, Dulles took a personal role in planning UN reforms for the dependent countries—and he spoke in the same universalist nostrums as did Chester Bowles and Henry Wallace, calling for a global Bill of Rights to deal with racial and sexual injustice.

Much of this was hot air for rhetorical effect. Dulles had a way of getting blown along by the atmosphere of the moment, of losing his intellectual moorings. While a delegate to the United Nations in 1946 and 1947, he suddenly got religion on the Soviet threat and started using the General Assembly as an anti-Communist forum; but again his public rhetoric sounded a good deal more zealous than his private opinions. Anger at the Russians, wrote Dulles, "*will* shock us, but it *may* shock us into doing what needs to be done." Like many liberals, he used communism as a goad to push Americans into taking positive action outside the Soviet bloc.

Another force that propelled Dulles was domestic politics. He was anxious not to run afoul of Republicans in the Congress; he wanted to make a good impression on middle America. So his method was to support the right wing in words while following an internationalist liberal line in his deeds. On foreign aid, for example, he and Eisenhower ended up in roughly the same boat as did President Truman. "Trade, not aid" was their slogan— but their foreign aid budget submitted in 1953 was scarcely any different from that of the Democratic administration. In fact, Dulles obtained a larger sum for India that year than any direct grant before or since.

In short, the Eisenhower team came in feeling uncertain how it ought to deal with the Third World, sharing some of Truman's doubts and problems at the tactical level. These doubts began to dissipate after mid-1953, when the President and Dulles started to hold wide-ranging discussions on foreign policy. Always their discussions came to the same conclusion: that the Cold War battleground had shifted to the underdeveloped countries, that America must do everything possible to keep them from going Communist. Massive increases in civilian aid were expensive, inefficient, and, for the time being, politically impossible. What remained was the expedient of giving military help, or else relying on direct action by the Central Intelligence Agency. A little CIA here, a little military aid there, might just do the trick. Eisenhower allowed the CIA to grow enormously under the directorship of Allen Dulles, and its covert operations were expanded—taking the form of coups d'état in Guatemala and Iran, where it looked as though anti-Yankee elements might be gaining control.[40]

In many instances, there was little the CIA could do about regimes that were neutral or anti-American. President Eisenhower knew that the United States could only swallow its pride and hope that some day they would pass. But not everyone felt so easygoing. By late 1955, pressure was mounting on the Republican administration to win friends and influence them through economic assistance. Ike's chief Democratic opponent, Adlai Stevenson, wanted more action by the United States: "Our Government is unprepared for this new Communist offensive, which has been in the making since Korea and the death of Stalin." Throughout South Asia and the Middle East, top Kremlin officials were promising all kinds of civilian aid. Nikita Khrushchev made a speech in Bhakra offering help for India's second Five Year Plan; then, in early 1956, Nehru revealed that the Russians intended to help build a steel plant and provide India with a variety of economic favors. A number of top Democrats, such as Stevenson and Harriman, said that Washington ought to do even more of the same thing.

"We need not get panicky because Soviet Communism displays itself in this new garb," responded John Foster Dulles. There should be no big increase in U.S. aid, especially for the neutral nations. In private, however, such new Soviet tactics threw the Secretary of State off balance. He hesitated to denounce the colonialism of his European allies—nor could he restrain himself from attacking Third World neutrality, calling it "an immoral and shortsighted conception."[41] On the other hand, Dulles went on approving aid programs for such nonaligned countries as India and Yugoslavia. His ambivalence finally was resolved at the end of Eisenhower's first term, when a Middle East explosion jolted the administration toward a more activist policy of anti-colonialism and financial aid.

In the Middle East and North Africa, nationalist tensions had been seething ever since World War II. Egypt was being ruled by a military junta—vehemently anti-Israel, anti-colonial, and impatient to end Great Britain's "imperialist" control of the Suez Canal. The Egyptian dictator, Colonel Nasser, also was making trouble for France's North African Empire. Angered by his help to the Arab revolt in Algeria, the French seemed to think that if Nasser were overthrown then their troubles would end.

Amidst all of this activity, American policy drifted, sometimes under the influence of big oil companies. Dulles worried about pushing the Arabs into Russia's arms, and yet he hated the idea of bidding with Communist sirens for the friendship of a non-aligned country. Genuinely neutral in the Cold War, Colonel Nasser appeared willing to accept help from almost any donor. In 1955 he made an arms deal with the Soviet Union—to which Dulles responded by having a "conniption fit" and withholding American civilian aid. In July 1956, Dulles and Eisenhower decided to renege on a U.S. commitment to help Egypt finance the Aswan Dam. Colonel Nasser hit back by accepting Russia's offer to build the dam and then went on to seize control of the Suez Canal Company.

President Eisenhower tried to warn France and Great Britain against taking any military action. If the British were so foolish as to invade Egypt, then the Third World "would be consolidated against the West to a degree which, I fear, could not be overcome in a generation." He also worried about its effect on his re-election strategy for that autumn. While the President issued his warnings, the Secretary of State went to London and shilly-shallied on the matter—confusing the NATO Allies about Eisenhower's real intention. Meanwhile, England, France, and Israel made secret preparations and launched a combined attack on Egypt in October 1956.

The invasion was a diplomatic blunder of major proportions. President Eisenhower decided—in the interests of America and his re-election campaign—to treat it as an act of imperialist perfidy. Along with Henry Cabot Lodge, Jr., U.S. Ambassador to the United Nations, he and Dulles denounced the entire venture in public. Dulles made a speech to the UN General Assembly, covering France and Great Britain with moralistic reproach. Then he introduced a cease-fire resolution that was adopted by a vote of sixty-four to five, with the United States voting against its European Allies. Ambassador Lodge called the White House to report that "never has there been such a tremendous acclaim for the President's policy. Absolutely spectacular." Small countries could hardly believe that America was supporting the Third World against its old friends in Europe. All of the Asian and African countries were overjoyed.

The Suez invasion had bogged down anyway. Using a mixture of military and financial clout, Washington soon pressured the Europeans and Israel to withdraw. But the Suez crisis has to be recognized as a diplomatic watershed. Although the United States had opposed colonialism in other parts of the world, generally it had not done so in public. Throughout the Middle East, America had been associated with British imperialism— and in Africa, especially, the State Department felt reluctant to make trouble for the NATO Allies. It was Suez that made Eisenhower decide to oppose colonialism openly and then gradually to liquidate it. Moreover, the United States must dramatically increase its civilian aid to the underdeveloped countries.

Right after Suez and his re-election victory of 1956, President Eisenhower put a task force to work on the most extensive review of foreign aid since the Marshall Plan. The conclusion, a few months later, was that more U.S. aid would lead to economic growth in the Third World. This, in turn, would encourage democratic reforms and political stability. To get the process started, America should extend government-to-government, long-term, "soft" loans. Eisenhower launched the program in his second inaugural address, declaring that "new forces and new nations stir and strive across the earth. From the deserts of North Africa to the islands of the South Pacific, one third of all mankind has entered upon an historic struggle for a new freedom: freedom from grinding poverty." Suez was only the most spectacular event in the break-up of European colonialism. All across the world the "winds of change" were blowing. And if conditions did not improve in the liberated countries, then the winds of change might blow them toward another form of tyranny.

Convincing his fellow Americans to give money was the catch—and Congress refused to go along with Ike. Trying every form of pressure, the President devoted most of his stag dinners to this topic and called up the politicians endlessly. But his request for a $2 billion loan fund, spread over three years, never had a chance on Capitol Hill; foreign aid increased only slightly from the average of his first term. In Eisenhower's opinion, such apathy reflected an "abysmal ignorance" among the American people. Never in his life had he felt more frustrated.

One person to whom the President confided his frustration was an old acquaintance, Chester Bowles. As Ike wrote to Bowles in 1956, "I thought that with the initiation of the Marshall Plan a few years ago we were definitely embarked on a long-term world policy and program that would find the vast majority of Americans in vigorous support"—but with regard to Third World aid, support from Americans was anything but vigorous. Bowles naturally sympathized, thinking only that Eisenhower ought to try harder. He himself was traveling America and the Third World over in a frenzy of writing and lecturing—always talking up his never-say-die optimism, his far-flung philanthropy, his eagerness for "progress," "improvement," and "change." And some of his fellow Democrats were moving in the same direction. One of them was the Democratic Party's two-time nominee for President, Governor Adlai Stevenson of Illinois.

Besides a devotion to Mrs. Roosevelt, Adlai Stevenson had quite a lot in common with Bowles. He was descended from a newspaper family, went to Choate and Princeton, and entered elective politics late, winning the governorship of Illinois unexpectedly in 1948. His first exposure to diplomacy had occurred during 1945, when he worked on selling the United Nations to an uncertain electorate; and he remained a UN booster for the rest of his life. Stevenson never actually worked or lived in a foreign country, going abroad only as a tourist or observer. But

he often was called a "citizen of the world" during the 1950s—
an era when that term was still regarded as a compliment.

There was something about Stevenson that did not add up. In
some ways he appeared a cautious politician, in others an ultraliberal dreamer who in any case could never make up his
mind. In the end his ruling passion turned out to be the poor
countries. After his defeat by Eisenhower in 1952, he took a trip
around the world and conceived a life-long interest in under-
development. In India, he was overwhelmed by Premier Jawaharlal Nehru—"Surely here *is* a remarkable man"—and asked
the 185,000 residents of one Indian city to become honorary
members of the Democratic Party. In Africa two years later, he
was much struck by the father of Ghana's independence and
went away feeling bullish on Africa's postcolonial future. In
Yugoslavia, he offered to go on a lecture tour of the United
States with Marshal Tito. That brief string of anecdotes gives us
more than a hint of Adlai Stevenson's world view—that the
non-aligned countries were what really mattered, that their leaders were decent and gentle people.

Not surprisingly, Chester Bowles was so impressed that he
devoted himself to a second presidential bid by Stevenson. Over
the next three years, he flooded Stevenson with letters, memos,
books, articles, invitations, and personal visits. "How the hell
have you the energy, time and wisdom to absorb and write so
much," complained Stevenson; "you depress me!" While the
candidate did not always agree with his new friend, some of
Bowles's advice found its way into his speeches and eventually
into the mainstream of Democratic policy.[42] "You are quite right
that we must find a way to present the modern version of Wilsonian idealism in terms of political realism," Stevenson affirmed. "I think it can be done, and I hope you'll keep at it."
Accordingly, Bowles kept urging him to attack Republicans for
their militaristic bluster and "warlike slogans," which did such
great harm to America's image. Adlai should push disarmament
and a nuclear test ban, then the tax money saved on weapons
could pay for an economic Bill of Rights: "In our cities, where
more than half of our people now live, we have what amounts
to a New Frontier."

Of course, the frontier that most fascinated Chester Bowles was the frontier where more than half of the world now lived—and that must be won with U.S. aid and understanding. Under a Stevenson presidency in 1957, he intended to initiate a broad re-examination of foreign aid, so as to make it "a far more effective instrument of policy." But Governor Stevenson spoke very little on foreign affairs during the 1956 campaign. The trouble for him was that this topic cut no ice politically. American voters wanted nothing except peace and resistance to communism, and President Eisenhower had both of those issues sown up. Except for ultraliberals like Chester Bowles, most Democrats had no serious quarrel with the President on foreign policy.

Not missing a beat after Stevenson was defeated, Bowles redoubled his effort to educate Americans in voice and in print. All through the 1950s, Stevenson fussed over a book on the Third World without ever finishing it; but Chester Bowles made good the loss. Besides his hundreds of speeches and lectures— he delivered ten speeches a month, and in almost every state of the union—he published six books and dozens of articles. Always more money and effort was what he wanted, a Marshall Plan for the world run by the United Nations, along with firmer denunciations of colonialism. We must be more positive. Zeal, always zeal. Third World politicians were like the American Founding Fathers: "The ideas and the passions that fired the revolutionaries of Concord, Valley Forge and Philadelphia have been recreated on every continent." From the continent of Africa, he reported on "the awakening of its 200 or more million people. After a long night the sleeper is stirring, blinking away his drowsiness, and stretching his limbs with all the eager, impatient spirit of youth approaching manhood." Bowles was not wholly naive on the awakening countries, some of which he realized might go sour. Yet he took it at face value when left-wing dictators spoke of being democratic. Treating them quite often as children, he found it easy to blame their misbehavior on some parental mistake.

Having learned a lesson from the Suez fiasco, the Europeans started to decolonize Africa in the late 1950s—a policy made easier, no doubt, because the terms of trade had turned against raw materials. Whatever the reasons for it, decolonization did help elevate Chester Bowles to greater power and influence. A huge number of newly independent states now would some-how—so it seemed—have to be dealt with, and policymaking elites in America felt ill-equipped to do so. Some of Bowles's speeches about Africa appeared suddenly quite relevant. Ul-traliberals seemed the only group with the vocabulary, with *any* vocabulary, to address certain related foreign and domestic problems.

It may sound odd thirty years later, but in 1960 the United States appeared more racist than did the European nations—including Russia. There was a tough popularity contest with the USSR, seen by Third Worlders as an anti-colonial, anti-racist, peasant, revolutionary state that had bettered itself through col-lective effort. And America seemed the opposite, especially in its treatment of blacks. As Bowles had pointed out, U.S. racism was "perhaps the greatest single success of the USSR in India," and it did the United States enormous harm elsewhere. He had become quite friendly with Martin Luther King, Jr., who was impressed by his articles urging a Gandhian strategy of non-violent struggle in the American South. To be successful in the Third World, Bowles argued, the United States must quickly end its own legalized racism. American whites owed special consideration and money to the newly liberated countries, just as they owed a special debt to American blacks.

The main cause of Bowles's elevation to power was the advent of a new and Democratic President. Bowles got himself elected a congressman from Connecticut in 1958 and, naturally, used his position to make contact with important Washingtonians of both parties. One of those Washingtonians was John F. Kennedy, a rising senatorial star who made a specialty of colo-nial liberation—Kennedy's criticism of the French colonial war in Indochina already had brought him together with Bowles. In 1957, JFK directed a blistering speech against France for resist-ing Algerian independence; he and Bowles co-sponsored bills to improve the foreign aid program; then, in 1959, Bowles became the first important ultraliberal to support Kennedy's bid for the

presidential nomination.⁴³ Early the next year, Kennedy asked
Bowles to function as his foreign policy adviser for the 1960
campaign.

By taking on Chester Bowles as an adviser, John F. Kennedy
gave himself more respectability among ultraliberals in the
party. Bowles assured his followers that the best way to support
progressive policies was to support JFK. When in due course
JFK was nominated—summoning fellow Americans to a "New
Frontier"—Bowles threw himself into the fray with all his usual
zeal. He saw this presidential campaign as the most important
of his lifetime, the start of a great political breakthrough. No
longer would he be living on the ideological fringe, for
Kennedy's moderate views soon would change with experience.
"As the leader of the kind of world-wide liberal movement which
I envisioned, a new American President would be faced with the
opposition of many powerful vested interests committed to the
status quo," Bowles believed. "But on his side would be all the
human forces for freedom, proclaimed in our own Revolution,
which had been gradually evolving and were now inspiring
young leaders in every corner of the world."

John F. Kennedy did not exactly win his race in a messianic
whirlwind. Running against Vice President Nixon, he was
elected by a hairbreadth margin, the narrowest of the century.
And it was clear before his inauguration that he wanted no basic
changes in foreign policy. Most of his top foreign policy appointees had been Republicans, or important players in the Truman
administration, or both. Another thing that many of them had
in common was an elusive element that Kennedy referred to as
"class."

More than most people, Jack Kennedy did not know who he
was. His family background was Irish, South Boston, and Roman
Catholic; and he resented the arrogance of such old Bostonians
as Ambassador Henry Cabot Lodge, Jr. On the other hand, he
himself had gone to the Choate School and Harvard College. He
inherited an enormous sum of money. This background seems
to have bestowed on him an inner conflict about his own identity. The class from which he sprang was tough, philistine, firmly

anti-Communist, and moderately liberal on most issues. Judged by his record in the White House, so was President Kennedy; he felt comfortable with the bipartisan consensus on foreign affairs. Nevertheless, his desire to be one of the emerging beautiful people may have helped lead him occasionally toward ultraliberal positions.

The United States is a land of many hierarchies and social elites. John F. Kennedy, as President, was the symbol of a new ruling class defined less by family background than by one's occupation and opinions. Ever since World War II, the "right" sort of opinions on U.S. foreign policy had come more and more to be opinions that were ultraliberal. President Kennedy's politics were in part the result of his desire to lead this New Class in the making—and, by leading it, to strengthen it. That was a very American solution to his problem. If the old system does not work for you, then bypass it and build a new, improved version. If your background is uncertain, then create a new foreground.

Kennedy's desire to look new and different also was the result of political opportunism. The New Class was strong in the public sector, universities, the arts, and news media—all of them opinion-making groups, where it was useful to be popular. Moreover, Kennedy wanted to strike an apparent contrast with the previous administration. Like the Republicans in 1953, he spoke a lot on breaking with the past without doing much about it; in the end, Kennedy trying to look more liberal was not much different from Dulles trying to look right wing. He appointed mostly moderate liberals, of whom many sprang from that elite with which the reader is familiar: an Old Class trying to blend in with the New, brightening up its style to fit the Kennedy image.[44]

In all fairness, party politics and social insecurity were not the only reasons why Kennedy's foreign policy sometimes had a fresh, new look. The President was an ambitious man in his prime who thought he could make a mark on his foreign affairs specialty, the Third World. He felt quite honestly that Eisenhower was failing—not so much in his analysis of the problem as in not trying hard enough. A recently published novel entitled

The Ugly American had a profound influence on Kennedy's Third World thought. Set in a fictional South Asian country—probably South Vietnam—the novel depicted U.S. diplomats as too insensitive, too cut off, too careerist, or too amateurish to be any match for the Communists. Kennedy meant to change all that with greater effort and imagination. Of course, everyone in Washington agreed on the need to "act" in the Third World— how and how much to act was another matter. Eisenhower was not at all certain; he believed in patience and firmness over hyperactivity. Kennedy, on the other hand, thought he knew some of the answers and soon would find out the rest.

So Kennedy did make a few changes that were real. One of them was a substantial increase in foreign aid. In his first year as President, he obtained from the Congress a much larger sum for Third World programs than any that preceded it. He also put through reforms in the way it was distributed. Chester Bowles, now Under Secretary of State, sought to establish a holistic approach—what he called a *"total diplomacy"* that blended economic, social, and political goals. To force a sense of discipline, Bowles emphasized loans over direct grants; stricter standards were set to qualify for aid; and he saw to it that military and civilian aid programs were formally separated. On anti-imperialism, too, the Kennedy team went farther than its predecessor. The President gave wholehearted support to decolonization in Africa, reflecting his stronger stand on civil rights at home.

Kennedy wanted to create a good atmosphere for innovation. With his encouragement, idea factories started to spring up in the American Northeast, manned heavily by members of the New Class. Out of them came batches of new Third World programs: the Alliance for Progress, to promote a "New Deal for Latin America"; the Peace Corps, to provide young Americans as teachers to the underdeveloped countries; the Green Berets, a military counterpart of the Peace Corps, for fighting Communist guerrillas. Some of these new programs were sustained by Democratic Party elders, brought back into power to lend it dignity and to repay political debts. One was Adlai Stevenson, who became Ambassador to the United Nations. Old Adolf Berle was exhumed from a law firm to help launch the

New Deal for Latin America. An even older Averell Harriman, still going on all cylinders, was made Ambassador at Large. From 1950 onward, Harriman had grown ever more partial to the ultraliberal view: "There is no such word as moderate or middle-of-the-road in the Democratic vocabulary." While governor of New York in the mid-1950s, Harriman fought hard for civil rights and scolded the Republicans for their halfhearted policy on foreign aid. He believed as strongly as Bowles did that more money was the answer, that America's aid system needed an overhaul, that the Marshall Plan's lessons could be applied to the Third World.

And Chester Bowles, in his job as Under Secretary of State, started moving so fast that he almost left the ground. He repeated Kennedy's flights of millenarian rhetoric, the calls to self-sacrifice and apocalyptic struggle; he spoke about the American Revolution as if it had been yesterday, predicted changes that might be centuries in coming. Bowles believed that Americans faced their Third Great Challenge—after Lend-Lease and the Marshall Plan—and every moment was one of ultimate crisis. "For many years to come, the Government of the United States must offer its people sweat and toil" . . . "We are approaching a watershed in regard to the world, our economy, and relations with nations" . . . "We are engaged in a titanic competitive struggle which will affect our destiny far into the distant future."

In another sense, too, Bowles fit happily into the Kennedy operation. We have seen that part of Kennedy's aim was to promote the new and different. Where Ike's approach to the Third World was defensive and skeptical, his would be joyful and geared toward youth. He wanted the symbolic Ugly American transfigured into someone beautiful and young—and Bowles was well qualified to make that happen. Along with his enthusiasm for dogs and cats and family life went an enthusiasm for children, for young people in general. He assumed that they agreed with his politics and, in the case of college graduates, that usually was true. He got along especially well with students of the liberal arts or social sciences, commanding a small army of devotees among them.

Bowles saw the missionary impulse of young Americans as a

hopeful sign in a deeply troubled world—"I see this hope in the enormous response to the Peace Corps, to the increasing ferment on college campuses." Young recruits to the Peace Corps and to the civil rights movement quite often were one and the same—like his own children, for instance. One of the Third World's most disturbing elements, as he saw it, was its overeducated and underemployed youth; this was becoming a problem for America too, but Bowles knew how to give a sense of purpose to disaffected people of a privileged caste. He would turn their energies to liberal good use by sending them down to the Deep South, into the inner city, and to foreign lands to develop joyfully a New Frontier.

If the story of Chester Bowles tells us anything, then America's titanic struggle was lost from the start. Soon after taking office, Bowles was excluded from influence and two years later was sent back to India—grievously disappointed by his failure at home. The first important ultraliberal to support John F. Kennedy, he was the first one to go.

Kennedy's main reason for limiting the role of ultraliberals was his basic disagreement with them; but in the case of Chester Bowles, there was another problem, too. Bowles was not a beautiful person himself. So pear-shaped and imprecise, he was an aesthetic misfit in Kennedy's Camelot. His style was old-fashioned and his politics were avant-garde, the reverse of a typical Kennedy man. Bowles had grown rich by means of a boosterism and verbal saturation that the President, who wanted wit from his advisers, considered tedious.

Besides getting cut off from the White House, Bowles did a lot to alienate almost everyone else. He made a mess of administering State and promoted too many ill-assorted ideas.[45] He liked to return his staffers' memos, telling them to rethink U.S. diplomacy from a peasant's point of view, and some of his own memos appeared bizarre. He advised the President to ask the Soviets for a six-month time-out on the Cold War; he recommended that the CIA be abolished or dispersed. As always, he was full of schemes for giant water projects. While governor, Bowles had wanted a dam on the Connecticut River, while ambassador a dam on the Ganges, and now he wanted to put up dams on rivers all over the world. Friends warned him to calm down, but he ignored them. In July 1961, he circulated a memo calling for a basic revision of American policy everywhere. The Secretary of State responded by asking him to resign.

That came as a shock. Bowles had hoped to become Secretary of State himself—or at least to be working under his friend Adlai Stevenson—but the President had taken care to keep them both out of key positions. Secretary of State Dean Rusk was a self-contained, tight-lipped man. He tended to sympathize with Europeanists in the Department, who resented the distraction of Third World alarums. Dean Acheson and David Bruce, for example, always worried about the effect of anti-colonialism on NATO. Now Ambassador to England, Bruce considered Bowles to be "a pleasant idealistic fellow, naive and wordy, and would think him better suited to the legislative than the executive branch of Government." At one point during 1961 the President asked Dean Acheson what was wrong over at State. Why was Foggy Bottom so inefficient? He got a straightforward reply—"Chester Bowles!"—and followed Acheson's advice. The Under Secretaryship was offered to Bruce, who declined it, and finally went to George Ball—another Europeanist who was quite uninterested in the colonial areas.

Scarcely believing what had happened, Bowles refused to go gracefully: "I was angry over the devious manner in which the situation had been handled, shocked at its suddenness and saddened." He was bought off for a year with a White House job, in the course of which he visited thirty-seven countries—a sign, perhaps, of Kennedy's desire to keep him out of town. Finally, he sent a letter of resignation to the President: "I fail to understand—and deeply deplore—the fact that no one in your Administration at a high level who is closely associated with you and has your full confidence has been giving priority attention to what is frequently referred to as the 'outlying areas.'" Campaign promises were being broken by Kennedy's advisers, who viewed the Third World with a "sense of exasperation" and "peevish reluctance."

Anxious not to lose Bowles entirely, the President asked him to return to India as U.S. ambassador. So he went back to New Delhi in 1963—convinced that he had been destroyed by the "experts" of Washington—and his decline from then on was uninterrupted. For six years he languished in India, where even the native government treated him badly. Starting to feel the symptoms of a degenerative nerve disease, he eventually was put on a drug that gave rise to nightmarish hallucinations. One recurrent nightmare featured a crowd of Washington lawyers and technocrats, surrounding Bowles and driving him into a corner of his living room. Another was of a crowd of little brown people in a Third World country. They were trying to chase Bowles down, angry at him because their revolution had gone astray.

At the height of his triumphalism in 1961, Under Secretary Bowles quoted in a speech from Shakespeare's *Julius Caesar*:

> There is a tide in the affairs of men,
> Which, taken at the flood, leads on to fortune;
> Omitted, all the voyage of their life
> Is bound in shallows and in miseries.
> On such a full sea are we now afloat, . . .

What did go wrong in the Third World, and why was Bowles so unnerved by it? Why was his own public life bound in shallows and miseries, and how did he so often manage to miss the right boat?

Perhaps his distress was the result of mortal disappointment. In 1953, Bowles prophesied that aid to the backward countries "will go down in history as the most creative idea of our generation." Eight years later, many liberals had come to agree. If ever there was a golden age of Third World aid it was the Kennedy administration. Civilian expenditures increased to twice the level of military aid, and they often were made according to Bowles's holistic plans. It was a time of monumental illusion: impressed by the progressive views of local politicians, Bowles predicted that in twelve years Africa's growth per capita would exceed that of Asia and Latin America. But by the 1970s, most of the Third World was doing terribly and most of Africa was a disaster; in fact, conditions were so bad that the colonial age started to look like a halcyon era. Elsewhere in the Third World, economic growth usually was lower than it had been twenty years before. The simple fact of overpopulation tended to upset the best laid plans—and success or failure had little to do with how much Americans spent, or how they spent it.

While the income gap widened between North and South, anti-Americanism also intensified. Bowles felt that American selfishness and racial prejudice were important causes of Third World hostility; and laissez-faire economics had little relevance to the needs of an underdeveloped country. Indeed, he believed that communism led to faster economic growth, but that Third World countries would be happiest under democratic social-ism.[46] As it turned out, the passage of civil rights laws in America and the failure of Marxist economics did nothing to diminish anti-American feelings; the United States became more hated than ever. Perhaps what Third World politicians really wanted was a scapegoat. Their troubles could be blamed on the United States, now identified in the United Nations as the ultimate "neo-colonial" power.

There were many reasons why Ambassador Bowles was so mistaken. One was his cheerful assumption that most people, given a chance, would prove as honest and virtuous as he. Bowles had a heart as big as the great outdoors and a very high opinion of his fellow man, especially foreigners. Yet he had no deep understanding of foreign cultures. If everyone had been like him, then his methods might have worked—maybe. And he assumed that everyone *could* be like him. At one point, he suggested a universal training program for young Americans, to prevent what he called "a militarized nation of 140,000,000 neurotics." The program should be designed "to develop enlightened public opinion," "to eliminate the racial prejudices," and to improve "the health of our people, mental as well as physical." Bowles was social chemist in some ways, wanting to treat people the way a kindly doctor might treat a patient. Folks who disagreed with him had an emotional problem that could to be cured.

Another mistake made by Bowles was to rely on false analogies. To some extent all liberals looked at models like democratic India, or like Europe in the 1940s, or like the United States itself during the Great Depression. And for many of them there existed an ideological dimension unknown to Woodrow Wilson. Influenced by the New Deal and its putative successes in rural America, ultraliberals hoped that incomes could be leveled on an international scale. They were influenced also by the civil rights movement. Equal rights for black people and public assistance to disadvantaged minorities—what might be called domestic foreign aid and domestic liberation—were expected to yield great economic advances and political tranquillity. After two decades they have yielded nothing of the sort.

Of course, the favorite model for Bowles, the lens through which he viewed much of the world, was Mother India. By extension, Mother India became a model for many of his admirers, who were deeply affected by his early experience there. The Peace Corps' India contingent was the largest in the world. The great subcontinent served as a last frontier for the secular missionaries of the United States. Like China before communism, it was a good place to uplift other people and thus to secure one's own salvation. It seemed as though America's faith in the common man, its Jeffersonian belief in people-to-people diplomacy, had been vindicated by Bowles in India. If only we could understand them and break down the barriers, Indians could be dealt with much like other Americans and so could all citizens of the Third World. Though Chester Bowles saw India as the "proving ground" of Third World development and democracy, India proved little about other countries. It has remained democratic and enjoyed a respectable growth rate because of cultural, historical, and geographic factors that are unique.

Factors such as these are what made possible the development of several Far Eastern economies, the so-called Little Dragons of Asia. Especially in Taiwan, the U.S. policy that helped them most was not foreign aid or socialism, but free trade. President Kennedy started a round of global tariff cuts which, at a time of First World prosperity and exceptional growth, was palatable to other American politicians. The Democratic Party made its free trade rhetoric into a reality, while U.S. business led the way in a vast multinational expansion of investment and commerce. Though far more important than foreign aid, this expansion went unnoticed or disapproved by many ultraliberals—and it shows something about Bowles's disciples that they gave it a relatively low priority. Free trade and investment meant less government action, not more. It went with capitalism and laissez-faire economics. Thus, it went against a basic instinct of ultraliberals, which was generally to encourage *more* government action.

However much the U.S. Congress disagreed with him, Bowles's faith in government action and expenditure abroad was shared to some extent by most American diplomatists. Moderate liberals fell into the same trap, if in a less spectacular way. While some spoke of how different the Third World was from Germany in 1947, few accepted that its problems were so different as to be insoluble by U.S. effort. Internationalist liberals were right in dreading where the Third World was headed—almost all of them erred in thinking that the U.S. government could do much about it.

New Frontier can-do-ism found expression in a variety of ways. Bowles was only one side of the liberal activist coin. It took the form of military and political ventures as much as it did foreign aid. Bowles constantly was warning President Kennedy to refrain from military meddling, especially in Southeast Asia. Over his objections, Kennedy enhanced the U.S. presence in South Vietnam to help fight a Communist insurgency there. It was in Vietnam that the Green Berets were most active; Kennedy supplied military advisers to the Vietnamese government; he sent huge amounts of money and military equipment. And it was largely because of the awful fiasco in Vietnam that ultraliberals—despite the failure of their own foreign policy offensives—emerged greatly strengthened from the 1960s. Eventually they came to dominate the national Democratic Party and, in that arena at any rate, Chester Bowles did win his war.

Bowles came close to being an outright pacifist. Always he spoke of the strength of "people" and "ideas" versus military power and armed force. His advice against armed intervention quite often was right for the wrong reasons. For example, Bowles thought that the Vietnamese insurgency was a case of pure nationalism, that North Vietnam "looked on the war in Southeast Asia primarily as a struggle for national independence and identity, not as a crusade to force their own or any other version of 'Communism' down the throats of their unwilling neighbors." He kept urging Kennedy to make a speech on television proposing that Southeast Asia be neutralized and then given large amounts of U.S. aid. Eventually we could create a "Southeast Asian Common Market" with a regional development authority, free trade throughout the area, and a dam on the Mekong River.

Mindful of Vietnam's importance, Bowles passed through Saigon on his way out to India in 1963. There he paid a call on the president of South Vietnam, Ngo Dinh Diem, and was treated to a four-hour monologue. "Diem is living in a world of his own and seems to be completely out of touch with the real situation," Bowles reported home. "Any attractive South Vietnamese brigadier general with a little courage and organization could, I believe, take this place over in twenty-four hours." Which is pretty much what happened a few months later. Acting on instructions from Washington, the new U.S. Ambassador to South Vietnam, Henry Cabot Lodge, Jr., gave the go-ahead for a military coup d'état. Diem was overthrown and murdered only weeks before the assassination of President Kennedy. Vietnamese politics were plunged into an even worse chaos, from which they never fully recovered until the Communist victory.

VII

A Third World War

1963–1968

The overthrow of President Ngo Dinh Diem is said to have been America's worst mistake in Vietnam, leading the United States down into a quagmire of political and military involvement. Perhaps the coup d'état was indeed a milestone of sorts, although South Vietnam under Diem had turned into a political basket case anyway. If America wanted to stop a Communist victory there, then the chance had to be taken that a new regime would be better. So President Kennedy and Ambassador Henry Cabot Lodge made a throw of the dice that failed.

An intriguing question is why South Vietnam had become such a mess, an ungovernable chaos that made it such easy prey for Communist guerrillas. The original trouble, in this case, can be blamed on colonialism. French Indochina—of which Vietnam was a part—had been one of the most brutally exploited colonies in the world. The exploitation naturally gave rise to a number of liberation movements, including one headed by a revolutionary named Ho Chi Minh. During the Paris Peace Conference of 1919, Ho Chi Minh had sent an appeal to President Woodrow Wilson, asking for democratic reforms and a constitution in Vietnam—to which President Wilson made no reply, as was suitable to his lukewarm attitude on colonial independence. Ho Chi Minh proceeded to become a Communist, deciding that the Russians were more likely than anyone else to give him serious help.

When the Japanese Empire enveloped Indochina twenty-two years later, Ho Chi Minh hoped that the United States would give his movement more backing this time around. President Roosevelt's statements on colonialism, though vague and contradictory, sounded far more encouraging than those of President Wilson. In fact, Indochina was one French colony that Roosevelt wanted to see independent. In 1943, he told one of his sons that he intended to do everything to frustrate "France's imperialistic ambitions"; he proposed a trusteeship for postwar Indochina, complaining that the French had "milked it for one hundred years." President Roosevelt's threats so worried General de Gaulle that he sent in military forces after the Japanese surrender and, with the help of local allied commanders, France did succeed in restoring a semblance of colonial rule.

Throughout the 1940s, America's policy toward Indochina continued to be muddled and inattentive. While Ho Chi Minh's guerrillas went on fighting the French, a standard argument arose between U.S. diplomats in Europe and U.S. diplomats on the colonial scene. The former urged support for colonial rule, mainly to keep France happy; the latter went on pushing for national independence.[47] France was told by the Truman administration that America recognized its claim to Indochina. At the same time, Truman refused to give any military aid to the war against Ho's insurgency. The result of Truman's refusal was a quiet reallocation of France's own resources; Averell Harriman later complained that "we were then giving the French about 900 million dollars through the front door and most of it going out the back door to fight the war in Vietnam."

It was the Communist triumph in China that quickened America's zeal to stop Ho Chi Minh. Insofar as they thought about Asia at all, U.S. policymakers had been thinking mainly about China. We have seen how William Bullitt did his best to stir up fears of a Red Chinese tide sweeping down to the Indian Ocean. In an effort to get the United States involved, he had started a diplomatic intrigue with France's puppet head of government in Vietnam. Bullitt's effort began to pay off in 1950, when Red China and Russia extended formal recognition to the Vietnamese Communists. The United States in its turn recognized the French puppet government, and Secretary of State Acheson persuaded Truman to provide $15 million for the Vietnam War.

Some officials claimed that this was Washington's payoff for France's support in the European theater. "We did it because we wanted to get the French to cooperate fully in NATO," Harriman says, "and in return for that we gave them this assistance, not only the money but also the arms. That was a tragic theory, and I was opposed to it." Tragic or no, it was the first important case of America recognizing a dictatorship mainly because it was anti-Communist. After the Red invasion of South Korea, the United States became ever more financially involved in Vietnam. By 1952, the French had lost more than ninety thousand soldiers in the war, while over one-third of their military budget was covered by Washington. The awful loss of life naturally mattered more to the politicians of France. Premier Mendès-France asked Ho Chi Minh for peace terms in 1954, and Vietnam soon was provisionally divided between a Communist North Vietnam and non-Communist South.

When the Eisenhower administration came in breathing fire and brimstone against communism in Asia, it was to some extent only political hot air. But there existed enormous pressure during 1954 for direct U.S. intervention in Vietnam, to prevent even a partial Communist victory. The American hysteria about communism made it hard to accept that the French cause was doomed. Even ultraliberals like Bowles attempted to turn Ike's discomfiture to their political advantage; Adlai Stevenson said that the "loss" of Indochina by Republicans was the "greatest disaster" to the free world since the "loss" of China. "I want to go on the record here," said Harriman, "that I think we ought to take steps to get troops—American as well as many others—into Indochina and the Red River Delta before this thing begins to go." Although President Eisenhower chose to ignore most of this talk, propping up the new government of South Vietnam was the least that American elites expected of him. Political pressure practically forced Eisenhower to take a position in southern Vietnam—warning that if this area were overrun, then the rest of Southeast Asia would "go over very quickly" to communism, like a "row of dominos."

Ike's other problem was that South Vietnam had too little legitimacy in the eyes of local nationalists. Most of them had fought with Ho Chi Minh, and almost all regarded the South Vietnam regime as a creation of Washington. Though personally a brave and austere man, President Diem did head a government that was narrowly based. Throughout the 1950s, he defied American requests to enact land reforms and broaden his base of political support. The only project on which he showed energy was the suppression of his non-Communist opponents. No doubt his tyranny was mild compared to that of Ho Chi Minh. North Vietnam's revolution resembled that of Red China, with economic stagnation and the murder of entire categories of people. Perhaps it was Ho's self-confidence and cruelty that made his government so respected—CIA attempts at subverting North Vietnam came to nothing. The Communists were far better at subverting the South, where they exploited a mounting discontent with President Diem.

By 1960, Diem's government was growing ever more repressive—and the United States, after sinking over $1 billion into South Vietnam, had less influence on him than ever. A prototype for so many other Third World countries, Vietnam was simply too corrupt for aid to be effective. Former backers began to plot against Diem; the number of Communist murders of his officials increased; an attempted coup d'état was put down with harsh reprisals. Conditions so deteriorated that guerrillas controlled the countryside wherever government forces were not present. North Vietnam had been reactivating Communist cadres in the South for several years. In December 1960, they made it official by announcing the formation of a "National Liberation Front"—its purpose being to overthrow the government of South Vietnam.

So matters stood when John F. Kennedy became President. At this stage, Kennedy had very few illusions about President Diem. Where he did have illusions was about how much America could do to improve things. In 1954, he had said that no amount of aid could defeat Ho's guerrillas in a colonial war—but he changed his tune soon after the French pulled out. Two years later, he was describing South Vietnam as "the cornerstone of the Free World in Southeast Asia, the keystone in the arch, the finger in the dike."[48] Behind his grandiloquence lay a lot of uncertainty, a reluctance to escalate into a bigger war. All the same, President Kennedy had no intention of "losing" Vietnam; so he just muddled along, secretly increasing U.S. military personnel. South Vietnam in 1961 already had the largest U.S. Embassy in the world. The number of American soldiers there rose from a few hundred when JFK took office to over sixteen thousand by the time he was assassinated.

Besides his worry about creeping communism, several factors were pushing Kennedy toward a deeper involvement. The one we already know about was his commitment to greater effort in the Third World. South Vietnam would be a testing ground of his civilian aid program, carefully coordinated with new "counterinsurgency" techniques. And a closely related factor was his huge military buildup, which made any sort of intervention seem easier and more tempting to White House civilians. The Democrats came in complaining that Eisenhower and Dulles, in their eagerness to cut military spending, had made the United States too dependent on nuclear weapons. Kennedy meant to rebuild America's conventional strength to deter a conventional war with Russia, and to make the United States more effective in a Third World war as well.

Perhaps a greater influence on Kennedy was the kind of advice he was getting. Almost no one in his administration seriously resisted his involvement in Vietnam, including the Secretary of State. Secretary Rusk had a temperamental bias which inclined him to defer to the Pentagon's wishes—and military intervention in Vietnam was supported not only by Rusk and the new Defense Secretary, but by many others who later would turn against the war. Averell Harriman, for example, said a lot in public to encourage American involvement. Listen to him in 1962, speaking at a convention of college professors: "The free countries of Asia are in the front line of the struggle against communism. The whole of the area, from Iran, Pakistan, Afghanistan, India, across Southeast Asia, Japan, and Korea, is in the front line against the Communist wall. The Communists are making a desperate effort to penetrate, to take over, through subversion, threat of force, or force itself." Proudly he promoted Kennedy's counterinsurgency Green Beret forces, already fighting in both Latin America and South Vietnam.

Like a number of others, Harriman used a lot of martial rhetoric while doubting in private whether force should be used. Certainly he detested the Saigon government, feeling that President Diem stood in the way of political progress. And in April 1962, he endorsed several points of a surprising memo to Kennedy: "We have a growing military commitment. This could expand step by step into a major, long drawn-out, indecisive military involvement." Therefore, we should "resist all steps which commit American troops to combat action." The Diem government was rotten to the core. Our presence in Vietnam made us look to its inhabitants, and to most of the world, like warmongers who wanted to replace French colonialism. We should distance ourselves from Diem and start pushing a settlement that would create a neutral Vietnam.

The trouble with this memo was that it assumed a settlement was possible. It assumed that once the United States got rid of Diem, and maybe did some other things too, then Averell Harriman could visit his friends in Russia, Jawaharlal Nehru could help make contact with Red China, and the diplomatic ball would start rolling. Somehow the idea of abandoning Vietnam, since America could not win at an affordable price, was unthinkable to anyone in Kennedy's administration. The mistake of most Democrats was not in assuming there was a "military solution," but in assuming there was any "solution" at all. Perhaps the ghost of Joe McCarthy, the political disaster of losing a country to communism, looked too fearful to overcome. The Democrats had faulted Eisenhower for the French pullout back in 1954—and no doubt the Republicans would fault a Democratic pullout in the same way. To most Americans, the idea that they could not win a small war if they tried hard enough seemed absurd. Therein lay Kennedy's political problem, and the chief reason for his ever-deepening commitment.

When he did send more men, money, and arms to Vietnam—accompanied by his warnings about holding the line—it only encouraged elite opinion to grow more determined. In part to compensate for his retreat from Communist Cuba, Kennedy doubled U.S. aid to Vietnam between 1961 and 1962. Meanwhile, he engaged in a certain amount of lying to the public which, significantly, the public did not mind. The buildup of U.S. troops was not officially acknowledged by Kennedy—and, in 1962, he lied at a press conference when asked if Americans were engaged in combat. No one seemed to care when, soon thereafter, TV pictures showed American soldiers fighting in South Vietnam. It was as though the American people, while supporting the Vietnam War, wanted it to be waged on the sly. The U.S. government did its best to oblige them.

Unfortunately, the rising intensity of rhetoric—along with the rising quantities of U.S. aid—also made an impact on President Diem, who started thinking that he must be indispensable. It became clear to the more perceptive Americans in Saigon that all he really wanted was a deal with the Communists, or else an inconclusive war that brought in plenty of U.S. aid. Needless to say, morale in the South Vietnamese Army was terrible. Its officers, chosen for their loyalty to Diem, tried always to rely on U.S. hardware while avoiding heavy fighting. In early 1963, a small confrontation with the Viet Cong turned into a major combat disaster for South Vietnam; President Diem started to explore an accommodation with Hanoi. Conditions deteriorated even further when Buddhist monks rose up in protest against his rule—sometimes burning themselves to death in public—and his government unleashed a series of repressive moves against them.

Meanwhile, a spate of decisions back in Washington helped to bring about President Diem's downfall and murder. By mid-1963, Averell Harriman had been promoted to Under Secretary of State for Political Affairs, and the Ambassador to South Vietnam was replaced by Henry Cabot Lodge, Jr. Under Secretary Harriman was worried that Lodge might not share his distaste for Diem, so a cable was sent to Saigon requesting that the ambassador draw up plans for a coup d'état in South Vietnam.[49] But to Harriman's relief, Lodge took an instant dislike to President Diem. The ambassador made public signals in Saigon that

Adlai Stevenson and former Senator William Benton (Bowles's advertising partner in the late 1930s) visit an impoverished family in Lima, Peru. (UPI/Bettmann)

Vice President Nixon and Nikita Khrushchev argue about the usefulness of kitchen automation at a U.S. exhibit in Moscow in 1959. Khrushchev displayed a self-confident disdain for free markets and American consumerism that Gorbachev probably does not share. Just behind Nixon and to his left is Leonid Brezhnev, who would oust Khrushchev five years later. (AP/Wide World)

The President and Mrs. John F. Kennedy patronizing the arts. (National Archives)

A Green Beret signs the guest register at the John F. Kennedy Center for Special Warfare. A poster in the background displays quotations from Kennedy's speeches. (National Archives/U.S. Army)

American Peace Corps volunteers in India during the 1960s. The Peace Corps was perhaps the most idealistic arm of American foreign policy in that era. (Library of Congress)

A Taiwanese technician checks a microcomputer board designed for the American market. While young Americans engaged in far-flung philanthropy, young Taiwanese were learning to outperform the United States in the global marketplace. There was some U.S. financial aid to Taiwan during the 1950s, but it was mainly free trade and home-grown discipline that enabled Taiwan to prosper. (AP/Wide World)

Vice President Lyndon Johnson lectures President Ngo Dinh Diem during a visit to Saigon in 1961. Johnson would refer to Diem as "the Winston Churchill of Asia" and opposed plans for a coup d'état against him. (Library of Congress)

An American "adviser" in Vietnam during the Kennedy administration, when Americans were not supposed to take part in combat. (Larry Burrows, *Life* magazine © 1963 Time, Inc.)

The explosion that blew up the Maine *in the Havana harbor was "hyped" by the U.S. press to encourage a war with Spain and to sell more newspapers. The cause of the explosion was never ascertained.* (Library of Congress)

Teddy Roosevelt goes to Panama, which was created and partially colonized by the United States. Roosevelt's visit was the first time a U.S. president ever left the United States during his term of office. (Library of Congress)

Henry Cabot Lodge on maneuvers in Louisiana in 1941, when he was a captain in the army reserves. (AP/Wide World)

(Below) *McGeorge Bundy and General William Westmoreland interview a soldier after a Viet Cong attack on a U.S. base in early 1965. Shortly after this experience, Bundy started to urge tougher action against North Vietnam.* (Library of Congress)

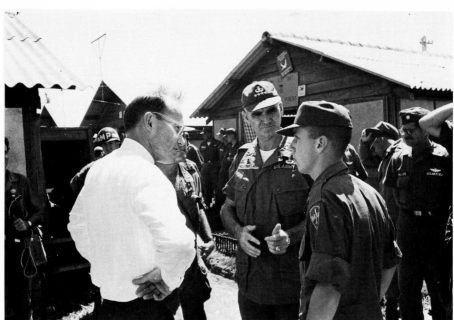

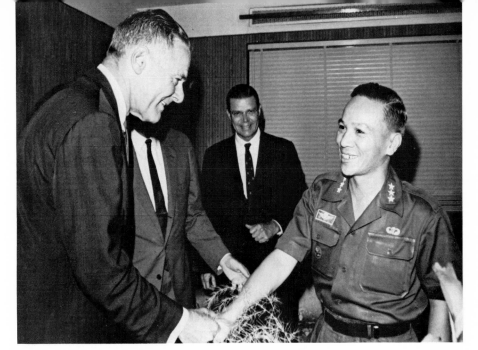

Lodge shakes hands with General Nguyen Van Thieu, a South Vietnamese strongman, after Lodge's return to Saigon as ambassador in 1965. Secretary of Defense Robert MacNamara stands between them in the background. (National Archives)

Ambassador Ellsworth Bunker looks at the body of a Viet Cong soldier after an attack on the U.S. Embassy during the Tet Offensive of 1968. (Dick Swanson, *Life* magazine © 1968 Time, Inc.)

Protest against the Vietnam War was intense and visible before 1968, but it generally was confined to marginal groups such as students. (Library of Congress)

(Below) An early meeting in October 1964 of the Senior Advisory Group to President Johnson—sometimes known as the "Wise Old Men." Most of the faces in this picture should be recognizable from earlier photographs. (National Archives)

Anti-war protesters taunt National Guard troops in Chicago during the Democratic National Convention of 1968. Earlier, city police and demonstrators engaged in a violent clash in which hundreds were injured. (AP/Wide World)

The Honorable Ellsworth Bunker, Ambassador to South Vietnam, at his desk in Saigon. (Library of Congress)

Jeering mobs in Caracas surround and stone Vice President Nixon's car during his visit to Venezuela in 1958. The sign says, correctly, that the United States was responsible for a "tragedy" in Guatemala. (AP/Wide World)

Khrushchev accompanies his new protégé, Fidel Castro, to a meeting of the United Nations General Assembly in New York. (Library of Congress)

The Alliance for Progress paid for schools, hospitals, roads, and the like—but at times it seemed that North America's direction of the program was a little too self-centered. (National Archives)

Ellsworth Bunker returns from an inspection tour during his long sojourn in the Dominican Republic after the invasion of 1965. (National Archives/U.S. Army)

In Air Force One during 1969. Clockwise from left: President Richard Nixon, Secretary of State William Rogers, Secretary of Defense Melvin Laird, General Earle Wheeler, General Creighton Abrams, Admiral John McCain, Henry Kissinger, Ambassador Henry Cabot Lodge, and Ambassador Ellsworth Bunker. (Defense Audio—Visual)

This prize-winning 1972 photo did much to bring home to America the random cruelty of war. Children are shown running along Vietnam's "Highway 1" away from an accidental napalm strike. (AP/Wide World)

(Above) *A political re-education center in Vietnam after the Communist victory.* (Gamma Liaison)

A flea market for Western goods in Saigon several years after the Communist victory. New economic policies in the 1980s suggest a shift by Vietnam toward a more loose, Western-style economy. (Gamma Liaison)

A giant poster of strongman Colonel Omar Torrijos behind a group of rioters in Panama. (National Archives)

Nicaraguan National Guard soldiers fire at Sandinista guerrillas during the last months of the Somoza regime in 1979. (AP/Wide World)

*A Salvadoran soldier holds a baby
and an automatic weapon shortly
after field operations against leftist
guerrillas in 1984.* (AP/Wide
World)

(Below) *Oliver North delivers a
pro-Contra briefing to members of
Congress during the 1987 hearings.* (AP/Wide World)

(Above) *A Toyota plant in Japan during the 1960s. Japan recovered from total destruction to take a place ahead of the United States in industrial competitiveness—due largely to free markets, free trade, and its own self-restraint.* (Library of Congress)

With the Statue of Liberty as a backdrop, George Bush, Ronald Reagan, and Mikhail Gorbachev pose on New York's Governor's Island in 1988. (AP/Wide World)

the United States might soon withdraw support for the regime; he started working through the local CIA to encourage Diem's opponents. As he cabled back to Washington: "We are launched on a course from which there is no respectable turning back: the overthrow of the Diem government."

Whereupon President Kennedy decided to give his ambassador full backing. He went so far as to repeat some of Lodge's warnings on prime-time television in America. The United States government was indeed up to its neck in South Vietnamese politics—just as, very soon, it would be up to its neck in the Vietnam War.

The man sent as viceroy to the world's "hottest spot," so called, had a host of similarities to John F. Kennedy—Boston, Harvard College, a mild liberalism—and one enormous difference. In contrast to Kennedy, the late Henry Cabot Lodge knew perfectly well who he was. The nineteenth-century Boston aristocracy whence he sprang was a self-defined, self-confident elite if ever there was one. Unlike other American elites, it could lay claim to literary and intellectual achievements equal to almost any in the world. New England culture soon would be eclipsed by immigration but it still appeared quite healthy around the turn of the century, when Henry Cabot Lodge, Jr., was born.

Young Cabot grew up among what must have seemed, to a child, rather ponderous company—such as that of the inevitable Henry Adams, who used to tell him that he looked like St. Thomas Aquinas. When his mother took him to go to school in Paris, it was Edith Wharton who made the arrangements at her home in France. And he remembered the outbreak of World War I on the Continent, the hasty retreat back home via England, and a visit to Henry James's house in Rye where, "finding the conversation rather heavy," he went out into the mulberry bushes to escape. His more permanent escape took the form of a passion for public affairs and an adoration of military men. Cabot's father may have been a poet, but the heroes of his life were often warriors: men like George Patton and General Frank McCoy, one of Teddy Roosevelt's comrades in the Spanish-American War.

But politics were just as important: "The discussion of political topics is one of the first things I remember." When his father died at an early age, it was natural that Cabot should come under the tutelage of his grandfather, Henry Cabot Lodge, Sr., a scholar-politician who headed the Republican Party in the U.S. Senate. Senator Lodge, Sr., had been case-hardened by party politics—but culturally he was descended from the Massachusetts mugwumps, a political caste that thought itself too pure for patronage and graft. Just as it was a Boston Brahmin's duty to serve his country, it was a government's duty to be morally bracing, to transcend the common man. "In becoming a Republican," Cabot Jr. remembers, "I thought I was joining something affirmative, evolutionary, and idealistic—which demanded sacrifice and generosity—not a party which said no to all proposals for change." Perhaps this was an early, more direct version of the New Class arrogance that arose after World War II.

President Theodore Roosevelt came as a mixed blessing for the mugwump liberals.[50] In domestic politics, his presidency marked a victory for reformist Republicanism that would not be repeated until the election of President Hoover. Roosevelt served as the chief inspiration even for the *New Republic* magazine, before it went over to Woodrow Wilson; in foreign affairs, however, Roosevelt's imperialism and protectionism was anathema to liberal purists. His view of America's mission abroad had far more in common with European colonialism and militarism than it ever did with Wilson's. There was an American mania for sports in the early part of this century, a mania exemplified by Roosevelt and his foreign policies. The Cowboy President promoted a strenuous, athletic life and encouraged a public impulse to flex America's muscles in the world. War and the exercise of power would help build the national character and enable Americans to return to a purer, more autonomous existence— both of them attractive themes for the Progressive movement. The anti-imperialist mugwumps, meanwhile, were dismissed by Teddy Roosevelt as a tribe of limp-wristed wimps and "perverse lunatics."

The result of Teddy Roosevelt's mission was the Spanish-American War and a U.S. empire that dared not speak its name.

"We shrink from the word 'empire,' " wrote Walter Lippmann in the 1920s, "and insist that it should not be used to describe the dominion we exercise from Alaska to the Philippines, from Cuba to Panama, and beyond." In fact, the war with Spain was welcomed at first by many anti-imperialists as a war of colonial liberation; it reflected a universalist view, typical of many isolationists, that foreigners were like Yankees or wanted to be. Other Americans saw the war as a means of spreading their benign, uplifting influence and, incidentally, of making a little money. There was some Anglo-Teutonic racism involved as well, shown in a contempt for the Spaniards and a patronizing attitude toward "liberated" peoples. Building a canal provided a legitimate excuse for the de facto colonization of Panama—in the Philippines, though, a sense of mission and moral advancement had to be cited as justification for the use of naked power.

Teddy Roosevelt's closest political friend and colleague was Senator Henry Cabot Lodge, Sr. The two of them bore a marked resemblance in their style of imperialistic bluster, their terror of losing out to Europe in an endless contest of strength and will. And they shared a fanatical partisan zeal. Senator Lodge hated Woodrow Wilson primarily for being a Democratic President. In 1915, he endorsed the bipartisan concept of a "League to Enforce Peace" and two years later zealously supported the declaration of war. But in 1919, he set out to destroy Wilson by delaying ratification of the Versailles Treaty—and to do so he was ready to make use of almost anyone, from the arch-isolationists to young Bill Bullitt. He demanded a punitive peace for Germany and prevented any effective system of collective security after World War I. The United States should be involved in world affairs, but only on a tough, "pragmatic," unilateral basis.

Taking his cue from this, Cabot Jr. did not come around to internationalist liberalism for another thirty years. From 1918 to 1924, he spent long evenings before his grandfather's fire being lectured to on current and foreign affairs. He took the senator's advice to go into journalism, by way of preparation for a political career, and worked hard at Harvard to graduate early. "I wanted to get going. I wanted to be a newspaperman." As such, he thumped against giving independence to the Philippines: the

Malay race was too ignorant, too passive, and too poor for democratic government. As for Europe, Lodge felt Americans should guard against any effort to trick them into guaranteeing the Versailles settlement. Behind his rhetoric, Lodge's world view was based essentially on racism, militarism, and above all a unilateral self-assertion.

By the late 1930s, Lodge had gone from American self-reliance to geographic isolationism—but at least he was no hypocrite about military preparedness. Hating the ad hoc nature of America's defenses, he spent most of his summers training in the army reserves; he liked to settle arguments with fisticuffs. Careful preparation and support for labor reforms also won him a U.S. Senate seat in 1936, which turned out to be less exciting than camp life. Young Lodge gave his casual backing to a lot of New Deal legislation, but by the time of Pearl Harbor he felt bored with politics. After a mission to North Africa and eighteen months of "grave thought," he became the first senator since the Civil War who resigned his seat to join up full time. He set off to take part in the D-Day invasion, feeling "confident that my political career was finished."

Of course, he was mistaken. In his military campaigns, Major Lodge won plenty of medals and returned a little less stuffy and parochial, winning back his old Senate seat by a very large margin. And by 1947 his politics had taken on a slightly new look, moving toward an internationalist stance just as fast as his self-respect would allow. His worm's-eye view of the world as a soldier, said Lodge, had proven his old attitude "100 percent wrong." This change was typical of many moderate Republicans, who were reacting to the Soviet scare and the American *Zeitgeist.* Lodge worked closely with others in his party to get the Marshall Plan through Congress and urged fellow citizens to join a global PR campaign: "An enthused America, speaking through its government, can make American democracy an article of export."

By 1949, Lodge was backing the entire Democratic program for Europe, pushing the Atlantic Alliance under one supreme commander and strategic plan. In order to have allies in a future war, America must work closely with like-minded countries, giving them economic and military aid. He allowed as how collective security was a difficult step for him—"But when we look at the fact of life, how can we doubt the wisdom of proclaiming a change which history itself has made inevitable?"

How indeed? Lodge had come a long way since the 1930s, but still he remained a black sheep in his own party. There was a presidential boomlet for him in 1947 that fizzled, and other Republicans in the Senate ignored him. So he tried a different approach four years later. He would sponsor a candidate for President who was independent of the party machinery, a war hero who could lead Republicans back to the White House after twenty years in the wilderness: General Dwight D. Eisenhower.

Having fought with General Eisenhower on the European battlefields, Lodge could make the kind of comradely appeal that no officer could ignore: that it was Ike's duty as a soldier to rescue America and the Republican Party. Certainly Lodge was the right man to manage Eisenhower's campaign for the nomination—he had grown up in the world of partisan intrigue and learned all the ropes from his grandfather. But the political game still bored Senator Henry Cabot Lodge, Jr. Beaten in his own re-election contest by young John F. Kennedy, he left senatorial politics once again with some relief.

It was fitting in 1953 that Lodge accepted the job of Ambassador to the United Nations. In the General Assembly, he was ahead of his time, giving speeches more to please his own compatriots than to achieve practical results. The military metaphor came naturally to him. He liked to use combative rhetoric against the Communists, comparing the French in Vietnam to an army of Spartans who were "fighting a modern Thermopylae—holding off the barbarian hordes who seek to impress free people into tyranny." Certainly he carried on with great theatrical flair; one night during the Suez crisis, he swept over from the Metropolitan Opera in white tie and tails to denounce America's allies, including France. Although he touted the UN all over the country, Ambassador Lodge had an impulse shared by many internationalist liberals: he believed in collective security just so long as the United States was strong enough to tell its allies what to do. The isolationist instinct never entirely left him.

With the face of a twenty-year-old, Lodge was something of a matinee idol by 1960, a new television star in the firmament. His spitting matches with Russia in the General Assembly became a popular alternative to the afternoon soap operas. It was primarily for this reason that Richard Nixon chose him as running mate in the 1960 elections: the U.N. ambassador could vie even with John F. Kennedy in youthful good looks and stylistic humbug.[51] Lodge personified some of the worst aspects of Ivy League taste as it had evolved by 1960—the pallid residue of New England culture, the *poshlust* of America's upper middle class.

President Kennedy bore a grudging respect for Lodge and several others like him, liberal Republicans from the Northeast who by this time were hard to distinguish from Democrats. They represented a mugwump remnant in the GOP, still looking to Henry Stimson as a patriarch and, even farther back, to Teddy Roosevelt. Being rich, northeastern, few in number, and a pain in the neck for other Republicans, they tended to know each other well. Perhaps it is not surprising that they soon declined as a political group or else joined the Democratic administration.

Lodge joined the administration. Urging the defeated GOP to get "more in tune with the times," he became director general of the new Atlantic Institute—a Kennedyesque think tank in Paris, touted by Lodge as "an idea factory for the Atlantic community." There he issued calls for an eventual American-European parliament, a new U.S.-British Commonwealth alliance, and a giant "free world forum" under a single high command. Multilateralism of that kind was Kennedy's way of institutionalizing U.S. influence, and so it was regarded by most Europeans.

In June 1963, when Lodge was at the White House sharing his latest North Atlantic ideas, President Kennedy asked him to become Ambassador to South Vietnam. Lodge already had made clear his desire to serve at a hardship post—and Kennedy probably wanted to implicate a Republican, just in case Vietnam turned into a political debacle. Although he had not volunteered specifically for Saigon, Lodge did not hesitate to go. "Americans were in Vietnam and were in combat. To accept, therefore, was a duty."

It is hard to say where by now Henry Cabot Lodge really stood. He appeared to have one foot in the past, another in the fashionable New Frontier—a unilateralist who touted the UN and NATO, a chavinist who cared about colonial liberation, a believer in old-fashioned military heroism who claimed a keen interest in modern counter-insurgency. Having learned something in the United Nations, he was far from a fool on the subject of Third World nationalism. Speaking of communism's threat to the Third World, he had warned Eisenhower's cabinet that most of the non-white peoples regarded capitalism as an enemy: "The U.S. can win wars, but the question is can we win revolutions." Through it all, Lodge retained an almost ultraliberal optimism about what America could do if it tried hard enough.

Like so many New Frontiersmen in Washington, Lodge also knew practically nothing about Vietnam. During the 1950s he had been kept out of the Indochina issue and rarely discussed it with Foster Dulles. What little he had said on the subject almost always was wrong: that the French would stand firm in 1954, that Ho Chi Minh would not compromise with them, that the South Vietnamese could be trained to fight a war on their own. The accelerating disintegration of South Vietnam was what made him decide in 1963 that President Diem must go, and there is little doubt that Kennedy agreed with this policy. In late October, the White House gave a "green light" to the coup d'état which then went forward without a hitch—except, perhaps, for the murder of President Diem. The murder allegedly horrified Kennedy, but Lodge assured the President that the prospect now was for a "shorter war."

The murder of Diem certainly did not horrify the Vietnamese, who were jubilant at the news. A carnival atmosphere swept through Saigon—with street demonstrations and burnings of symbols of the old regime—and Ambassador Lodge emerged a hero of the piece. The Vietnamese assumed that he had organized the coup; a number of them asserted that if an election were held, Lodge would become president of their country by a landslide. Of course, no election was held and the successor government was no better than Diem's. At Lodge's instigation, a second coup d'état occurred in January, bringing an atmosphere of violence and intrigue back to Saigon.

So Lodge's throw of the dice had failed, and his recovery attempt had failed even more. Early in 1964, he reported to President Lyndon Johnson that development projects in South Vietnam were collapsing and the war was going even worse than before. His advice to Washington was to send more money. He shared the conviction of most liberals that a broadly based approach to foreign aid—coordinating military assistance with a carefully balanced civilian program—could ward off communism. This method had worked in Europe and a number of Third World countries; with enough time and sacrifice, it would work even in Vietnam. Lodge's weekly reports galvanized the White House. Although Saigon already had the biggest U.S. aid mission in the world, President Johnson went ahead and increased the quantity of financial assistance.

Meanwhile, Lodge carried on with a daredevil bravado. After breakfasting each morning on a mango or papaya, he would shove a .38 revolver into his shoulder holster and set out in a white suit, with his bodyguards, for the embassy. "I can see him sitting at his desk with a pistol in the drawer, and a heavy Magnum in the open safe," reported a witness in *Time* magazine. He used to talk about defending the Chancery as enthusiastically as a Knight of St. John." Publicly he proselytized, warning Americans that Red China wanted to take over all of Southeast Asia. The war could not be won just by military means—we must get Vietnamese nationalism on our side—but "at this rough and dangerous stage, both for the Vietnamese and for Americans, there is no substitute for force." Like St. Thomas Aquinas, Lodge believed in just wars, and at this point most Americans enthusiastically agreed with him.

Moreover, Lodge's position at the front lines of the Cold War made him look very good in the United States. Pressure was building on him to come back and seek the Republican presidential nomination. His claim that Vietnam was too dangerous, too critical, for him to leave it only made him look more heroic. Almost incredibly, he won the New Hampshire presidential primary by a write-in vote. He easily was first choice among Republican voters, most of whom felt he had the best chance of beating President Johnson in the autumn. So, in June 1964, Lodge returned to the United States for a last, futile attack on the GOP right wing.

Liberal Republicans wanted mainly to stop the nomination of a horrifying upstart, Barry Goldwater—despised as much for his background as for his right-wing politics. "What in God's name has happened to the Republican Party?" said Lodge on his return; "I hardly know any of these people." As in Joe McCarthy's day, a social contempt for the right wing persisted even among certain Republicans, and conservatives returned the compliment. They resented Lodge's halfhearted effort in the 1960 campaign, his eagerness always to copy establishment policies. At the 1964 convention, Lodge urged that the federal government undertake a "reawakening of America. Indeed, we need another Republican-sponsored Marshall Plan for our cities and schools."[52]

Moreover, he refused to say anything helpful about Vietnam. "I don't see how Vietnam can be a part of this campaign. It involves the Eisenhower Administration and the Kennedy and Johnson Administration and the Truman Administration. As a matter of fact, foreign policy often is not a good subject for politics." That sort of remark irritated even moderate Republicans, who needed some tough talk that could be used against the Democrats. President Johnson's political strategy was to keep Vietnam on the back burner until after the 1964 election, in which task he was brilliantly successful. Barry Goldwater was nominated and it disappointed few people in Washington when Johnson beat him by a landslide.

Lyndon B. Johnson seems, in retrospect, a political paradox—a mixture, less unusual in those days, of hard-liner abroad and liberal enthusiast at home. One reason he wanted to win very big in 1964 was to push through a massive program of domestic liberal reform. Like so many ultraliberals, he regarded certain areas of foreign policy as an extension of American politics, which in his case meant Texas politics. Your opponents might be tough—sometimes you even had to rough them up a little—but in the end they would make a deal, if you had something to offer. That was how he thought of Ho Chi Minh.

Despite his senatorial background in military affairs, Lyndon Johnson's prime concern was not foreign policy. He knew little about foreigners and cared less—and yet he wanted to avoid losing the Vietnam War for the sake of his domestic "Great Society" programs. He feared that a congressional debate on "that bitch of a war" would do harm to "the woman I really loved—the Great Society"; he worried that right-wing politicians would destroy him for "losing" South Vietnam, just as they had destroyed Truman for "losing" China. In fact, he once declared that allowing another country to go Communist would be even worse than losing his social programs at home. Johnson's war would become a demonstration of America's true grit before the world.

After succeeding to the presidency, Johnson had come quickly to the conclusion that much more money and force would be needed in Vietnam. Increasingly pessimistic reports from Lodge and McNamara in early 1964 worried him and his advisers—as did the need for a second coup d'état early that year. Although Johnson had warned that "I don't want any more of this coup shit," the next year and a half saw a steady succession of coups in Saigon. The Vietnamese generals who succeeded Diem proved even more corrupt and inept than he was. After a lull in the fighting in late 1963, the Viet Cong moved forward to control ever larger amounts of territory. Little of Johnson's extra aid money in 1964 ever reached its intended destinations, but it was enough to delay a total collapse of South Vietnam.

Perhaps because of a comparative disinterest in foreign policy, and a desire to keep it going smoothly, Lyndon Johnson retained most of Kennedy's foreign affairs team. In effect, this meant continuing the internationalist activism that characterized the Kennedy administration. Among such people, President Johnson had no trouble obtaining a consensus on Vietnam, inasmuch as they wanted a deeper involvement. The Secretaries of State and Defense stayed on in the cabinet, and neither one of them did anything to alter this trend. Even had they wanted to, the locus of policy planning was shifting toward the National Security Council, where McGeorge Bundy continued as National Security Adviser. "Mac" Bundy typified liberal Republicans from the Northeast almost as well as did Lodge. He had been Jack Kennedy's classmate at a grade school near Boston; he had gone to Groton and Yale, assisted Henry Stimson in the writing of his memoirs, and later had spent seven years as dean of Harvard College. Bundy intended some day to write a book on the conflict between what he called "Wilsonian idealism" and the exigencies of power—though for him this conflict had been satisfactorily resolved. He had few doubts about his own, and America's, ability to control events in the Third World.

McGeorge Bundy also had a strong ally in his brother, William, a former Assistant Secretary to McNamara who was now in charge of the Far East desk at State. After some careful preparation by Bill Bundy, President Johnson managed in August 1964 to obtain a congressional stamp of approval for his war. On the basis of two alleged attacks on a U.S. ship by North Vietnam, Congress passed a resolution giving Johnson the right to take any actions needed to protect U.S. forces in Southeast Asia. Congress acted with only two dissenting votes, and 85 percent of the American people were behind the President on this issue. After the resolution passed, Bill Bundy took the lead in urging more pressure on North Vietnam; he drew up a plan for regular bombing of the North, scheduled to commence at the beginning of 1965. Over the next few months, a governmental consensus was reached in accordance with Bundy's plan. The U.S. military now was ready to go along, demanding much tougher action and Americanization of the war. All that was needed was another provocation from the Communists and a suitable fear of catastrophe in the South.

Neither of those developments was long in coming. Viet Cong strength in South Vietnam doubled during 1964; and their attacks, including terrorist attacks in Saigon, also intensified—leading to the massacre of hundreds of South Vietnamese at a time. Over the first few months of 1965, U.S. bombing was stepped up and contingents of U.S. Marines sent in to bolster the Saigon regime. The news was muffled through what Johnson's advisers called "a policy of minimum candor," but in any case it caused hardly a ripple in the United States. Polls showed a broad support for what the President was doing, and Congress continued to back him overwhelmingly. Meanwhile, a bombing pause brought no diplomatic response from Hanoi, even as South Vietnamese forces continued to disintegrate. To prevent a total collapse, the South Vietnamese government and the commander of American forces, General William Westmoreland, asked for intensified bombing of the North and a massive new infusion of U.S. troops.

In Washington and Saigon, support for this policy was almost unanimous. The ensuing discussions involved no basic examination of the goals and consequences of a further buildup in Vietnam. The questions asked tended to be "how" and "how much," not "why." President Johnson, in any case, only went through the motions of seeking advice. Already he sensed that Vietnam would need more than half a million U.S. soldiers. He held a series of meetings in July 1965 to obtain a consensus and as usual had no difficulty doing so. The civilians present included Rusk, McNamara, the brothers Bundy, and Lodge; George Ball, the token dove, registered his dissent but was not taken seriously.[53] President Johnson proceeded to make a muffled announcement that he was sending the extra troops requested to Vietnam, up to 125,000 men.

Almost no one before Kennedy—not William Bullitt, not even General MacArthur—had urged the fatal mistake of sending troops to Indochina. Now Johnson was making that mistake on a massive scale. It was the most important decision of the Vietnam War.

Henry Cabot Lodge was among those most firmly behind the decision. During the previous year, he had traveled all over the world for Johnson, trying to drum up support for the war in Southeast Asia. His warnings against the appeasement of Asian communism met with little success in the European countries. But at one White House meeting in July 1965, he made a strong and convincing plea to congressional leaders that they should give General Westmoreland what he wanted in Vietnam. Immediately, Lodge returned to Saigon for a second tour as ambassador. "Something brave, something noble is going on out there under your leadership, Mr. President. I am grateful to have a part in it."

In his own way, Lodge embodied what the President needed in the Ambassador to Vietnam: experience in military requirements, sympathy with soldiers, propaganda skills, a familiarity with civilian development theories. He still exuded an amazing cheerfulness and optimism—and a patriotism, too. When his old outfit, the First Cavalry, arrived in Vietnam in 1965, Lodge felt a nostalgic thrill. Praising a slain hero of the outfit, he quoted Pericles: "We survivors may pray to be spared their bitter hour, but must disdain to meet the foe with a spirit less triumphant." Certainly Vietnam would do much to destroy the triumphalist spirit among American liberals, whether they were peaceful or militaristic.

Lodge attempted to be both. For all his martial enthusiasms, he knew that victory would depend partly on non-military progress. After a year of thought back in the United States, he decided that this would be accomplished by a program of "Pacification" in the Vietnamese countryside. Lodge was devoted to Pacification and pushed it harder than any other aspect of the war, describing it to President Johnson as "the heart of the matter" in South Vietnam. The program set out to encompass the political, military, and foreign aid methods of building democracy at the village level. Inevitably it involved almost every civilian agency of the United States then operating in Vietnam, as well as the U.S. Army and the Vietnamese government. American experts in agronomy, engineers, teachers, doctors continued pouring into the Vietnamese provinces. It was a Bowlesian, holistic approach run rampant, involving counter-insurgency and civilian development under one administrative heading. Lodge's task was somehow to braid it all together.

Washington also saw Pacification as a top-priority item. The meaning and theory of this program became a subject for endless, mandarinesque debates—America's method of "winning the hearts and minds" of the South Vietnamese, whose passivity was the main problem of the war. Yet it never was entirely clear to anyone, including Lodge, exactly what Pacification should be. Originally it was a brainchild of technocrats in Washington—people like McGeorge Bundy and Walt Whitman Rostow, who replaced Bundy in 1966 as National Security Adviser. Having entered government with the New Frontier, Rostow was a development economist with elaborate theories on what armed force and civilian aid could do for the Third World. The trouble was his theories often broke down in practice. Except among American civilians, the attitude toward non-military programs was cynical. U.S. Marines summed it up by saying, "Get the people by the balls, and their hearts and minds will follow." For all its American expertise, the Pacification program was creaking and inefficient—short of local manpower and training—and its Vietnamese officials lived in constant fear of assassination. The Vietnamese government treated Pacification primarily as a method of dispensing patronage and collecting bribes, as they did every program they had anything to do with.

The story of America in Vietnam from 1954 onward is a story of varying dimensions of corruption, among the South Vietnamese, the American military, and American civilians—first in Vietnam, and then finally Washington. Ambassador Lodge had thought in 1964 that what South Vietnam needed was a better leader, but the problem went far deeper. When he began his second tour in 1965, he found what he called a "madhouse" in Vietnamese politics—"a fantastic situation, almost verging on the insane." To restore the country to political stability would be his second concern, which for him meant above all coherence among the Vietnamese military. "The military is the chief nation-building group in the country. It has education, skills, experience and discipline which no other group can offer." In point of fact, the Vietnamese military was almost as corrupt and incompetent as the rest of the country, but it seemed to be all that Lodge had left to work with.

The chief concern of Vietnamese officials, whether military or civilian, was how to extract as much money as possible from

America without appearing too obviously like puppets. That kind of demoralization in South Vietnam had an indirect effect even on the ambassador. Less and less could shock him. In spite of great pressure from Washington, he gave up on corruption at the higher levels in Saigon—better to let graft and inefficiency slide than push the government too hard. Like a banana dictator in Central America, the Saigon rulers knew that the United States was stuck with them anyway. So Lodge found himself drawn into supporting the regime against legitimate challenges to its rule, including outright revolt. Buddhist monks started burning themselves to death again, and this time Lodge showed less sympathy, seeing their protest as helpful only to the Viet Cong. To his great credit, he also tried to work toward developing some form of constitutional government and arranging elections in Vietnam. It was a struggle even getting this process started, and what is surprising is that Lodge had any success at all.[54]

Perhaps the worst influence on Vietnamese morale was the overwhelming presence of hundreds of thousands of foreigners—mostly U.S. soldiers—and the massive amount of money that came with them. Prosecution of the war forced the migration of four million peasants to the cities, which in turn brought about some profound changes in urban life. Foreign soldiers produced a vast increase in drug smuggling and prostitution, as well as black marketeering. The influx of Japanese and American consumer goods destroyed native industries so that, by 1967, much of the urban population was employed in servicing the U.S. presence. Absolute dependency on America tended to corrupt absolutely South Vietnam's entire culture and economy.

The enemy, meanwhile, was the opposite of the South Vietnamese and their government, showing high motivation and devotion to a cause. They regarded the American presence as just another form of European imperialism—defections from the Communist side were almost unheard of. Air strikes against North Vietnam went on almost daily from March 1965 to November 1968. But the bombing had almost no effect on North Vietnamese infiltration of the South or on imports of Soviet arms to North Vietnam. Indeed, it probably did a lot to strengthen nationalist feelings among the Communists. American soldiers fought hard against a tough and elusive enemy, but inevitably the nature of this struggle started to undermine their honesty and morale as well.

With its great numbers and firepower, the U.S. Army did succeed in preventing the disintegration of South Vietnam. The "kill ratio" in most engagements was very much in its favor. And yet little discernible progress was made in reclaiming lost territory or reducing the level of violence. In mid-1966, the Chiefs of Staff decided that over the next eighteen months, they would have to boost U.S. forces up to half a million, a request that was approved by President Johnson. But then, in early 1967, General Westmoreland already was asking the President for yet another 200,000 troops—still unable to explain exactly when and how the war could be "won."

In February 1968, when Johnson still was wondering whether to grant this request, the Viet Cong suddenly struck hard at South Vietnam in what would be known as the Tet Offensive. The offensive came as a complete surprise; it stunned President Johnson and General Westmoreland. Communists hit cities and towns throughout the country in suicide attacks, especially symbols of the United States and the government of South Vietnam. Their goal was to bleed American soldiers further and to drive a wedge between them and the South Vietnamese. Atrocities were committed on a massive scale, especially by the Communists; the slaughter of Vietnamese on both sides was enormous; over twelve thousand civilians were killed and a million refugees created. The United States proceeded to counterattack effectively. Fifty thousand Viet Cong died, compared to about two thousand Americans and four thousand South Vietnamese soldiers. In strictly military terms, the offensive was a disaster for the Viet Cong and was so regarded by Hanoi.

The Tet Offensive did, however, prove to be a propaganda victory for North Vietnam and it turned the tide in the Vietnam War—indeed, in all American foreign policy for at least twelve years. Mainstream American opinion was not much affected by Tet. But seeing such dramatic Communist successes after so much American effort—the U.S. Embassy compound was briefly occupied by Viet Cong—made a critical impact on certain American elites. This was especially true of those within the Johnson administration. The pervasive demoralization in Saigon now was spreading back to policymakers in Washington itself. In late March of 1968, Lyndon Johnson made the surprise announcement that he would not seek re-election as President, that he would limit the bombing to only 10 percent of North Vietnam, and that Averell Harriman had been authorized to start talking with the Communist side.

This announcement was the culmination of a process brewing since 1965, when President Johnson first sent army regulars to Indochina and started to bomb North Vietnam. Congressional dissent on the war had been insignificant until 1968, as we have seen.[55] The U.S. Congress followed public opinion, not vice versa, and public opinion supported the President. Except among college students and other fringe groups, there was little domestic opposition until mid-1967, when war taxes started and draft calls went up. By then most Americans had decided that the Vietnam War was a mistake and started to question Johnson's leadership. Even in 1967, however, a huge majority opposed withdrawing from Vietnam and wanted much tougher action against the enemy.

Surprisingly few stirrings had been evident in the press either. Perhaps the most significant opposition came from Walter Lippmann, still a columnist with unusual influence on Washington's inner circles. After a trip to Latin America, Lippmann had decided that America's Third World policies were far too concerned with stopping communism, instead of the twin scourges of poverty and despair. Lyndon Johnson had promised him that the Vietnam War would not be escalated. Therefore, Lippmann felt cruelly deceived by the military buildup of 1965, just as he had been by Woodrow Wilson at the Paris Conference—except that this time it was worse because whenever he criticized the President's policies, the President criticized him right back. Johnson kept making fun of him in a series of devastating and obscene little jokes. Lyndon Johnson, he opined, was "the most disagreeable individual ever to have occupied the White

House." In fact, the jokes became so hard to take that Lippmann eventually left Washington entirely—laughed, as it were, out of town. He died a few years later in New York.

Any kind of dissent from his war policies irritated Johnson, though in truth he had few powerful critics in America. What finally changed his strategy was disaffection at the highest levels of his own administration. Within the government, where before 1967 dissent on the war had been close to zero, there had existed little desire for negotiations with the Communists. In his effort to get peace talks started, Averell Harriman's first important backer in Washington turned out to be Secretary McNamara. In late 1965, the Secretary of Defense urged the first in a series of bombing pauses that would give Hanoi a "face-saving chance" to sit down and start talking. Other advisers of Johnson urged the same thing, if only because it might make for good propaganda, show the world that America was trying and strengthen support for new military efforts.

Johnson had good reason to feel suspicious. He already had offered Ho Chi Minh massive development aid—including a giant water project on the Mekong River—in exchange for a quick settlement of the war.[56] As usual, he saw the thing in personal terms: "Old Ho can't turn me down, old Ho can't turn me down." But old Ho did turn him down, and this time Johnson doubted whether Hanoi had any desire for a compromise. After much hesitation, Johnson decided to play along and started a bombing pause on Christmas Day—sending Harriman, Mac Bundy, and Vice President Hubert Humphrey out on a "peace offensive" to fifty different countries. The President's doubts were verified. There was no response from Hanoi, and so the bombing was resumed.

Over the next two years, several other serious attempts were made to bring Hanoi to the table. Harriman was put in charge of "peace feelers" at State, while others in various parts of the world joined him in what was called a race for the Nobel Prize. In 1966, Ambassador Lodge thought Hanoi had given signals that it would negotiate if there were an end to the bombing, but the White House decided that this was a trap. Another attempt was made in England, by Ambassador Bruce and the prime minister during early 1967, to get peace talks started through the Russians—but Johnson and his advisers again felt too skeptical of Hanoi's sincerity to cooperate. Later that year, an unofficial *démarche* by Professor Henry Kissinger scarcely got off the ground. Johnson's skepticism probably was justified. The evidence now indicates that Hanoi never was serious about negotiations until the end of 1967, and even then intended to use them mainly as a propaganda platform.

In December 1967, Hanoi stated publicly that it would begin negotiations if the bombing were ended. And by this time, dissent among liberals within the Johnson administration had grown more widespread. Various officials had left government as the ship of Vietnam began to sink: first Mac Bundy, then George Ball, and then, most importantly, Bob McNamara, who started to lose heart after the resumption of bombing in 1966. He confided his doubts to journalists and made contradictory remarks in public—dovish urgings toward retrenchment and restraint. At one point he told Congress that Pacification might take ten years or more. By mid-1967, he had become an embarrassment to the White House and a serious annoyance to the Pentagon brass. When he told the Senate that bombing North Vietnam was achieving nothing, LBJ decided to get rid of him.

So McNamara was replaced in February 1968 by Clark Clifford, an old Johnson crony who was hawkish on the war. But Clifford also was a fabulously successful attorney in Washington, an influence peddler who had been Truman's chief of staff and a personal lawyer for Jack Kennedy. Very much an entity in his own right, the new Secretary of Defense owed nothing to Johnson; he felt capable of challenging his new boss. Immediately he was presented with General Westmoreland's request for 200,000 more troops and asked for a recommendation in less than a week. "Give me the lesser of evils," Johnson told him.

Secretary Clifford turned for help to a group of Pentagon civilians, most of them demoralized liberals who shared McNamara's dovish views. They produced a report for Clifford that attempted to turn him against military escalation—making the usual points about the impossibility of "winning" in Southeast Asia, advocating retrenchment and "Vietnamization" of the war. Added to this was an extraordinary argument that further military expenditure, in place of spending on domestic social programs, "runs great risks of provoking a domestic crisis of unprecedented proportions." In other words—how else can one interpret it?—Pentagon monies should be reallocated so as to dissuade Americans from rioting. This report was perhaps the first significant example of isolationist liberalism penetrating the upper counsels of government since the 1930s. It foreshadowed an important trend of the next two decades.

The Joint Chiefs of Staff objected vigorously to this report, but they could not for the life of them offer good arguments of their own; after all, the war strategy never had been justified to *them* by civilians. For Clifford, who had begun to harbor private doubts the previous year, this experience settled the matter. He submitted his own recommendations to the President, suggesting a call-up of reserves for contingencies worldwide but not for Vietnam. There was no reason to believe that the Viet Cong could be beaten by "an additional two hundred thousand American troops, or double or triple that quantity." General Westmoreland should be ordered to retrench and the South Vietnamese Army warned to improve its performance.

A number of other developments and changes of heart finally decided President Johnson, who was worried about political setbacks later in the year. Dean Rusk suggested a bombing halt in exchange for negotiations; the rest of the administration accepted Clifford's report with little debate. When word of General Westmoreland's new troop request also was leaked to the press, even hard-liners on Capitol Hill resisted it. A hundred and thirty-nine congressmen called for a Vietnam policy review; public approval of the President's handling of the war plunged back to the lows of the previous year. On top of all this came the defection of news anchorman Walter Cronkite, who after a visit to Vietnam during the Tet Offensive expressed serious doubts on network TV: "To say that we are mired in a stalemate seems the only reasonable, yet unsatisfactory conclusion." When Johnson was almost beaten in the New Hampshire presidential primary by an opponent of the war, Senator Robert Kennedy immediately entered the campaign on his own anti-war platform.

Exhausted and unnerved, Lyndon Johnson asked Clark Clifford for a "peace proposal." He told the Joint Chiefs that he would send only another thirteen thousand troops to Vietnam and Saigon must begin to draft people into the South Vietnamese Army.

A major problem persisted. Johnson still hesitated to curtail bombing, a move which Clifford knew was essential to get peace negotiations started. So he persuaded the President to call a meeting of his senior paladins, a group known variously as the "Usual Suspects," the "Wise Old Men," or simply the "WOMs." Organized by Mac Bundy in 1964, this group had "advised" Johnson before on Vietnam. They had supported his decision to send in U.S. troops during 1965; and then again they endorsed his war policies two years later, urging him to intensify the bombing. In reality, the WOMs had given only casual, rubber stamp approval to decisions already made.

The WOM meeting with Johnson on March 26, 1968, was one of those melodramatic set pieces that occur every so often in the making and unmaking of American policy. This particular tableau included Dean Acheson, Averell Harriman, Cyrus Vance, George Ball, McGeorge Bundy, Henry Cabot Lodge, Douglas Dillon, Robert Murphy, and several military elders. Dean Acheson did the most talking and was blunt: both Johnson and the Saigon regime had too little support for the war effort. The United States could "no longer do the job we set out to do in the time we have left and we must begin to take steps to disengage." Several of the generals present demurred—the old war horse, Bob Murphy, declared himself "shocked" by this proposal of a "giveaway" to communism—but most of the Wise Old Men more or less agreed with Acheson.

President Johnson was even more shocked than Murphy by the change of heart: "The establishment bastards have bailed out." Never had he expected such a major switch in just four months. Even Henry Cabot Lodge felt demoralized by Tet. "If they had been so deeply influenced by the reports of the Tet offensive, what must the average citizen in the country be thinking?" wrote Johnson, which was very bad reasoning. Elites were quicker to change their minds about the Vietnam War than was the average citizen. In any case, Clifford's machinations and Acheson's rhetoric had their desired effect. The establishment bastards may have overreacted to the Tet Offensive and misread the public mood; nevertheless, their general advice on Vietnam was correct and it is well that Johnson accepted it.

Like the war in Korea, the Vietnam War was less important in and of itself than for its effect on U.S. policy worldwide. By 1968, it was beginning to destroy internationalist liberalism, that global enterprise which had preoccupied Washington for over twenty years. American liberalism already had achieved a certain sterility both at home and abroad; the liberal zeal for economic development had gone sour. But the enterprise might have recovered had some of its military initiatives in the Third World been more successful. They were not. America's package of development programs and military intervention failed disastrously in Vietnam. Partly because of the Vietnam debacle, intervention was failing in Latin America too—and still other dramatic failures were yet to come.

Chester Bowles's experience has shown that these failures often stemmed from overoptimistic goals. In most Third World cultures, the basic lessons could be learned only through bitter experience over many decades. Even where free trade and U.S. aid sometimes raised a GNP, the local economy was so distorted that political morale collapsed. Democratic development became almost impossible in such countries—where, in any case, it was hard to create a democracy without strong indigenous roots. Military intervention, likewise, was fraught with unforeseen complications. The very presence of U.S. soldiers tended to demoralize a country, especially one fighting against nationalist guerrillas.

But America's failures had as much to do with declining morale at home as they did with flawed policy. Losing even a small war has a debilitating impact on any country—and the impact of Vietnam on America's self-confidence was critical. After all, Third World intervention had not always been ineffective. Where the United States was sufficiently strong and determined, such policies sometimes could work for a time. Many liberals came to office in 1961 having learned their lessons not just from the Marshall Plan but from successful anti-guerrilla programs under Truman. In 1964, Henry Cabot Lodge cited Greece, Korea, Malaysia, and the Philippines as valid precedents for the Vietnam War: "Some have said that despite this effort the war in Vietnam cannot be won. Yet recent history shows that we have been fighting wars of this sort for the past 20 years and the record is creditable." Communism could be stopped, and democracy encouraged, by a subtle blend of military and civilian intervention. In his enthusiasm, Lodge was distorting the record; but America was so strong and prosperous that his argument sounded plausible in 1964. Three years later it seemed more likely that, with an overinvolvement of resources in Vietnam, the great American republic had gone too far.

This overinvolvement was more a liberal than an anti-Communist phenomenon. It is significant that liberal activism abroad began to overheat in 1965, at about the same time as liberal activism at home. Always more was better. If equality in civil rights was good, then more-than-equal rights for some would be better. If foreign aid and military intervention had worked well before, then more of it in Vietnam would work better. But the resources, both material and psychological, simply did not exist. After huge increases in domestic and military spending, Johnson refused to raise taxes until 1967—and even after that, the public deficit went on growing. Money was printed to keep interest rates down. Inflation started gradually to gather speed. Each of these closely related mistakes contributed to the accelerating effect of the other, until by the late 1970s prices were skyrocketing and American morale was at a nadir.

The loss of national confidence already was under way by 1968, after a series of race riots in American cities and the growing frustration of the war. Therefore, the Tet Offensive hit the United States at a vulnerable moment. It was the first dramatic setback since Kennedy's abortive invasion of Cuba. Washington was stunned by this spectacular, though minor, event and probably yielded to the Communists a great deal more than they expected. One week after the President announced that he would curtail the bombing, Hanoi made it clear that it was ready to start talking. Although Johnson had said that Harriman would go anywhere for peace talks, it took another month of bickering for a venue to be chosen. Finally, both sides accepted an offer by President Charles de Gaulle to host the negotiations in France.

Over the previous ten years, the United States had received no help on Vietnam from the august president of France, beyond some good advice. Knowledgeable about Indochina, de Gaulle warned President Kennedy that a war out there would trap him in "a bottomless military and political swamp." He tried in 1963 to arrange an accommodation between Diem and the Communists. In 1968, perhaps the old general was relying on the strange, inspirational effect that the City of Light sometimes has on U.S. officials. Accompanied by Cyrus Vance, one of McNamara's Pentagon civilians, Averell Harriman left for Europe with his peace delegation in early May. The delegates arrived in a mood of high euphoria, expecting that the Vietnam War might end after a few months of diplomatic talk—in Paris.

VIII

The Last Wilsonian

1968–1988

While decisions on Vietnam were made up in the stratosphere
of Washington politics, the netherworld of America seemed to
be falling apart. Black ghetto riots had been an off and on thing
in the United States since 1965—a sinister aftershock of the civil
rights movement, a counterpart to the chaos of colonial liberation. America's violence culminated in the Washington riots of
April 1968, which destroyed entire neighborhoods only a few
blocks from the White House. Martin Luther King, Jr., and
Robert Kennedy both were assassinated that spring. Student
uprisings, building seizures, and busts meanwhile became a
standard feature of northeastern and West Coast colleges in the
United States. In the first half of 1968, two hundred campus
demonstrations erupted to the sound of such slogans as: "Hey,
hey, LBJ, how many kids have you killed today?" Almost every
aspect of U.S. government policy was being vilified by America's
young—not just in Vietnam, but all over the world.

Many parents and grandparents of these students felt deeply
impressed by all the protest and turmoil, the most prominent
examples being liberals in the Johnson administration already
demoralized by the Vietnam War. It was around this time that
an upper-middle-class, intellectual, and under-class coalition
began its quixotic struggle against the rest of American society.
Inasmuch as the new coalition comprised at best about 20 percent of the country, most Americans regarded it with indifference or hostility.

In some respects, 1968 can be seen as a uniquely national happening, a climax of American political vulgarity, a public washing of the country's linen. But other countries were going through political turmoil as well. Averell Harriman arrived in Europe to find there something even more dramatic than what was happening at home. Student riots had brought Paris and much of France to a standstill. Marxism was at the height of its middle-class vogue in Western Europe, where large portions of the bourgeois youth were denouncing the United States as an imperialist monster. As for older Europeans, they had been patronized for decades by America on account of their colonial wars—now that America was suffering its own debacles in the Third World, the temptation to patronize back proved irresistible.[57]

All of this made a strange coda to the North Atlantic drama begun at the Paris Conference nearly fifty years before. In those days, Western liberals and socialists saw the European powers as bulwarks of imperialism and the U.S. president as a clean, bright hope. Now, during 1968, student demonstrators sensed a new dawn in young men's hearts that would overwhelm the evil American Empire. Bemused by such attitudes, Harriman refused to play the bogeyman role assigned to him. In an odd sort of way, he and his staff felt their own sophomoric exhilaration—bliss was it in that dawn just to be alive, if no longer young. North Vietnamese delegates, likewise, were confused but intrigued by the Paris événements—anything anti-American might be useful to their cause. They maintained a "patient anger" toward Averell Harriman and expected a long wait in Paris: "We know the enemy very well, and we brought our barber here."

The American delegates came to their senses quickly. They set up headquarters on the fifth floor of the Hotel Crillon, then moved to cheaper rooms and sent for their wives after realizing they were in for a long wait. It would take another six months of discussion even to bring the disputants to the table. Before engaging in formal talks, Hanoi insisted on a total bombing halt; but President Johnson was determined not to offer that sort of concession. As he ominously suggested, Johnson preferred to be succeeded even by Richard Nixon than by a fellow Democrat who would not stand firm on Vietnam.

Averell Harriman felt hemmed in by President Johnson. He wanted a generous opening offer, fearing perhaps that Johnson's refusal to end the bombing endangered not just the peace talks but something more precious: Democratic control of the White House and Harriman's own job. The Democrats' presidential campaign went badly from the start. Their national convention of 1968, where Vice President Hubert Humphrey was nominated for President, saw the worst protest rioting of the Vietnam War era—aggravated by the brutality of Chicago's police force. Harriman and Cyrus Vance tried to persuade Hubert Humphrey to make a conciliatory speech at the convention, "to reach out to those who had been beaten and jailed and to the whole peace movement." But Humphrey held back until the end of September, when finally he broke loose from White House policy and called for a total bombing halt.

Hanoi leaders responded to Hubert Humphrey by offering, in exchange, to include in the conference both the Saigon government and the Viet Cong—at that point, a serious parley could begin. Pressured into going along with Humphrey, President Johnson announced a total halt in the bombing just before election day. It seemed that the peace talks might soon start in earnest, that Johnson's latest maneuver might help Humphrey win the presidency by getting out the "peace vote." Then Saigon's rulers suddenly spoiled his new initiative. Egged on probably by Richard Nixon, President Nguyen Van Thieu of South Vietnam refused to send delegates to Paris until further conditions were met.

Many Democrats believed that President Thieu had scuttled their initiative so as to ensure the electoral victory of Richard Nixon. Certainly Averell Harriman was furious. He blamed the whole fiasco on administration hawks—especially Ellsworth Bunker, an old crony from Yale and Wall Street who had replaced Lodge as Ambassador to South Vietnam. Harriman felt that Bunker's malign influence and a "ridiculous performance" by the Saigon government had made Lyndon Johnson more rigid. In fact, Harriman was so fed up that he seemed almost to prefer the Communists to the Saigon regime. When he returned home to Washington, friends gave him a welcoming party spread among no fewer than three Georgetown houses—and of course the chit-chat included much talk of recapturing the White House in 1972. Communist Vietnam was not much worse than the Republicans. Nixon was an uncouth right-winger from southern California. Liberal Georgetown would rise again.

In one sense Johnson had been right on the peace talks, and Harriman wrong. The Communists were not interested in a real compromise, or in any further concessions without a U.S. pull-out from Vietnam. Harriman's replacement in Paris, Henry Cabot Lodge, would achieve practically nothing, either; in fact, the talk-fest in Paris would accomplish little for another four years.

Under President Richard Nixon, the steady shift of power away from State and the Pentagon toward the White House became nearly total. The new President and his National Security Adviser, Dr. Henry Kissinger, took foreign policy almost entirely into their own hands—a return to Franklin Roosevelt's methods, only more so. Dr. Kissinger revamped the National Security Council to keep other departments out of its deliberations; eventually he created an apparatus to evade even the Secretary of Defense, going directly to the Chiefs of Staff. Kissinger's tenure in office was the high point of White House control over foreign affairs.

President Nixon himself was an old McCarthyite from the 1950s, but in some ways his world view had evolved with the Washington *Zeitgeist*. From a lifetime of pragmatic dishonesty, he emerged looking like a liberal Democrat in some of his foreign and domestic policies. One exception perhaps to his political pragmatism, where his old instincts had not left him, was the war in Southeast Asia. Nixon remarked in 1967 that "whatever one may think of the 'domino theory,' it is beyond question that without the American commitment in Vietnam, Asia would be a far different place today." Determined not to appear the loser in Vietnam, he felt every bit as sensitive to criticism on this subject as Lyndon Johnson. Like LBJ, he would get more than his share of criticism, too—and his paranoid reaction to it led eventually to his downfall as President.

As for Henry Kissinger, he did not follow any partisan tradition, having curried favor with both Republicans and Democrats for more than twenty years. He shared Nixon's view of diplomacy as a matter for personal prestige, power, and realpolitik— to a degree unequaled by any other administration in this century. Policies of détente toward the Soviet Union and Red China may have appeared ultraliberal, but they arose mainly from pragmatic calculations. On the whole, the 1970s should be seen as a transitional era in American diplomacy. Moderate, internationalist liberalism continued to influence in a weaker form; ultraliberal "détente-mindedness" had grown far more prevalent; and reactionary unilateralism also was on the rise. Perhaps Nixon's realpolitik was not such a bad response to these conflicting trends in Washington.

Outside Washington, Americans during the Nixon era entered a period of diplomatic confusion—a conflict between following their isolationist instincts and doing what obviously was required. With the decline of internationalist liberalism, a natural consequence in the United States would have been a reversion to geographic isolation. That is the stance that comes most easily to U.S. citizens after a setback. But for all the talk of détente with Russia, there persisted a vaguely felt fear of expanding Soviet power—and besides, America's sheer size and the magnitude of its commitments made even a tempered isolation impossible.

The Vietnam War itself remained a debilitating commitment for Nixon and Kissinger. Both of them knew that military victory was unlikely. But both believed that they might pressure Hanoi into allowing an exchange of prisoners and an "honorable" U.S. withdrawal. The South Vietnamese regime appeared stronger than ever before in early 1969; with firm U.S. backing, President Thieu might be able to hang on indefinitely. Part of their strategy was effective negotiations and diplomacy, combined with a punishing air war against North Vietnam. More important was the slow withdrawal of U.S. troops while strengthening the Vietnamese government and army—what would come to be called "Vietnamization" of the war.

The chief proponent and symbol of Vietnamization was Ambassador Ellsworth Bunker, who had gone to Saigon in 1967.

One of Nixon's similarities to Johnson was that he hated the Ivy Leaguers who had run American diplomacy and looked down on him for so long. During the 1952 campaign, for example, Nixon had referred to Adlai Stevenson as a Ph.D. graduate of "Dean Acheson's Cowardly College of Communist Containment." But also like Johnson, Nixon had a grudging respect for such people and even kept a few on. The most important among them was Ellsworth Bunker, one of the last great paladins of internationalist liberalism. Over the next five years, Bunker would have more influence on Nixon's Vietnam policy than anyone except Henry Kissinger himself.

Nor was this surprising. When he went to Vietnam as ambassador, Bunker had the well-earned esteem of nearly everyone in Washington, the highest reputation of almost any U.S. diplomat. Probably he was the most skillful and accomplished mediator that American diplomacy has produced—and he possessed an ideal personality to go with it. Lytton Strachey, in a bitter mood, once described the characteristics of a Victorian official rather like Bunker: "His temperament, all in monochrome, touched in with cold blues and indecisive greys, was eminently unromantic. He had a steely colourlessness, and a steely pliability, and a steely strength. . . . His views were long, and his patience was even longer. He progressed imperceptibly; he constantly withdrew; the art of giving way he practised with the refinement of a virtuoso. But, though the steel recoiled and recoiled, in the end it would spring forward."

Certainly Bunker's tall, gray-haired, bespectacled appearance was the stereotype of a Yaleman in his generation. It sometimes surprised people to hear that he had spent thirty-five years in the sugar industry before switching to public service. How could someone so successful in business have emerged such a perfect gentleman? Probably because his father owned the National Sugar Refining Company before Ellsworth joined as dockyard hand and "worked his way up." His good business sense was thus rewarded without the usual compromise of manners and gentility.

Ellsworth Bunker was a prominent and active interventionist just before World War II—a self-identified "Wilsonian liberal"—but not until 1950 did he enter government service. At age fifty-seven, he was asked to serve as Ambassador to Argentina by Dean Acheson, an old friend who had coached "Elly" on the Yale freshman crew. Bunker's expertise in hemispheric affairs was based mainly on his savvy as a sugar baron. Not that this had differed much from the outlook of the State Department; Bunker had joined his father's company in an era when the U.S. flag followed capital, when State operated in the Americas mainly to help trade and investment. And the sugar business reflected an unquestioned fact of life in the hemisphere: that Latin America provided food and raw materials in exchange for U.S. manufactured goods. A system of economic dependency on the United States had developed, especially in Central America and the Caribbean, a system that was strengthened by U.S. military power. Almost all of this area was, theoretically, open to trade and investment from anywhere—but the United States intervened often to prevent the "nationalization" of U.S. assets or the establishment of European business beachheads. It was the kind of relationship that existed, in a somewhat different form, between the European countries and many of their own dependencies.

Interference in Latin America has been perennial throughout most of U.S. history. It continued under Woodrow Wilson, who sent troops into the Caribbean area more often than any other U.S. President. Wilson did so to defend the Panama Canal and impose what he thought was good for the natives—a system of economic freedom and political reform, combined with military coercion whenever the system backfired against U.S. interests. When Wilson suffered one of his frequent digestive ailments, he would refer to it as "Turmoil in Central America." That area was for him an organic part of the U.S. security and defense, albeit a rather sickly one.

Latin America's comparative advantage in cash crops and raw materials led steadily to a higher concentration of resources in the hands of a few more efficient producers, a cooperative oligarchy of local magnates or absentee Yankees. Later on, the Green Revolution would push this trend even further. Although free trade and cash cropping may have helped raise the various

GNPs, it often deprived the peasantry of what little land it possessed. Moreover, U.S. interference turned some Central American countries into not just economic dependencies but outright military protectorates, which only made it harder for a democratic center to develop.

During the presidencies of Hoover and Franklin Roosevelt, an effort was made to end this pattern of armed intervention and improve the economic relationship somewhat. "That is a new approach that I am talking about to the South American things," Roosevelt said in 1940. "Give them a share. They think they are just as good as we are, and many of them are." He had put Sumner Welles and Adolf Berle in charge of a "Good Neighbor" policy that unfortunately made little difference to the South American things. U.S. intervention gradually was replaced by local, surrogate forces to put down anti-Yankee revolutions; dictators were accepted and democratic change generally resisted. Moreover, the bigger share given to Latin Americans of their own economies went almost entirely to the richest few percent. The beginnings of U.S. financial aid did very little for democracy—Central America was ruled by economic and military oligarchies that owned nearly everything not owned by Yankees. The oligarchs proceeded to run things in their own and North America's short-term interest.

In 1956, when John Foster Dulles needed a token Democrat for a Third World post, it is not surprising that he turned to Ellsworth Bunker. Their temperaments and world views were in many ways identical. Both Dulles and Bunker were cold, firm diplomatists, with a Wilsonian conviction that free trade and commerce was an important route to political and economic progress; both of them had worked for U.S. business in Latin America before entering government; and both shared a certain Wilsonian confusion about that part of the world. For instance, it was only natural that Bunker wanted his own business protected from free trade. He encouraged laws to restrict the importation of refined sugar, laws which helped his own refineries in the United States but harmed Latin America and U.S. consumers. Moreover, Bunker thought that Wilsonian principles must be backed up by U.S. intervention and pressure, especially south of the border.

As Ambassador to India, Bunker made a stark contrast to Chester Bowles's hearty style—although he had the sense to build on Bowles's achievements. He oversaw a lot of aid programs and did a good job mediating between the moralistic Dulles and the self-righteous Nehru. Returning to private life in 1961, he found that his wife was mortally ill; he might easily have retired forever to the sugar maples on his Vermont farm. Instead, he did some work on the Peace Corps and performed two special assignments for JFK. In both Yemen and Indonesia, he had to mediate an armed confrontation; and in each case he let the most intransigent side have its way, while enabling the loser to save face. Crown Prince Faisal, the loser in Yemen, said later that only his personal confidence in Bunker had made him yield. In fact, Bunker's extraordinary presence often instilled a respect, verging on trust, in foreign potentates. Perhaps he was what so many Third World rulers secretly wished to be: the rich, handsome, gentlemanly representative of a powerful democracy.

Even Lyndon Johnson was impressed by the mystique. Just before his assassination, John F. Kennedy secretly appointed Bunker as U.S. representative to the Organization of American States (OAS); as president, Johnson approved the appointment, which became official in 1964. Kennedy had wanted to show that the OAS could and should be the hemispheric equivalent of the United Nations—which the United States still dominated. Kennedy's policy in Latin America, as in so many other areas, reflected a zeal to transform the New World into a dynamic and optimistic entity like himself.

We have seen how parts of Latin America, by 1945, already suffered from the same economic pathology that would afflict most of the newly liberated Third World. As elsewhere, primitive traditions and statist interference were the main causes of this disaster; in Central America, however, the United States itself bore some of the blame. Economic and military involvement by the north may have done a little good, but it also had taken an awful toll on local morale. After World War II, the

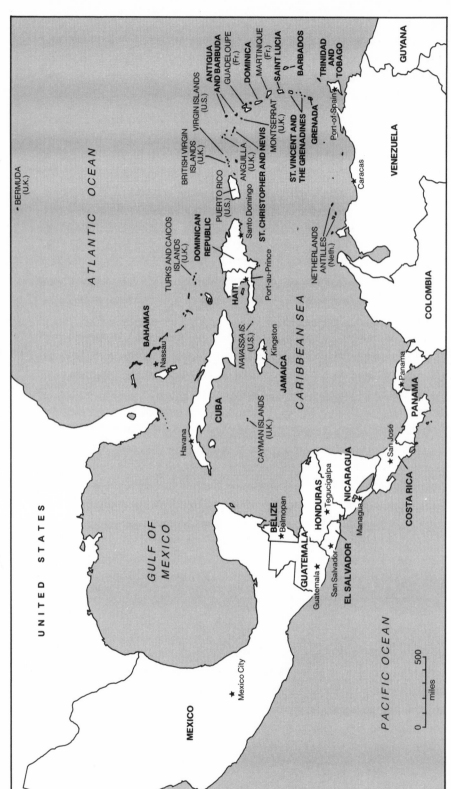

Central America and the Caribbean

picture was muddied further by multilateral efforts to oppose
the Communist threat. The Rio Pact was signed in 1947 and
supplemented by the OAS the following year—intended as a
combination of NATO and the United Nations that would function as a security organization for Latin America. Unfortunately,
the degree of economic dependence on North America only
increased, even as military cooperation tightened further in the
1940s and 1950s.

During the fifties, Latin America had been considered relatively safe by the United States—safe enough in fact to receive
under 5 percent of U.S. civilian aid to the Third World, less than
any other major region. Pentagon and CIA involvements did
intensify—Washington functioned as though Central America
were a U.S. colony—but there were no direct interventions
other than the overthrow of a government in Guatemala.[58] The
coming to power of a Communist regime in Cuba and the election of John F. Kennedy seemed to augur a more positive approach, a new effort to promote development south of the Rio
Grande. The Eisenhower administration had warned that massive aid programs for Latin America might well be dissipated in
corruption and inefficiency, after raising false hopes. In Central
America, capitalist investment was so resented that it would be
seen only as delaying a needed revolution. Nevertheless, President Kennedy went ahead and inaugurated such a program.

The "Alliance for Progress," launched in 1961, was perhaps
the greatest example of Kennedy's coordinated approach to
Third World development. The President declared his vision
for turning Latin America into "a vast crucible of revolutionary
ideas and efforts" during the critical, twilight decade of the
sixties. The American nations, he said a week before his death,
must "use every resource at our command to prevent the establishment of another Cuba in this hemisphere." Pursuant to the
theories of Walt Rostow, the Alliance was to employ CIA intervention and internal security programs to stamp out communism; this would be combined with land reform, education, and
industrial investment to bring each country to a "takeoff stage"
of democratic capitalism and self-sustaining growth. Alliance
officials in both Washington and Latin America were united by

their passionate faith in statist economic policies. Typically, Averell Harriman likened the Alliance for Progress to the Marshall Plan, especially in its goal of lowering intracontinental barriers to trade.

As in Southeast Asia, the Alliance for Progress only proved the ineffectuality of massive aid programs for corrupt, statist, or backward economies. Policies that accomplished so much for European middle-class democracy could do little for democracy in Vietnam and Latin America. The "revolution of rising expectations," combined with a temporary jump in incomes, tended even to encourage anti-Yankee upheavals. Rapid population growth brought further dislocation. Moreover, there existed a dark side of the Alliance for Progress in its U.S. interventions and security programs. This was demonstrated most blatantly by military meddling in Guatemala and other countries of the region.

Already, when Bunker became Ambassador to the OAS, the bloom was off the rose of the Alliance for Progress—programs that trained soldiers for "internal security" had become its most significant aspect. During the early 1960s, military juntas took control of nine Latin American countries, several of them headed by officers trained under the Alliance. As the threat from Castro's Cuba appeared to recede, President Johnson felt forced by such priorities as Vietnam to cut back on the Alliance's economic side. His emphasis went into backing the local status quo, which usually meant continued rule by military and economic oligarchs.

Nevertheless, Ambassador Bunker's speeches remained those of an optimistic industrialist. He promoted Latin American "economic integration, which may well prove to be the most important development in the hemisphere since the American nations achieved independence." To his eternal discredit, Bunker also approved of various OAS programs "designed to enhance the internal security capabilities of the military and police forces of Latin America so that they may be better able to cope with threats of violence and subversion."

Right after joining the OAS, Bunker had to help pacify Panama following some riots directed against U.S. rule in the Canal

Zone. Implying that the riots were largely the work of Communists, Bunker warned that they might provide an issue for Fidel Castro to exploit. Panama was the first overseas test of the Johnson administration. Nationalist riots there called further attention to anti-Yankee sentiment in the Americas, and certainly they deepened Washington's fears about the Communist threat in Southeast Asia. U.S. politicians felt the new President ought to show that these little countries could not kick him around, and Johnson was ever sensitive to congressional feelings.[59]

Another overseas test soon occurred on Ambassador Bunker's watch. Bunker had approved of what he called "OAS intervention," meaning almost always United States intervention. "Since the Rio Treaty was concluded in 1947," he said, "the OAS has intervened some 30 times in situations which involved threats to the peace and security of the hemisphere." Accordingly, U.S. Marines were dispatched to the Dominican Republic during 1965, where President Johnson worried that Castro was coopting a progressive revolution. After the Marines landed, a dictatorship took over once again, and so Bunker arrived at the head of an OAS committee to negotiate a compromise regime. The President felt skeptical—the OAS "couldn't pour piss out of a boot if the instructions were written on the heel"—but after a year of patient effort and frightful risks, the impossible was achieved. Bunker put together a moderate government that would secure Dominican stability for another twenty years. The leader of the Dominican left finally conceded, "I have the respect for that man that I have for my own father"—and a right-wing general agreed.

Lyndon Johnson agreed, too. Bunker often had echoed LBJ's remarks during the Dominican crisis, and the President began to introduce him as his personal mentor: "Ellsworth Bunker showed up every morning on the palace steps down there and held that new government together with his bare hands!" When the man of steel returned from his year-long assignment, Johnson offered him practically any diplomatic post he wanted. Even some ultraliberals who deplored all military intervention admired this Mr. Fix-It for the Third World.

Actually, Bunker's success in the Dominican Republic had some bearing on the President's decision to go full tilt into Southeast Asia. U.S. Marines entered the Dominican Republic soon after they first went ashore in Cam Ranh Bay—and just a few months before Johnson's most fateful decisions on the Vietnam War. In both theaters, Johnson hoped, a dramatic victory would silence his critics. Ellsworth Bunker personified this determined presidential optimism, and it should have come as no surprise when suddenly Johnson made him Ambassador to South Vietnam.

Much has been written about the effect of the United States's failure in Vietnam upon its subsequent policies, or non-policies, in Central America. Far less is understood about the effect of the United States's experience in Latin America on its policies in Vietnam, which the Dominican crisis so well illustrates. It was primarily in Central America and the Caribbean—not Asia or Africa—that North Americans had learned their formative lessons on Third World intervention. And in the mid-1960s, despite the failure to overthrow Castro in Cuba, many of those interventions could be seen as tempered successes. Armed force and civilian development in Vietnam would comprise two parts of an old liberal package—a package pushed in Latin America by Bunker and many like him.

In South Vietnam, Ambassador Bunker shared none of Lodge's soldierly panache. His initial effort was simply to increase the efficiency of U.S. operations. Working seven days a week and fifteen hours a day, he ran the vast bureaucracy like a good business—though in this case ignoring the question of its basic profitability. One reason for sending him to Vietnam was to apply some Alliance for Progress methods to the Pacification program. He agreed with Ambassador Lodge's view that Pacification was what counted: "Like my predecessor, I regard revolutionary development—often termed pacification—as close to the heart of the matter in Viet-Nam." This meant braiding the program more closely together "by unifying its civil and military aspects under a single management concept."

In some respects, Vietnam did resemble parts of Latin America. The democratic center was almost nonexistent. The United States had to rely on corrupt landlords and generals. However, Bunker regarded the poor morale of South Vietnam as a problem that might be solved by American effort rather than an inevitable result of dependence on the United States. Always he urged patience—his kind of Sisyphian patience—and said in 1967 that Pacification was just getting off the ground. The Viet Cong were under more pressure, the South Vietnamese Army was improving, corruption was being rooted out, and democracy was advancing. By late 1968, a lot had indeed been done by Thieu on inflation, but new problems were emerging and many of the old ones remained. In private, Bunker knew that corruption was worsening and that land reform, especially, had seen little progress.

If anyone had the strength and determination to reform South Vietnam, it was Bunker. Recently remarried at the age of seventy-three, he commenced a second middle age, and his reports struck a cautious but endlessly optimistic note. When the Tet Offensive erupted in 1968, Bunker was forced to fend off an enemy attack on the U.S. Embassy. But he decided right away that the main purpose of the offensive was psychological, to hurt morale in the South and to strengthen the Communist hand in negotiation. Advising Lyndon Johnson at Camp David that April, he agreed with Walt Rostow that the Tet Offensive had weakened the Viet Cong. To the press he declared, "If Tet was a psychological and political success abroad, it certainly was a resounding military defeat for them in Viet-Nam." He asserted, moreover, that the South Vietnamese troops had fought well in the crisis.

Bunker certainly was doing all he could to "Vietnamize" the war. He had opposed adding large numbers of fresh U.S. troops after the Tet Offensive, urging instead that Americans should help build up the South Vietnamese Army. Throughout 1968, he made a steady effort to implement Vietnamization. Soon it became an integral part of the Pacification program, which President Nixon tried to accelerate. Bunker stated in 1969 that the South Vietnamese military performance was improving and "the pacification program this year has made steady progress."

As he put it later that year, "We have sought to prevent the North Vietnamese from taking over the South by force, and, to the extent that we have been able to frustrate these efforts, we have been successful. This may not be a victory in the usual sense of the word, but it is nevertheless a success."

This was true up to a point: by 1970 the countryside was indeed more secure than it had been since the war began. South Vietnam was starting to show some signs of self-reliance, and Vietnamization proved successful enough to stalemate the conflict for a while. But long neglect had made Vietnamization a very slow business and, in any case, the South Vietnamese quietly resisted the whole thing. Meanwhile, after Ho Chi Minh's death in 1969, the North Vietnamese grew more determined than ever to win. They retrenched by switching to small operations and a protracted struggle.

Ambassador Bunker went on worrying that "the American people have not kept up to date with what is happening in Vietnam. It is almost as if many people had stopped reading about Vietnam after Tet, 1968, and reached their conclusions at that time." Still, he managed to feel optimistic about the American anti-war media. "As I discovered in the Dominican situation," he wrote to a friend, "there is always a time lag until the facts catch up with the reporting." His problem was that the crucial facts did not justify his optimism. It is true that the suicidal Tet Offensive had destroyed the South Vietnamese insurgents as an effective fighting force; from then on, soldiers infiltrated from the North would have to bear the brunt of Communist fighting. But none of this could alter the basic weakness of a corrupt and dependent South Vietnam, or the fanatical determination of northern Communist guerrillas.

Meanwhile, another kind of fanaticism intensified back in the United States—what fittingly was called anti-war hysteria. President Nixon throughout his first term kept implementing large troop withdrawals from Vietnam, and in October 1969, the public approved his war policy at a rate of 71 percent. But tremendous pressure against him mounted in the Congress and major print media, where neo-isolationism was growing more prevalent. After the Tet Offensive, even television coverage had become quite critical of the war.

Anti-war demonstrations also continued. Student protest enjoyed a big revival during the spring of 1970 because of Nixon's decision to extend the ground war into Cambodia, South Vietnam's western neighbor. At the urging of Bunker and the U.S. military, the United States had been bombing Cambodia secretly for over a year in massive B-52 strikes. In early 1970, Cambodia entered a state of chaos—the combined effect of American bombing, an anti-Communist coup d'état, and an insurgency backed by North Vietnam. Tense and defiant, Nixon worried that Cambodia would "go down the drain" if he did not intervene there.

The President unveiled his decision to invade Cambodia in a television address—whereupon, articulate elites in the United States erupted into an anarchy of protest, especially on college campuses. At Kent State University in Ohio, the National Guard reacted to campus disorder by firing on a group of protesters, killing four of them and giving rise to a nationwide "student strike" against the war. A hundred thousand demonstrators gathered in Washington, and many older groups joined in. Incredibly, two hundred State Department employees registered their public dissent from the President's policies. Like some of Johnson's advisers, one member of Nixon's cabinet was not immune to the influence of his own college-age children: the Interior Secretary publicly objected to the Cambodia invasion and was fired.

One reason why Nixon had invaded Cambodia was to show protesters, and a hostile Congress, that he would not be swayed by their pressure tactics. But still he was taken aback by the breadth of his opposition, which touched off a paranoia that led ultimately to Watergate. "Within the iron gates of the White House, quite unknowingly, a siege mentality was setting in," one of Nixon's aides later said. "It was now 'us' against 'them.' Gradually, as we drew the circle closer around us, the ranks of 'them' began to swell."[60]

Anti-war protests had an equally unfortunate effect on the other party. Student unrest in the United States subsided rapidly after 1970, but political turmoil continued among intellectuals, the "prestige media," and most Democratic politicians. Congress voted symbolically in June 1970 to rescind its own 1964 resolution of approval for the war; and politicians started to consider a "War Powers Act" to restrain presidential powers of armed intervention abroad. It took only four years after 1968 for the Democrats to revert to a self-critical form of New Deal isolationism, from which they still had not recovered twenty years later.

One example of this trend was to be found in Averell Harriman. Most Democrats left Nixon alone during his first hundred days in office, although Harriman fulminated in private—"President Nixon is following the advice of people that got President Johnson into the deepest mud in Vietnam, and not following the advice of those that helped get him onto the hard concrete, which he was on January. And I'm afraid that includes Ambassador Bunker, who's committed to Thieu." Ambassador Harriman felt "in a state of almost frustration" over the way the negotiations were being handled by his successor in Paris, Henry Cabot Lodge. The United States should show more respect for the opinions of mankind, emulate the restraint of North Vietnam, restore its great popularity in the world.

In mid-1969, Harriman, Clark Clifford, and Cyrus Vance started to criticize Nixon openly for implementing the policies which they had urged privately six months before. Clark Clifford called for a total withdrawal by the end of 1970 and, one year later, Averell Harriman went farther. "To me the Vietnamization of the war is an immoral thing," he said to group of college students. "We have no right to perpetuate the fighting. Every effort should be made to end the human tragedy that is going on in Vietnam." He singled out students and journalists for special praise, asserting that U.S. reporters had provided "much better evidence than we've gotten out of Lodge as to what these people feel" in Hanoi. Harriman felt heartened by student protests against the war—and wasn't it a shame that President Nixon had "scorned student opinion on Vietnam."

In late 1970, Harriman continued to accuse Nixon of making no serious effort to reach an agreement with Hanoi. He and

Clark Clifford went on calling for total withdrawal. The experience of Vietnam led both of them to question the premises of U.S. policy worldwide, especially those of Soviet-American relations. Harriman wanted more emphasis on East-West trade and détente with Russia; most American troops should be withdrawn from Europe, where they never were meant to stay so long. He was proud of having returned to his accommodating stance of 1944—unlike, say, his old comrade Dean Acheson—"What annoys me beyond belief are these old cold war warriors who pull out their rusty armor and bring out their broken swords and charge into battle." America's main difference from Russia was not in economic systems, Harriman felt, which would some day converge as the United States moved closer to Swedish-style socialism.

The leadership of the Democratic Party agreed with most of these views and often went farther. Much of this was a long-delayed reaction against the intense red baiting of the McCarthy era. The Vietnam War produced an upsurge in the Democratic Party similar to the right-wing upsurge of the Korean War. McCarthyism had been, among other things, a wave of resentment against the control of policymaking by a ruling aristocracy—against the political corruption of eastern cities and foreign entanglements. So was the reaction against Vietnam.

As in the case of McCarthyism, certain politicians like Averell Harriman started to trim their sails and move with the times. Other Democrats had different motives. American intellectuals and subintellectuals had been for the most part anti-Communist, but they had felt uncomfortable in the Cold War atmosphere of the fifties. So when America's foreign policy elite stumbled in the late 1960s, they naturally seized an opportunity. Certainly it was fitting that their most prominent exemplar, Senator George McGovern, had been a Henry Wallace delegate in 1948. And George McGovern found among the sixties adolescents an effective cohort of supporters. Though his moralist isolationism was too much even for Harriman, Senator McGovern had little trouble winning the Democratic nomination for President in 1972.

*   *   *

McGovern and his congressional colleagues were right in sensing that the silent majority of Americans wanted their boys back home without delay, despite the popular support for Nixon in 1970 at what seemed a moment of crisis. Later that year, Congress almost passed a bill to repatriate all GIs by the end of 1971 and, in some respects, the army brass was starting to agree with anti-war politicians. Declining morale in Vietnam, a serious problem since 1968, now was damaging the entire U.S. military establishment. Decisions reached in Washington after the Tet Offensive soon made U.S. soldiers realize that they were fighting only a holding operation; nor did the war back in America do much to stiffen their morale. There was a growing use of drugs in the ranks; racial tension, racketeering, and even the killing of officers increased. And just when the student protests started to subside in 1970, returning GIs started to take part in anti-war demonstrations.

Meanwhile, the government and army of South Vietnam still had no capacity to survive without massive U.S. backing. In June 1970, Bunker said on American television that "what is important, I think, there and in many of these small countries, is the development of effective government. Effective government is what people want and what they will support, and this is what Thieu is trying to do." But Thieu was trying to do nothing of the sort. His attitude was reflected in the conduct of South Vietnam's army—now a big fighting force, but still the same repository for political cronies and grafters that it had been under Diem. In early 1971, South Vietnam invaded southern Laos and was completely routed by the enemy. An idea mainly of Bunker's, this operation only demonstrated the poor morale of South Vietnamese soldiers, most of whom hated the Thieu regime. And in civilian life, the popular attitude was similar. It did not say much for South Vietnamese democracy when Bunker had to beg candidates to run against President Thieu in the 1971 "election," an election that Thieu eventually "won" unopposed.

The Paris peace talks went exactly nowhere during the first three years of Nixon's presidency. Secret negotiations continued under the guidance of Harriman's successor, Henry Cabot Lodge—but Hanoi was stalling, demanding the ouster of

Thieu and a coalition government that included the Viet Cong. It would not even agree to a mutual withdrawal of troops. Dismissing Nixon's proposals in 1969 as a "farce," the Hanoi delegation vowed to sit in Paris "until the chairs rot"; then when Lodge quit in frustration, top Communist negotiators pulled out of Paris as well. Secret discussions between Henry Kissinger and Hanoi officials did not get serious until two years later. Though stymied on the battlefield, the Communists still hoped to achieve some advantage in negotiation and insisted on Thieu's ouster before any other agreement could be reached.[61] Their patience paid off. By 1972, under greater time pressure than the Communists, Kissinger began hinting at some important new concessions.

President Nixon had decided that, in addition to these concessions, some new forms of military and diplomatic pressure on Hanoi might lead to a peace agreement. His authority was bolstered by his revelation of Communist intransigence in the secret talks, as well as by his personal visits to Russia and China—Americans felt that their President was making serious efforts toward peace. Triangular diplomacy also proved effective. Anxious for a détente with the United States, the two Communist giants now could be relied on to push fraternal North Vietnam into softening its terms. At first resisting such pressure from its patrons, North Vietnam struck heavily against the South in early 1972—to which Nixon responded, for the first time in his presidency, with massive B-52 raids and the mining of North Vietnamese harbors. At the same time, he delivered a conciliatory speech that said Americans would withdraw within four months of a cease-fire and the mutual release of prisoners. He made no demands for a similar Communist withdrawal and said a political settlement could be worked out by the Vietnamese later.

Nixon's package of military force, concessions, and the backing of other countries had its intended effect at the bargaining table—and some unintended side effects elsewhere. No longer faced with a demand for their withdrawal from the South, the North Vietnamese decided to reach a settlement—or the appearance of a settlement—in Paris. In mid-1972, Kissinger offered them a "standing cease-fire," and after that the secret talks

moved forward quickly. President Thieu had pretended to ac-
quiesce in everything. But when a treaty was produced for his
signature in Saigon he went on strike, endlessly refusing to meet
with Bunker or Kissinger. True to his old form in 1968, Thieu
publicly denounced the treaty a few days before the 1972 elections in America—which did not prevent Nixon from winning a
landslide victory over McGovern, even so.

After the American elections, there unfolded another three
months of argumentation, changes of heart, and haggling
before a treaty was signed and the POWs returned. North Vietnam, for example, walked out of the discussions just before
Christmas and Nixon responded with the unrestricted bombing
of Hanoi—the heaviest of the entire war. Hanoi promptly returned to the table and resolved all differences in a day. Meanwhile, Thieu was handed an American ultimatum and finally
caved in. Looking across his desk at Bunker, he said: "I have
done my best. I have done all that I can do for my country."
Soon after his second inauguration, President Nixon felt that he
could tell his fellow Americans that "we have achieved peace
with honor."

The most important point of honor in the agreement—besides the immediate return of six hundred American prisoners—
was that it allowed South Vietnam at least a "decent interval"
between America's departure and a Communist victory. Thieu
would be supported by American arms, bombs, and money so
as to give him one last chance to get his government and army
in shape. Unfortunately for him, the Democratic Congress immediately set about passing bills to disengage the United States
totally; and the Watergate scandal further weakened the Nixon
administration in its Vietnam policies. The rapid communization of Laos and Cambodia made the war look ever more hope-
less, but the U.S. Congress probably would not have gone on
helping an inept and corrupt Saigon government anyway.

An important symbol of America's departure was a sudden
diminution of the U.S. Embassy in Saigon. A few months after
the agreement with Hanoi, Ambassador Bunker returned home
to be replaced by a nonentity. Pretty soon the South Vietnamese
economy started to fall apart. President Thieu went right on

spurning advice to broaden his political base and instead cracked down on dissidents. Of course, this was the continuation of a very old story. He could not reform his regime without destroying the entire system of graft that guaranteed support and kept him in power. His government was 85 percent financed by U.S. aid and comprised one-third of the economy. While American aid receded, Vietnamese corruption and inflation went completely out of control, soon degenerating into a collapse which resembled that of China in 1948.

Congressional cuts in aid were not the only reason for the military debacle. The Communists were in bad shape militarily, but slowly they prepared for a massive invasion of South Vietnam. Twelve thousand miles of road were built to replace the old infiltration trails; an oil pipeline net three thousand miles in length was constructed to provide fuel for a mechanized offensive. The Soviets and Chinese increased their military support for Hanoi, no doubt vying for influence after what seemed an inevitable Communist triumph. The invading army of North Vietnam—for that is what it was this time—struck in March 1975, moving through the major cities and south toward the capital. One million refugees fled before it, but America was too weary to give any further help. Amidst a final frenzy of political intrigue, President Thieu left the country in April and Saigon quickly fell to the Communists.

As might be expected from such a debacle, the fall of South Vietnam gave ammunition to both political extremes back in America. Both the right wing and the left felt vindicated by what happened. Anti-war spokesmen could point out that the victory of North Vietnam did not cause the collapse of other dominos throughout Southeast Asia—few of the nearby countries objected to America's retreat from Indochina. Furthermore, mainland China had long since split from the Soviet Union, so a Communist Vietnam did not entail the expansion of an Asian Communist monolith.

On the other hand, conservatives could argue that the rest of Indochina soon came under the control of Hanoi. Vietnamese communism remained a singularly nasty tyranny, forcibly moving urban populations, taking 200,000 political prisoners, executing thousands. More important to the United States, all of Vietnam was now allied with Russia. That meant a significant addition to the Kremlin's sphere of control, the more so because of its apparent permanence. Once a Marxist-Leninist regime took control of any country, it never could seem to change or be overthrown by rebellion—still a major worry for American conservatives.

Nothing fails like failure, and the failure in Vietnam undermined U.S. influence everywhere. Movements under way for years were encouraged by the defeat, which further hastened the breakup of America's foreign policy consensus. To this was added a sense of economic decline and political malaise back home. Different institutions were affected in different ways. To some extent the State Department came under the influence of Democratic "reformers," speaking endlessly of the need for a more open and populist diplomacy. But populist diplomacy could cut from another direction. In the Republican Party there arose a very populist, right-wing backlash reminiscent of Teddy Roosevelt's unilateral adventurism. President Gerald Ford and Henry Kissinger had to navigate their way through these competing movements.

Changes in the bureaucratic *Zeitgeist* made an impact even on the steely Ellsworth Bunker. When he left Saigon in 1973, it seemed at first as though the harrowing experience had not softened his old toughness: "I have always said that countries like Vietnam, and the countries in South America, should not be expected to model themselves on us and our democratic form of government." He remained optimistic even about the country he was leaving. "As far as the US in Vietnam is concerned, the degree of progress is that we can work ourselves out of a job." At the age of seventy-nine, Bunker wanted to spring forward into a new job of his own.

And Henry Kissinger, now Secretary of State, wanted to give him one. Bunker soon was asked to resume negotiations on the Panama Canal Treaty—a good example of Washington's deepening troubles in the underdeveloped world. Perhaps the most important result of the Vietnam War was its effect on the behavior of Third World politicians. Any dictator now felt that, by imitating North Vietnam, he could challenge the self-confidence of Western democracy and the United States itself. General Omar Torrijos was a vaguely leftist, populist strongman in Panama. Having repudiated the new Canal Zone treaties—initialed in 1967—he went on to threaten guerrilla activity against the United States.

In 1972, Torrijos suddenly decided to take his case to the world at large—or, rather, to the Third World at large. This meant every Third World forum he could find, especially those of the United Nations, where he told his spokesmen to "let the gringos have it." Panamanian rhetoric drew a parallel between European colonialism and the Yankee "occupation" of the Canal Zone. The original Panama Canal Treaty was indeed the prime example of Teddy Roosevelt's arrogance in the Caribbean; and the Third World, naturally, was receptive to complaints about what seemed a heaven-sent case of U.S. colonialism. Torrijos's onslaught reached a climax at a UN Security Council meeting held in Panama in March 1973, which denounced the United States and nearly ruined all hope of a peaceful settlement.

But the outcome was exactly what Torrijos wished: enormous pressure on Washington to make further concessions, and the start of a new phase in the dispute. When Ellsworth Bunker resumed work on the negotiation, he found it "the most difficult and complex" he had ever conducted. Giving way on several issues, he managed to establish some common ground between the Pentagon and Torrijos. Early in 1975, a new Panama treaty was almost complete.

Then a more serious problem arose back in the United States. Egged on by candidate Ronald Reagan, Ford's rival for the GOP nomination, a movement took hold across the land that resisted any concession to Panama. Saigon had just fallen to North Vietnam. Reagan called the new treaty another example of weak wills in Washington retreating before communism. Of course, Reagan's resistance to the Panama treaty also was related to the Vietnam debacle; some Americans had grown more eager to give way and to withdraw, while others had grown more rigid in reaction.

The tactics of Omar Torrijos made things worse. He took a

propaganda trip all over the world to push his case. Serious left-wing violence broke out in Panama itself—a typical 1970s scenario for a Third World country. Bombs went off in the Canal Zone, and the U.S. Embassy was attacked; native politicians blamed the United States for a deteriorating local economy. In 1975, Panama joined the Organization of Non-Aligned Countries, a gaggle of Third World states united mainly by their anti-American, anti-Western, and anti-democratic stance. Naturally, Torrijos also worked on winning support from other Latin American governments. Neighboring politicians became his advisers, and he flirted with Fidel Castro. Asserting that the Canal was part of a much bigger problem, Torrijos started to complain about U.S. "imperialism" throughout all of Central America.

Caught between Torrijos and Ronald Reagan, Ambassador Bunker underwent a radical change in his style. "In the past, when serving as a U.S. negotiator, I have made it a habit to keep my mouth shut publicly while negotiations were in progress." Things would be different this time around. To push his treaty through, he made seventy-five appearances in twenty-one states to deliver speeches and answer questions, all the while enduring harassment from anti-treaty protesters. Bunker's usual argument was that, without a new treaty, there might be so much violence in Panama that the U.S. Army could not keep the Canal open anyway.

This, of course, was largely a post-Vietnam *angst.* We have seen how disturbances in Latin America helped to encourage an interventionist policy in Vietnam. Well, now it was time for the reverse. In 1964, the idea of a Central American dictator threatening guerrilla actions against the United States would have seemed almost laughable. Ten years later, it did not sound funny. As Bunker said, "We should bear in mind that the Canal is vulnerable to sabotage and terrorist acts. We would find it difficult, if not impossible, to keep the Canal running against all out Panamanian opposition. The problem—in my opinion—simply will not go away. Attitudes—not only in Panama but in the Hemisphere at large—have changed." And Ambassador Henry Cabot Lodge, that old Teddy Rooseveltian, shared almost exactly the same fear.

Meanwhile candidate Reagan, as he rode toward the 1976 campaign, found that Panama got better electoral results for him than any other issue. Desperate to win the Republican nomination, he became shrill and demagogic: "When it comes to the canal, we bought it, we paid for it, it's ours." President Ford responded lamely that an unrevised Panama treaty might mean guerrilla warfare—hardly an argument to use on people who were smarting from Vietnam and aching to win a fight.

Throughout most of the campaign, Ellsworth Bunker kept quiet and the treaty talks bogged down; but when Jimmy Carter took office in 1977, he put Panama at the top of his presidential agenda. A new treaty was initialed after one last bout of demagoguery from Omar Torrijos, who made a promotional trip to visit Colonel Qaddafi in Libya. Not that the issue ended there. All the spleen, bile, and vinegar of America's defeat in Vietnam kept welling up among U.S. conservatives, who were assured by Ronald Reagan that "the fight has just begun." Ambassador Bunker had to spend another six months soothing Panama's nerves and placating politicians during the senatorial debate, one of the most rancorous in decades on a foreign issue. The treaty finally squeezed through by only one vote.

This was a Pyrrhic victory for the foreign policy establishment. Opponents of the Panama treaty started to rally around some ever more popular issues. The winds of Reaganism blew stronger, even as President Carter blundered from one disaster to another. Carter and Bunker may have been right on the Panama Canal treaties, just as Eisenhower had been on the Suez invasion. But the application of Carter's doctrine to other Central American countries appeared far more doubtful.

As Stalin once remarked to Ambassador Harriman, "communism starts in the cesspools of capitalism." Perhaps that is the best way to sum up Central America. Most Great Powers, through sheer negligence or disillusion, tend to leave certain territories to the lowest elements of their private and public life—to the most unscrupulous businessmen, to the least capable diplomats. In Central America, the Alliance for Progress was designed to provide more carrot and less stick, but old habits proved almost impossible to break. Rather like a welfare ghetto in the United States, no amount of financial aid could solve the neighborhood's problems. Foreign investment, loans, and grants only prolonged a cycle of dependence and corruption.

As in the North American cities, all of this happened amid greater prosperity. Though far poorer than Panama, the rest of Central America had enjoyed some of the highest growth rates in the Alliance for Progress. Such rapid growth could achieve few of Washington's political aims; rising expectations and birthrates only made the region more unstable. President Kennedy's pledge of a great ten-year effort, so difficult to sustain, led to a pervasive feeling of hopelessness and betrayal. An absence of social and land reforms helped to create a widening disparity of incomes and worsening destitution. Moreover, the Central American Common Market, by which the Alliance for Progress hoped to reproduce the success of Western Europe, made little difference in these primitive economies.

Then, during 1965, the U.S. Marine landings in Santo Domingo revived the image of North America as an enemy of socioeconomic change. The first overt U.S. invasion of Latin America in forty years, it naturally gave encouragement to the Latin American Communists. Fidel Castro hoped that, with the United States mired down in the Vietnam War, he could start some similar wars in Latin America and open a second front against the Yankees. With his encouragement, several Marxist insurgencies soon got under way. These failed almost everywhere except in Central America, where they went through a quiescent period and then came back with a vengeance in the late 1970s.

The most direct U.S. response occurred in Guatemala. Green Beret forces helped in fighting guerrillas there, adding to the culture of savagery between left and right—in the ten years after 1966, more than fifty thousand Guatemalans died in political violence. During the same period, twenty-eight U.S. soldiers were killed, culminating in the 1968 murder of a U.S. ambassador. A large Peace Corps contingent and huge amounts of civilian aid made little impact; like the urban underclass of North America, many Guatemalans took to criminal behavior such as trafficking in drugs. Washington's handouts were replaced by further "get-tough" law enforcement and Alliance for Progress programs superseded by further military supplies.

Meanwhile, leftist guerrillas everywhere took heart from the success of North Vietnam. One example was an insurgency in the Philippine Republic, that Oriental cousin of Central America. As the Philippine Communist Party put it, "Indochina has demonstrated that with the help of the Soviet Union one can achieve national liberation without threatening either world peace or détente." And U.S. opposition to such movements was weakened, first by Watergate and then by the diplomacy of President Carter. Carter wanted to make human rights an acid test in his foreign relations, with both friend and foe alike. This test was applied most pointedly to Central America, where the President threatened to withhold military aid and questioned the legitimacy of U.S. client regimes.

Political violence in Guatemala continued, but the first country in the region to fall to an insurgency was Nicaragua. President Carter decided during 1978 that the days of the hereditary U.S. client dictator in Nicaragua were numbered. He pushed for a compromise regime, before the political center was destroyed by a prolonged civil war. Unfortunately, the struggle in Nicaragua gave rise to further conflict in Washington. A fight broke out in the Congress between politicians who wanted to cut off aid to the Nicaraguan dictatorship and politicians who wanted to send even more.[62] Sure enough, the moderates in Nicaragua were weakened while Marxist-Leninists grew stronger within the "Sandinista" insurgency.

Most Latin American countries showed the same indifference to communism as had the countries of Southeast Asia. Many regretted their acquiescence in the Dominican invasion, believing that the danger from Cuba had been exaggerated. The most militant of the Sandinistas' supporters probably were the Panamanians—but democratic Costa Rica also was providing bases to Sandinistas and sending them Cuban arms. When Carter tried to create a multilateral force of OAS troops to oversee a transition, the Latin American governments refused to join up. Later, the OAS extended its formal backing to the Sandinistas.

The danger from Marxist-Leninists proved more real this

time than it had been in the Dominican Republic. After taking control of Nicaragua's capital in 1979, the Sandinistas proceeded to declare themselves "non-aligned"—which meant, as usual, both anti-United States and anti-democratic. Members of the new junta made a triumphal visit to Cuba, where they denounced U.S. support for the dictatorship of neighboring El Salvador. In an attempt to make his peace with the Sandinistas, President Carter proposed a $75 million aid package for Nicaragua. But he had lost his influence over an anarchic Congress and the package was delayed on Capitol Hill. Although it finally was passed in June 1980, Carter's relations with Nicaragua continued to deteriorate.

While the Sandinista government clamped down at home, it also lent support to guerrilla movements elsewhere in this war-torn region. Walt Rostow once had argued that U.S. success in Vietnam and Latin America would discourage the "romantic revolutionaries" and lead to political "pragmatism and moderation." And his reasoning was correct in that the U.S. failure in Vietnam tended to discourage moderation everywhere—including Central America. President Carter tried at first to pressure the military juntas of El Salvador and Guatemala to disband their death squads and mend their ways. But fears were on the rise in Washington that the communization of Nicaragua would have a domino effect throughout the Caribbean basin. Carter felt that he had no political choice but to continue supporting both of those governments.

Pressure on Carter came mainly from politicians who had criticized him on the Panama Canal. In his rhetoric, Ronald Reagan said that Central Americans were being subverted by communism, which threatened their freedom and endangered the United States. As President, he was determined to back "friendly" governments—whether democratic or otherwise—and to encourage anti-Communist "freedom fighters" all over the world. Convinced that Nicaragua was no exception to the century's experience of Marxist-Leninist regimes, he would make it the acid test of his new policies.

Critics of Reagan had some valid points. A period of honest and centralized governments might be needed, they argued, before an enlightened, local business class could emerge in Central America. They felt that Reagan oversimplified the problem, which was true. On the other hand, they too oversimplified it. Certainly these insurgencies had arisen not because of foreign subversion, but because the peasantry was poor, oppressed, and wanted change—*any* change. Even so, people had remained just as poor and oppressed after similar revolutions elsewhere and were quickly disillusioned—with an added problem that the new regimes were friendly to the Soviet Union, hostile to the United States, and almost impossible to overthrow.

Soon after entering the White House, President Reagan cut off financial aid to Nicaragua. By the summer of 1981, his spokesmen were accusing the Sandinistas of moving closer to the Soviet bloc and creating a police state. This accusation seems just. With Soviet help, the Sandinistas started building up a 50,000-man army; they moved sharply leftward when U.S. aid stopped and their economy went further downhill. The Roman Catholic hierarchy and moderates in Nicaragua cooled toward the revolution as Marxist-Leninists took control of the revolutionary junta. Umberto Ortega, Defense Minister and brother of the top Sandinista, had put it bluntly enough in a secret speech: "We do not fool ourselves. Our Revolution has a profoundly anti-imperialist, profoundly revolutionary, profoundly class character. We are anti-Yankee, we are against the bourgeoisie. . . . We are guided by the scientific doctrine of revolution, by Marxism-Leninism."

Like Carter, President Reagan also worried about Nicaraguan aid to nearby insurgencies. White House officials warned in late January 1981 that Nicaragua's support to leftist guerrillas in El Salvador had better stop, or else. One month later it did appear to have stopped—but U.S. aid to Nicaragua was cut anyway, and the arms flow from Nicaragua resumed. To counter this, massive amounts of U.S. arms were shipped to El Salvador, which started to resemble South Vietnam in its absolute reliance on Yankee money and advice. The guerrilla army grew from about three thousand in early 1981 to ten thousand in 1984, while millions of U.S. dollars disappeared into governmental corruption.

In a time-honored U.S. fashion, Reagan tried to promote new

economic solutions for Central America—although economic aid never had worked before in these countries. In August 1983, he appointed a bipartisan commission on Central America, supplemented by calls for a Central American "Marshall Plan." Inevitably, there was also talk of a new Central American Common Market. Headed by Henry Kissinger, the commission issued a report in January 1984 urging an $8 billion aid package and free trade in the Caribbean—a similar package was urged later on for the Philippines. Perhaps Reagan did not mind very much when the Caribbean Basin Initiative bogged down in Congress.

Despite little public interest, Reagan's effort in Washington was successful in bringing aid to El Salvador. Indeed, his determination may have staved off a Soviet client dictatorship where the Democrats would have caved in. But this dubious success was not enough to win U.S. support for a counterrevolution in Nicaragua. Fearing another Vietnam, many top U.S. military officers opposed Reagan's policy of building up a "Contra" army to wage guerrilla war against the Sandinistas. Their outlook was shared by most intellectuals and journalists of influence—and the secular intellectuals had some new allies. The U.S. Roman Catholic hierarchy—once a supporter of the Vietnam War—condemned Reagan's efforts in the strongest terms.[63] Most of Latin America and Western Europe did the same. Almost all of young Europe and much of the old reacted even more intensely against the Contra war than they had against Vietnam.

By far the most effective critic of Reagan was the Democratic Party in Congress. As an Assistant Secretary of State put it in 1985, there were two things that most Americans did not want in the Caribbean—"they do *not* want a second Cuba, and they do *not* want a second Vietnam"—but it was Vietnam that preoccupied most Democratic politicians. There were a few Bill Bullitts among them, ever hopeful and even eager to befriend a revolutionary regime. More broadly, many Democrats could oppose Reagan's intervention in Nicaragua with the same political opportunism with which he opposed the Panama treaties. Opposition to aiding the Contras benefited from a very popular disaffection with almost any kind of land war abroad, even one waged by surrogate troops. Vietnam remained a more potent symbol than Cuba and it went well with the astonishing ignorance of U.S. voters, few of whom even knew or cared where Central America was.

When a peace proposal suddenly was agreed to in 1987 by five Central American countries, Democratic politicians quickly jumped on board. Indeed, they more than jumped on board; the Democratic leadership in Congress took charge of the entire ship, meeting privately with Sandinistas in Washington to discuss the new proposal. Asserting that the peace agreement would be respected by Nicaragua, Congress voted in February 1988 to suspend all military aid to the Contras. It took only a few months to prove this wrong. After a brief show of keeping the agreement, which called for political amnesty and democratic rights, the Sandinistas cracked down once again on political dissent. Meanwhile, Soviet advisers and arms—$2.5 billion worth since the revolution—continued to pour into Nicaragua.

As we saw during the 1930s, intellectuals and politicians usually prepare to fight the previous war or, more often, to prevent it. World War II may have resulted from a zeal to avoid repeating World War I; the Vietnam War was a misplaced attempt to prevent another World War II or Korea. Will the desire to prevent another Vietnam lead to something similar in Central America? While the Contra army disbands in Nicaragua, subtle pressure is building in Washington to withdraw support from the Salvadoran government, still under attack by leftist insurgents. Perhaps an intensified guerrilla war will follow in Guatemala. The outcome of all this is hard to predict, but efforts to stop communism through military intervention are in obvious decline—suffocated by a new form of isolationism in the United States.

Epilogue
Götzen-Dämmerung

U.S. foreign policy has passed through some vast pendulum swings since the Spanish-American War. Great crises have led to new political splits and then, without much delay, ended in a new political consensus. Popular support—or just popular deference—has helped American presidents to act with some consistency and internal logic. Since the 1970s, however, that kind of support has been radically divided. For the first time in this century, there exist many separate pendulums in U.S. policy, and none of them is moving at all.

This is a condition that arises from American irresolution and malaise since 1968: political demoralization after Watergate, military demoralization after Vietnam, a sense as early as 1973 that the U.S. economy no longer was the world's engine. Foreign policy setbacks have provoked different reactions in the great political parties. Republicans and Democrats each have sought refuge in some venerable, but rather archaic, forms of isolationism.

All of this can be seen easily enough in the views of such party leaders as Jimmy Carter, Ronald Reagan, and Michael Dukakis. American politicians tend to regard their limitations as virtues; while none of those three is an exception, perhaps the most egregious example is Mr. Carter. A bright but simple soul out of rural Georgia, he won a narrow victory in 1976 as a man who compared well with the cynical Washington establishment. His rural background had instilled in him a semi-pacifism and strong religious convictions—a belief that American Protestant ideals could be exported through arms treaties, international law, respect for human rights, and an honest effort in such multilateral forums as the United Nations.[64] His successors at the head of the Democratic Party still are influenced by those assumptions.

Nevertheless, the Democrats have problems that go beyond the policies of their leaders. President Carter's feeling that the world might be improved by moral example, exhortation, and embargo went quite easily with the fecklessness of his party. Liberal anti-communism almost ceased to exist, with moderates being coopted either by ultraliberals or by conservatives on that issue. The Democratic Party remains torn on foreign policy because so many of its members have reverted to a traditional American stance in disappointment: political and military isolation.

Isolationist liberalism has returned with an interesting new twist since 1968: America should withdraw from the world not because of its superior virtue, but because of its unique wickedness. The twenty years after 1947 are seen not as a halcyon era of economic growth and preservation of liberty—on the contrary, they were a bizarre period of harsh, warmongering rigidity engendered by World War II, Korea, and Vietnam. Perhaps because the United States now is regarded as a villain rather than redeemer, the Democratic stance is more extreme in a geographic sense. Rarely has isolationism excluded U.S. involvement in the Caribbean and Central America. But now even that area is considered out of bounds.

The Democrats' defeat in 1980 resulted partly from a perception of their weakness and vacillation in the face of anti-American advances—something that goodwill and negotiation could not stop. And Ronald Reagan's victory seemed a mandate for the party that had a clear and coherent policy, the party that had adopted much of the program of internationalist liberalism. The feeling among Democrats that the United States could not af-

ford the old liberal agenda, that it was not working in the Third
World anyway, was unacceptable to most Republicans. Furthermore, they meant to do something about it. The right wing long
had scorned "containment" and called for a rollback of communism; in the 1980s, this conviction took the form of U.S. support
for anti-Communist insurgencies throughout the Third World.
Elsewhere, there existed longstanding U.S. commitments that
only the GOP was ready to back up. Clearly, Republicans had
not lost that feeling of U.S. exceptionalism that is essential to
success in almost any foreign enterprise. Many of them also had
an advantage that the liberal leadership usually lacked—a belief
in God and God's sanction for America's mission in the world.

But if it seemed that all positive zeal had gone over to Republicans, perhaps they were asserting their own brand of isolationism. Most Republicans have rejected the legal and moral internationalism implied by human rights criteria, the United
Nations, the International Court, and the Law of the Sea—dismissing them as ineffectual and harmful to the national interest.
Ronald Reagan also took NATO less seriously than almost any
other president since its inception. He earnestly promoted the
concept of a Star Wars defense that might make possible the
self-sufficiency of Fortress America, a fortress that would not
need any foreign allies.

Moreover, the GOP suffers from a crucial disadvantage. Con-
certed action abroad requires a sense of community at home—
Reaganite individualism is ill-suited for getting Americans to die
fighting in large numbers. Like a yeoman farmer, the mythical
American cowboy might be a more honest and virtuous type
than the city slicker. But he also is freer, more individualistic,
more violently heroic. He does not engage in the steady cultivation of traditional agriculture. Perhaps that is why Republicans,
though sometimes more eager than Democrats to acquire an
empire, are less interested in maintaining it. Ronald Reagan and
most Republican presidents naturally have preferred limited,
unilateral forays—with a very quick finish—to broad, institu-
tional, liberal commitments: the sort of liberal mission that has
sustained United States in almost all of its major wars.

President Reagan was not drawn into any major wars, but his

unilateral forays sometimes had their own foolishness or futility. However much the opposition of Congress helped bring it about, the Iran-Contra affair was an exercise in individualist heroics and religious naivete, a unilateral initiative that rejected the need for allies at home and abroad. Like the bombing of Libya, the initiative seemed a case of armed posses in action or a southern filibuster, not part of a broadly conceived, global strategy. In Reagan's defense, perhaps he felt the meddling of a Democratic Congress left him with no other choice in Central America. Certainly the episode comprised a perfect illustration of the Democrats' isolationism and opportunism, of a flaky Republican unilateralism, of partisan gridlock.

The problems of American foreign policy went too deep to be cured by partisan change in the White House during 1981. There exists a division not just between the parties—or within the Democratic Party—but within the government structure itself. A largely Democratic Congress is at constant odds with the President. During Eisenhower's era of good feelings, a Democratic majority in Congress supported the President on foreign policy—just as a Republican majority had supported Truman in the 1940s. Democrats were willing to be firmly anti-Communist, as well as activist abroad; Republicans were willing to be activist abroad, as well as firmly anti-Communist. By the mid-1970s, all this had changed. More politicians saw foreign policy not just as a method of winning elections but as a matter for profound personal conviction. Some of them assumed diplomatic authority themselves, making it almost impossible for the White House to follow through on its initiatives.

The breakdown of cooperation went with a breakdown of trust. The President grew less willing to give Congress a hearing, while the Congress grew more eager to interfere. The CIA became a congressional obsession, a permanent target for opponents of a strong foreign policy. Very little that characterized Congress in the late seventies is much different ten years later. Such is the strength of ethnic and interest group factions that they have a veto on many foreign policy initiatives. Coherent U.S. policies in the Middle East are made impossible by the oil and Israel lobbies; other such lobbies influence U.S. policy from

Greece to South Africa. Church groups, left and right, help shape policies against population control or the Contra army in Nicaragua. Even America's feminists have gotten into the foreign policy act, pushing such "women's issues" as disarmament and peace—it is Mrs. Roosevelt's old coalition, newly refracted into the eighties.

But it is isolationism, too. For such behavior rests on a solipsistic assumption that the United States and its dependencies embrace the entire world. Congress legislates for the great American electorate as though it were legislating for all humankind.

How does this state of affairs look to America's chief allies and adversaries? West Europeans and the Soviets agree in finding American foreign policy quite bizarre—but the Soviets also have learned how to manipulate it. The Kremlin, for example, rightly perceives that Congress's growing role in foreign policy has weakened U.S. policy toward the USSR. Since the 1970s, Moscow has abandoned America's leftist fringe in favor of cultivating mainstream groups that can influence the U.S. legislature.

One "mainstream" group that Moscow manipulates to considerable advantage are the NATO allies in Europe, where there is a cultural sympathy for Russia and a chronic weakness toward it. West Europeans always have wanted a détente that they can control, one that reduces tensions and fosters trade with the Communists. From 1947 to 1968, the Cold War dragged on with occasional interludes—such as Khrushchev's trip to the United States in 1959 and the Nuclear Test Ban Treaty four years later. Although de Gaulle helped to start a détente with the Soviets, it was the Germans who lent it momentum. In power by 1969, West Germany's Social Democrats gave the Soviet Union all that it asked for in Central Europe in exchange for the "normalization" of West Berlin. While East-West trade increased enormously, the political and economic advantages of détente went primarily to the USSR.[65]

Meanwhile, the Soviet Union encouraged a West European tendency to impede U.S. policy, within and without the NATO area. One area of disagreement was Central America. The Middle East was another. During the Arab-Israeli War of 1973,

NATO countries refused to provide facilities for provisioning Israel; after the Arab oil embargo, they again declined to cooperate with the United States. U.S. intervention in Grenada and Libya was excoriated in Europe, but by far the most serious dispute was over NATO defense strategy. With some justification, West Europeans felt that democracy in Eastern Europe would come only from gradual changes in Russia itself—direct pressure on the satellite countries might just make things worse. However, any form of pressure against Russia they left almost entirely to the United States.

The high point of Russia's efforts to manipulate NATO occurred during Carter's presidency. Moscow called on Europe to end its "complaisance" and "appeasement" of America, which endangered world peace. This call found a ready audience among the leaders of France and Germany, who continued pouring money into the Soviet bloc—partly as a form of tribute—and who switched their decisions on nuclear weapons in response to Soviet complaints. For a while, Moscow could count on Western Europe to restrain the United States from almost any foreign initiative. Toward Soviet initiatives, such as the invasion of Afghanistan, Europeans reacted as though Americans were the threat; protest against the Afghan War was strong nearly everywhere except Western Europe, which did not want its trade with Russia disturbed. The same was true of the Solidarity uprising in Poland, regarded like Afghanistan as a serious danger to détente and East-West commerce.

If the Soviets could not obtain backing from Europe, then they could get it from the Democrats. Their most useful weapon, perhaps, was a growing assumption in the Democratic Party that the Soviet Union would be pacific if it feared no outside threat. During the Watergate episode, Congress was hostile to virtually any White House initiative. President Carter hoped that the Soviets would appreciate his rejection of Nixon's immoral realpolitik, his abandonment of right-wing client regimes, his restraint in defense spending. Meanwhile, Democrats in the Congress had worried more about White House imperialism than Soviet imperialism—a useful point in party politics that would not be so useful for steering the ship of state.

To some extent, Western Europe's appeasement of Russia

can be seen as a prudent adjustment to such new American weaknesses. Unfortunately, the demoralization of the West presented some dangerous temptations to Moscow. This was especially true in the Third World. Marxism-Leninism made significant gains among the peasantries, religious movements, and lumpenproletariats that Karl Marx would have scorned but the Soviets found useful. Through Cuban surrogates, they moved into Ethiopia and Angola, while the Congress prevented any U.S. response. Moreover, it seemed that no U.S. client anywhere in the world could rely on Washington's backing unless it was democratic.

Under these circumstances, an administration like Reagan's became almost a necessity—and his policies toward Russia have to be seen on the whole as a success. Reagan knew when to be firm. He accelerated a huge arms buildup which, given the dismal state of U.S. defense after Vietnam, was largely justified; the United States had been maintaining a military posture that it was unwilling to pay for. Against enormous pressure, Reagan also put intermediate nuclear missiles in Europe which proved perfect bargaining chips in negotiation. Ultimately, he knew when to take Mikhail Gorbachev's initiatives seriously and accept a new Soviet-American détente.

The latest détente does reflect some genuine changes in the Soviet system.[66] Gorbachev's desire for reform springs from a practical concern over "objective circumstances" that almost every Russian shares. It is accepted that weakness in the civilian economy is dragging the military economy down. On the other hand, Gorbachev has been even more skillful than his predecessors at manipulating Western opinion, and a great deal of Leninist brutality remains. For all of his glasnost, the new generation of Russians is nationalistic and expansionist, still seeing the world as a battleground of military and political power. Soviet leaders waiting in the wings feel that they must seek a form of expansion that will appeal to Russian patriotism and legitimate their rule.

Despite Gorbachev's fears and Reagan's modest success, the future for America does not look bright. The two developments most helpful to U.S. policy—the failure of Russia as a rallying point for other countries, because of its political cynicism and economic stagnation; and the U.S. détente with China, which underscores an image of Soviet irrelevance—have not been enough. If the Soviet economy is a failure, then so perhaps is the American. U.S. fears of Asian communism have been replaced by fears of Asian capitalism. Japan and some other Oriental economies are seen as having succeeded through a blend of dynamism, industriousness, and self-restraint that American culture can scarcely hope to equal.

While the Far East performs far better economically, Russia still looks formidable militarily. And while the attractions of capitalism and democracy have increased even in the Third World, respect for American power has declined at the same time. In the late 1980s, it still seems to be all that Washington can do just to stop the rot at home—not Marxist rot obviously, but numerous other examples of social, political, and economic decay. In his concentration on drug abuse and educational standards, President George Bush appears vaguely aware of the larger problem and approaches it by urging people to be more like himself. Something of a Marquand figure like Henry Cabot Lodge, Jr., perhaps President Bush knows who he is a lot better than what he stands for.

If the present looks so grim, why does the past look better? Perhaps because the "past" is an era when America was geographically so remote that it hardly even needed a diplomacy or defense—or else, after World War II, an era when the United States enjoyed enormous power and authority throughout most of the world. Foreign involvements could be avoided or controlled; diplomatic compromise and material sacrifice was less necessary. American power also profited from a twenty-year extension of the attitudes of World War II. Because of their involvement in that war, Americans learned something about the outside world and had a keener sense of its realities. Those lessons were not passed on to their children.

American international behavior after World War II was governed by a cadre that took charge at a crucial moment. In fact, internationalist liberals were the closest thing to an American ruling class since the early nineteenth century. They did not, however, rule on their home territory. Lacking their own political base, they had the consent of a large Middle American majority that no longer exists—for democratic pluralism has reimposed itself on foreign policy. Moreover, they relied on constant success to stay in power, and their luck ran out in the 1960s.

They filled not just a functional but a political and intellectual void. Theirs was an idea that emerged from the progressivism of Theodore Roosevelt and Woodrow Wilson, answering a need long felt in U.S. politics. The Progressive movement flourished at a time when America's frontiers were being closed and its territory rounded out, an ominous change which seemed to threaten political stability and to necessitate domestic reform. So the internationalist liberals turned their attention to foreign policy, looking outward to maintain the civic virtue of Americans and a sense of national unity.

Fear of political entropy has ever been a concern of American elites. It is no coincidence that a classical text of internationalist liberalism was *The Education of Henry Adams.* Edited by, of all people, Henry Cabot Lodge, Sr., this autobiography was published posthumously at a perfect moment—October 1918. For more than a year it remained the most popular non-fiction book in the United States. The author was a mugwump patrician who disdained the mass culture of America and who, in his old age, felt dubious about how much political reform could accomplish. Adams supported free trade and regarded Teddy Roosevelt's imperialism as repugnant to American principles. At the same time, he thought that a more active, non-imperial diplomacy, enacted by a strong central government, might help bring an end to the incoherence of U.S. politics—and for thirty years after 1940, that is more or less what happened. Fear of communism and a positive mission in the world did indeed bring a greater sense of purpose to the republic.[67]

The elements of this purpose were to be found in Woodrow Wilson's original program. Liberals never entirely forgot that agenda: free trade and investment, economic aid, arms control, democracy, national autonomy, and multilateral institutions to maintain the system. Furthermore, it was a deeply felt set of beliefs—utopian in some respects, but more than just a figleaf for powermongers and cynics. The original intent of the League of Nations was limited cooperation among similar countries. Although the United Nations proved a great disappointment, this intent was partly fulfilled in a set of alliances and international organizations. On the question of arms control, total disarmament still is seen as a utopian goal—but the United States has made some important breakthroughs since the Cuban missile crisis.

The two essential components of Wilson's program, causes as old as the republic itself, were freedom of trade and anti-imperialism. Free trade was the acid test for internationalist liberals, central to almost everything they wanted—such as the end of imperialism and colonialism, the destruction of despotism in all its forms. This cause enjoyed a tremendous success in the 1960s. But it always is easier politically for economies on the rise to support free trade; in times of economic decline, special economic interests become stronger and more demanding. Fears of decline in America have led to an abandonment of this bedrock principle by many liberal Democrats.

As for anti-imperialism, there has been in one sense progress on this issue. Scores of new countries have been "liberated" since World War II. However, most of them suffer under far worse governments than before, and the cause of anti-imperialism has backfired against the United States. After the mid-1960s, commentators started arguing that the self-styled anti-imperialists of 1918 were running a de facto empire themselves—not just the old U.S. empire of nearby colonies and protectorates, which predated World War I, but a global empire of military dependencies, multinational corporations, and monetary control.

Empires, in one form or another, may be inevitable—nor was this kind of empire entirely new in human history. And certainly the internationalist liberal system, any international system, requires a dominant currency and military power. Like so many imperialists before them, internationalist liberals felt that their system had its own special nature and justification—and perhaps they were right.

On the other hand, post-World War II "expansion" has been attacked by many Americans as a new form of powermongering. Obviously, it did involve some very brutal and high-handed actions. The cruder form of U.S. military interference reached a climax in 1961–68, a period that saw a decline of faith in American military force. But this soon was followed by a decline of faith in almost every kind of foreign venture; ultraliberals rebelled against the whole enterprise. Like the early Progressives, like Senator Joe McCarthy, many Democrats started fighting what they considered a wicked aristocracy, corrupted by the eastern cities and by foreign entanglements.

Thus it was that a movement that took shape under Woodrow Wilson became by the 1970s an empty intellectual shell, an overall confusion and reaction to defeat. Leading Democrats were left with the sense of running a rather un-American Empire, without any intellectual movement to legitimate it. Former internationalist liberals—*vide* Averell Harriman, Cyrus Vance, and Clark Clifford—were as badly split and confused as the nation itself. Having been foolish in their pride, they became foolish in their humility.[68] What has occurred since Vietnam is an effort by many liberals to return to the Arcadian normalcy before World War II, to America's beloved role as a neutral mediator. At one point, President Carter even tried to mediate the Sino-Soviet dispute. Such politicians forget that pre-World War II America was very remote from other powers—so remote that it could play the role of mediator and eschew normal diplomacy.

Not all internationalist liberals lost their nerve. One reason the movement died is simply that its fathers started to die; its sons never had been so sure of its ideals or so practical in pursuing them. The fathers reached maturity in a time when the idea of a modern United States, with all of its attendant problems, still had not entirely sunk in. They grew up in an industrial, urban America but were not entirely of it—and to some extent that socioeconomic milieu dictated their beliefs. Internationalist liberalism was a world view developed by educated, cosmopolitan, third-generation mugwumps—most of them earnest gentlemen who retained a slight connection with the land

and a settled belief in God. When such people ceased to exist, their movement probably had to change or go with them.

On a broader level, internationalist liberals were the carriers of certain cultural norms long upheld by the Western upper bourgeoisie. Their traditions were rooted in those of the eighteenth-century British entrepreneurs—moralistic, rationalistic, puritanical, acquisitive, the sort of people who sustained the Industrial Revolution. We have seen how the young Wilsonians possessed a Victorian earnestness that their European counterparts lost in World War I. Like the Protestant, North European, upper middle class, they had a sense of civic duty that was potent when combined with American pragmatism and dynamism. Just as important, they also were true believers in some old political icons. Lacking enough stature to serve as idols for their children, they had the emotional advantage of worshipping certain idols themselves.

The paladins of U.S. diplomacy after World War II comprised perhaps the last generation to feel a spiritual tie with the Founding Fathers of the republic. The writer of these lines finds it easy to sympathize with the Victorian earnestness that motivated them. Their initial admiration for President Wilson is likewise not difficult for him to comprehend. He must, however, confess that he cannot see, or rather *feel,* with them much farther back than that. Many of the idols that internationalist liberals worshipped were much older than Wilson, and it is there that the author parts company with his subjects.

Most internationalist liberals thought of the eighteenth century the way an eighteenth-century intellectual thought of antiquity—as a normative age, as a source of inspiration. *The Education of Henry Adams* looked forward to an era of greater world involvement for the United States, but what gave the book its bearings was its presumption of relative unity in America during the late 1700s. Adams's autobiography was an elegy to the eighteenth century, suggesting a link between the American Revolution and the events of the Progressive Era. Of course, Adams's spiritual children interpreted the norm in different ways. When John Foster Dulles and Chester Bowles kept referring to the

ideals of the American Revolution, each of them read its significance as he liked. David Bruce saw in eighteenth-century America a way of life that nurtured the right civic virtues: personal
autonomy—affirmed by landed wealth and maintained by inher-
itance—upheld liberty; and dependency corrupted, whether dependency on capitalists or on the U.S. government. In the same
vein, Averell Harriman felt that his money and independence
improved his effectiveness as a servant of the republic. And
Henry Adams's belief that the better class of people were born
to lead revolutions was a conviction that William Bullitt shared
to an astonishing degree.

But there was a more basic reason for this fixation on the
American Revolution. If the late nineteenth century was the
Golden Age of the bourgeoisie, the late eighteenth century was
its Heroic Era. That was a time when even the Parisien intellectuals supported the middle class. America was seen by many
educated Europeans as the hope of mankind—in the same way
that Soviet Russia, then China, then Cuba would be seen by
intellectuals of the twentieth century. Enlightenment *philo-
sophes*—the effete snobs and nattering nabobs of their era—
assured the rising business classes that, in a world of growing
interdependence, political restraints on commerce were absurd.
Intellectuals lionized the bourgeoisie, asserting that it represented the vanguard of history, that its fight was the fight of all
mankind. As soon as the manacles of imperialism were thrown
off, then peace would guide the planets in a free trading world.

It followed from all this that, in a world governed by reason
and by law, the practice of diplomacy would be utterly transformed. Realpolitik was immoral, treaties and alliances led to
war, and secrecy in negotiation only hid the wickedness of diplomats. After the triumph of the bourgeoisie, negotiations would
be frank and open, diplomacy would follow the same mores as
personal relations, and commerce based on a few simple rules
would do it all. And a single measure, Free Trade, would usher
in the Fundamental Change—especially if it were accompanied
by its natural partner, Democracy.[69]

An already virulent utopianism in America was encouraged by
these views. American revolutionaries developed some mil-

lenarian notions about the effect that they might have upon the nations of the earth. Thomas Jefferson, especially, thought that a new spirit was emerging in the world and bliss was it in that dawn to be alive. As he put it to James Madison in 1789, the rules of realpolitik "were legitimate principles in the dark ages which intervened between ancient and modern civilization, but exploded and held in just horror in the eighteenth century. I know but one code of morality for man whether acting singly or collectively." Energized by the Paris *événements* during the French Revolution, Jefferson wanted to give fraternal assistance to this new republic in Europe. The world did not need cynical diplomacy, but rather simple commercial relations and occasional help between fellow democracies.

In the tradition of the Enlightenment, Thomas Jefferson was an inveterate meliorist, uncomfortable with the notion of permanent conflict—and his revolutionary comrade, John Adams, at first saw things much the same way. Adams recoiled from old-fashioned diplomacy, referring to hopes of a "reformation, a kind of protestantism, in the commercial system of the world." But as they grew more powerful and secure, America's Founding Fathers tended to follow the same path as would some of their twentieth-century descendants. While president, John Adams fell comfortably into the belief that natural aristocrats of reason and virtue—the best and brightest like himself—were born to lead the American republic. Perhaps it was natural that he also inclined more and more to the classical mode of diplomacy—that of realpolitik and the free market system in power relations, wherein great and small countries pursued their own interests without any notions of romance or idealism.

The system of realpolitik—espoused by people as diverse as George Kennan, Charles de Gaulle, and Richard Nixon—never has held much appeal for American voters. On the other hand, it does not necessarily clash with their elemental prejudices. One of the most influential statements in U.S. history, President Washington's Farewell Address, has been identified with a doctrinaire isolation from Europe. In actual fact, the Farewell Address pushed a policy of pure realpolitik and national interest, while managing to present this policy in idealistic terms. The address was clothed in appeals to isolationism, free trade, neutrality, peace among Great Powers, and American exceptionalism; at the same time, it allowed for the expansion of a U.S. hegemony in the New World that would maintain a profitable commerce with the Old. It postponed the era of international involvement, America's mission to redeem Europe, to a more propitious age that would dawn when the United States attained its destiny as a Great Power.[70]

After a false twilight during World War I, dawn finally broke following World War II and the future arrived. It is rare in a country's history for the economic and political possibilities to seem limitless—but to many Americans they seemed so then. Over the next twenty years, America was so powerful that most countries could be treated as an extension of it. Allies never were quite accepted as sovereign states. The crucial debates took place within the U.S. government, not with foreign entities. "Nothing can stop us," exulted Harriman, "except our own doubts as to our own ability to accomplish the unlimited," and such statements among American politicians became the norm.

So much power and enthusiasm made it possible for U.S. diplomats to operate on a global scale and interpret their actions in idealistic terms, with no basic sense of contradiction. They found acceptance by an electorate that did not have any natural enthusiasm for international programs. As citizens of the first truly global power, American voters could support an "internationalist" agenda without entirely abandoning their instinctive isolationism.

The decay of America's supremacy, because of economic competition and losing the Vietnam War, has made U.S. diplomacy a more difficult task. But this change of status may offer its own compensations to the United States. And perhaps Americans' feeling that their global effort was temporary, their very isolationism, now provides the best hope for an orderly and peaceful adjustment to decline.

Bibliographical Note

The bibliography of American foreign relations amounts to an ocean of intractable material, even excluding the unpublished documents. As Strachey once said of the Victorian era, "the industry of a Ranke would be submerged by it, and the perspicacity of Gibbon would quail before it." It is my aim simply to present some of the more important and interesting sources that were used for this book and the accompanying TV programs, especially sources that may be of interest to non-specialists. Readers in need of a more thorough bibliography should consult *The Universal Reference System, Vol. I, International Affairs,* a project that attempts to cover almost everything.

There are several short general histories of American foreign policy in this century, the most accessible of which probably is *America, Russia, and the Cold War* by Walter LaFeber; another, more controversial sketch is *Rise to Globalism: American Foreign Policy since 1938* by Stephen Ambrose. A somewhat longer study is *American Foreign Policy* by Thomas Paterson, J. Garry Clifford, and Kenneth Hagan; and LaFeber recently has published *The American Age,* a survey of U.S. foreign policy since the eighteenth century. Two general commentaries from a quasi-Marxist perspective are *The Tragedy of American Diplomacy,* an influential work by William Appleman Williams, and *The Roots of American Foreign Policy* by Gabriel Kolko. Though not specifically about U.S. foreign policy, Paul Johnson's *Modern Times* is successful in presenting a conservative perspective on important issues.

A number of published primary sources have been especially helpful in the research for this book. Of course, *The Education of Henry Adams* provided me with a far clearer understanding of the larger culture from which many U.S. diplomats of this century sprang. The autobiography that first drew my interest to American foreign relations is *Witness to History, 1929–1969* by Charles E. Bohlen. *On Active Service in Peace and War* by Henry Stimson and McGeorge Bundy and the memoirs of U. Alexis Johnson also are valuable over much of the same period. Two excellent diaries covering the subject since the 1920s from a liberal perspective may be found in *Navigating the Rapids, 1918–1971: From the Papers of Adolf A. Berle* and *The Journals of David E. Lilienthal.* However, the best of all published sources for original material is *Foreign Relations of the United States,* an annual compilation of important State Department documents and correspondence.

Secondary sources on specialized aspects of U.S. foreign relations are almost beyond counting. *Congress and Foreign Policy* by Robert Dahl is one of the best books on its subject, although the subject deserves a new study since the recent congressional involvements in this sphere of government during the 1970s and 1980s. *Foreign Policy and Presidential Elections, 1940–1960* is a superb study of that topic by Robert A. Divine. *A New Isolationism: Threat or Promise?* by Robert W. Tucker examines another important aspect of U.S. attitudes toward foreign affairs. *The American Style of Foreign Policy: Cultural Politics and Foreign Affairs* by Robert Dallek puts America on the couch and tries to give a psychoanthropological cast to this subject. Two books that proved useful to me in exploring the eighteenth-century roots of this country's international conduct are *The Machiavellian Moment* by John Pocock and *To the Farewell Address; Ideas of Early American Foreign Policy* by Felix Gilbert. Some obviously helpful books examine U.S. foreign policy through the lives of particular groupings of people. *The Best and the Brightest* by David Halberstam contains many factual inaccuracies and minor distortions; it was nevertheless an important document of its times and probably the first to focus on the cadre of diplomats who helped run the show after World War II. Other examples of history through biographies are *Architects of Illusion; Men and Ideas in American Foreign Policy, 1941–1949* by Lloyd C. Gardner; *The Cold Warriors:*

A Policy-Making Elite by John C. Donovan; and *The Wise Men* by Walter Isaacson and Evan Thomas. *The Agency: The Rise and Decline of the CIA* by John Ranelagh is the most comprehensive history of U.S. espionage/intelligence and is crucial to an understanding of this aspect of American international behavior.

On U.S. foreign policy and politics in the early part of this century, there are many excellent secondary works. *The Age of Reform* by Richard Hofstadter is a path-breaking work on the Progressive movement that makes a good companion to the Henry Adams memoir. A lively book on mugwumpery and Teddy Roosevelt's imperialism is *Twelve Against Empire: The Anti-Imperialists, 1898–1900* by Robert L. Beisner. *The Crossroads of Liberalism* by Charles Forcey takes a fascinating look at early progressive impulses, the *New Republic* magazine, and Woodrow Wilson. For a slightly disenchanted biography of Walter Lippmann, see *Walter Lippmann and the American Century* by Ronald Steel.

The best books on Woodrow Wilson are the various biographical studies by Arthur Walworth and Arthur Link. Walworth has written an excellent study of Wilson and the American delegation at the peace conference, *Wilson and His Peacemakers,* which can be supplemented by *Peace Without Victory; Woodrow Wilson and the British Liberals* by Laurence W. Martin and *Political Origins of the New Diplomacy, 1917–1918* by Arno J. Mayer. A strong general history of the Versailles Conference is Arno Mayer's *The Politics and Diplomacy of Peacemaking; Containment and Counterrevolution at Versailles,* although the author probably gives the peacemakers too much credit or blame for farsighted anti-Bolshevism. On the specter of Bolshevism at the peace conference, see *The American Liberals and the Russian Revolution* by Christopher Lasch and *Russia, Bolshevism, and the Versailles Peace* by John M. Thompson. George Kennan's *Russia and the West under Lenin and Stalin* provides a convincing reconstruction of Soviet foreign relations, especially in the early period of the Soviet state.

The most interesting published diaries and memoirs by Americans at the peace conference are those of Charles Seymour, James Shotwell, and Robert Lansing, but surely the most comprehensive is a twenty-one volume marathon by David Hunter Miller. *The Intimate Papers of Colonel House Arranged as a*

Narrative are indispensable, and another important but belated witness is Herbert Hoover in his *The Ordeal of Woodrow Wilson.* William Bullitt's Senate testimony has been published as *The Bullitt Mission to Russia;* other primary sources that also were influential documents of their times are *Peacemaking, 1919* by Harold Nicolson and *The Economic Consequences of the Peace* by John Maynard Keynes, the latter published originally in the *New Republic* during 1919. Dean Acheson's memoir, *Morning and Noon,* includes an elegant description of how things looked from the Washington home front.

A Pretty Good Club by Martin Weil is gravely oversimplified but presents some interesting information on the Foreign Service during the 1920s and 1930s and the New Deal view of it. An excellent series of scholarly essays on the diplomacy of the 1930s may be found in *The Diplomats, 1919–1939,* edited by Gordon Craig and Felix Gilbert. *The Origins of the Second World War* by Arnold Offner makes a good general study. *The Challenge to Isolation* by William Langer and S. Everett Gleason is still authoritative on official reactions in America, but see also *Roosevelt and the Isolationists, 1932–1945* by Wayne S. Cole. On the diplomacy of Roosevelt himself, see *Economic Aspects of New Deal Diplomacy* by Lloyd Gardner; *Franklin D. Roosevelt and American Foreign Policy, 1932–1945* by Robert Dallek; and, for a more critical view, *Wind over Sand: The Diplomacy of Franklin Roosevelt* by Frederick W. Marks.

Two important primary sources for interwar diplomacy are *Turbulent Era* by Joseph C. Grew and *For the President: Personal & Secret: Correspondence between Franklin D. Roosevelt and William C. Bullitt,* edited by Orville Bullitt. The memoirs of Cordell Hull make heavy going but are a useful source for the 1930s; so probably are Herbert Hoover's memoirs. *After Seven Years* by Raymond Moley describes some of the flakier aspects of early New Deal economics and diplomacy; the diaries of Felix Frankfurter and Harold Ickes are interesting but limited looks at the Roosevelt administration by insiders, as are the memoirs of Francis Biddle. The diaries of Jay Pierrepont Moffat and Breckinridge Long are more directly relevant to foreign policy and are illuminating by their omissions.

The standard book on Roosevelt's policy toward Vichy France

and North Africa is *Our Vichy Gamble* by William L. Langer, but a number of interesting original sources have appeared. *Adventure in Diplomacy* by Kenneth Pendar throws a sidelight on the events in Vichyite North Africa. One also should consult the war memoirs of Winston Churchill, Harold Macmillan, William Leahy, and Charles de Gaulle. Of course, the most useful memoirs for me were those of Robert Murphy, *Diplomat Among Warriors.* On the "Wilsonian" revival during World War II, see especially *Second Chance: The Triumph of Internationalism in America During World War II* by Robert Divine, a brilliant study of this phenomenon. Diaries that are directly relevant to this subject are those of Henry Morgenthau, Jr. and Henry Wallace. But perhaps the most pertinent primary sources that have been published are three works of Sumner Welles: *World of the Four Freedoms, Seven Decisions that Shaped History,* and *The Time for Decision.*

There are innumerable studies of the origins of the Cold War. Some interesting ideas on Soviet-American relations that were highly instructive to me may be found in *Roosevelt and World War II* by Robert Divine. *Churchill, Roosevelt, Stalin; The War They Waged and the Peace They Sought* by Herbert Feis sometimes is referred to disparagingly as the "authorized" history of this subject in its early years—but perhaps that makes it a good place to start. A huge number of histories attempting to "revise" Feis's approach began to come out in the mid-1960s, beginning with *Atomic Diplomacy: Hiroshima and Potsdam* by Gar Alperovitz. *The Limits of Power: The World and United States Foreign Policy, 1945–1954* by Joyce Kolko and Gabriel Kolko takes a strongly revisionist and vulgarly Marxist view. *The Diplomacy of Silence* by Hugh De Santis tries rather naively to show that the social and cultural prejudices of U.S. diplomats played a large part in creating the Cold War. A wistfully revisionist history of the Cold War's origins is *Shattered Peace: The Origins of the Cold War and the National Security State* by Daniel Yergin; but the best summary of the subject is *The United States and the Origins of the Cold War, 1941–1947* by John Lewis Gaddis. *The New Left and the Origins of the Cold War* by Robert J. Maddox makes some successful jabs at Cold War revisionism, which has indeed been generally modulated since the early 1970s. The revised standard version of revisionist orthodoxy is that the Cold War was inevitable, with both sides equally at fault—ideologizing a rather reductionist view advanced as early as 1967 by Louis J. Halle in *The Cold War as History.* Tang Tsou's *America's Failure in China, 1941–50* is the most comprehensive work on the Chinese aspect of the early Cold War.

Many personages of the early Cold War have written their own recollections, including Averell Harriman, with the help of Elie Abel, in *Special Envoy to Churchill and Stalin, 1941–1946. Mission to Moscow* by Joseph Davies comprises a fascinating cultural document by a friendly American who believed everything he was told. *The Strange Alliance* by John R. Deane is a good study by one of Harriman's subordinates—but far more important are the memoirs of another member of the embassy staff, George F. Kennan. Truman's memoirs and those of Dean Acheson, *Present at the Creation,* also are essential to any bibliography of the Cold War. The most important published diaries and personal papers are those of James Forrestal and Arthur Vandenburg. Henry Wallace's diary, again, provides an interesting dissenting view, and so does a more influential work by Walter Lippmann, *The Cold War.*

For America's relations with Western Europe, the bibliography is somewhat less extensive than for the Cold War with Russia. Several valuable biographies are quite relevant to this topic, including the last volume of Forrest Pogue's biography of George Marshall, Stephen Ambrose's biography of Eisenhower, and Ronald W. Pruessen's biography of John Foster Dulles up to 1953, which I hope will soon be followed by a second volume; meanwhile, interested readers must unfortunately rely on *The Devil and John Foster Dulles* by Townsend Hoopes for an account of Dulles's secretaryship. *The Origins of the Marshall Plan* by John Gimbel gives a standard interpretation of that subject, while Alan Milward offers a strong dissenting analysis in *The Reconstruction of Western Europe, 1945–51.* A lively general history of Western and Eastern Europe since the war may be found in *Europe Since Hitler: The Rebirth of Europe* by Walter Laqueur as well as *The Recovery of Europe, 1945–1973* by Richard Mayne. On French postwar diplomacy, see *The Reluctant Ally: France and Atlantic Security,* an excellent study by Michael Harrison; on Germany, *The Rise of Western Germany: 1945–1972* by Aidan Crawley;

on Great Britain, *The Special Relationship: Anglo-American Relations Since 1945* by William Roger Louis and Hedley Bull. David Calleo's book on North Atlantic relations, *The Atlantic Fantasy: The U.S., NATO and Europe,* harshly analyzes the new problems that developed during the 1960s. The most important reminiscences are those of Truman, Eisenhower, Acheson, Macmillan, Monnet, Khrushchev, and Lucius Clay. And one should also consult *The Papers of General Lucius D. Clay: Germany 1945–1949,* edited by Jean Edward Smith.

On the general subject of America's official conceptualization of the Third World, perhaps the best summary is *Liberal America and the Third World* by Robert Packenham. On more specific topics and areas, see *Warriors at Suez* by Donald Neff; *Island China* by Ralph N. Clough; and *Modern India: The Origins of an Asian Democracy* by Judith M. Brown. Biographies of Adlai Stevenson and John F. Kennedy, including Arthur Schlesinger's *A Thousand Days,* certainly should be consulted. A crucial document of those times is *The Stages of Economic Growth* by Walt Rostow, but another equally important viewpoint is expressed in three books by Chester Bowles: *Ambassador's Report; The Conscience of a Liberal: Selected Writings and Speeches;* and *Promises to Keep: My Years in Public Life, 1941–1969.* In this connection, one should also look at *Of Kennedys and Kings* by Harris Wofford as well as the memoirs and journals of John Kenneth Galbraith. On the failure of foreign aid and the effects of international trade and investment, see *Dissent on Development* by Peter Bauer; *U.S. Power and the Multinational Corporation* by Robert Gilpin; *Trade Policy and the New Protectionism* by David Greenaway; and *Leading Issues in Economic Development* by Gerald Meier.

The Vietnam War now has an enormous literature, best summarized in *The Wars in Vietnam, Cambodia, and Laos, 1945–1982,* a bibliography compiled by Richard Dean Burns and Milton Leitenberg. Certainly the best general history is *Vietnam: A History* by Stanley Karnow, but a good shorter synthesis may be found in *America's Longest War: The United States and Vietnam, 1950–1975* by George C. Herring. *America in Vietnam* by Guenter Lewy helps to explode some of the favorite myths of anti-war dissenters, while Gabriel Kolko's book on Vietnam looks at the war from a quasi-

Marxist perspective. Some interesting but more limited studies certainly are worth consulting, such as *Kennedy in Vietnam* by William J. Rust and *Planning a Tragedy: The Americanization of the War in Vietnam* by Larry Berman, which examines Johnson's crucial decisions of 1965. A rather plodding but worthy book on bureaucratic inertia behind the war is *The Irony of Vietnam: The System Worked* by Leslie H. Gelb and Richard K. Betts.

Surely the most important published primary source is the multivolume edition of *The Pentagon Papers*. The reader should also look at *The Vantage Point: Perspectives of the Presidency, 1963– 1969* by Lyndon B. Johnson. Two novels that had a considerable influence on public opinion on the war are *The Quiet American* by Graham Greene and *The Ugly American* by William Lederer and Eugene Burdick—the former tending to discourage American involvement and the latter having an opposite drive. The model for Greene's "Quiet American" is said to have been Edward Lansdale or Roger Hilsman. Hilsman's own memoirs of the Kennedy administration, *To Move a Nation,* do reflect the mindset of American officials who relied on past successes in Third World wars.

The best short summary of U.S. relations with Latin America, *The United States and Latin America: An Historical Analysis of Inter-American Relations* by Gordon Connell-Smith is colored by a strongly anti-U.S. viewpoint, which seems to be true of most books on the subject. *The New Empire; An Interpretation of American Expansion, 1860–1898* by Walter LaFeber is a good study of U.S. expansion to the turn of the century. This can be usefully supplemented by *Pan-American Visions: Woodrow Wilson in the Western Hemisphere, 1913–1921* by Mark T. Gilderhus and *Roosevelt's Good Neighbor Policy* by Edward O. Guerrant. *The Hovering Giant: U.S. Responses to Revolutionary Change in Latin America* by Cole Blasier is a good general study of this topic after World War II. A personal statement from the field, so to speak, may be found in Penny Lernoux's *Cry of Freedom* and, from the U.S. official perspective, *The Making of a Public Man: A Memoir* by Sol Linowitz. On the Alliance for Progress, see especially *The Alliance That Lost Its Way* by Jerome Levinson. A useful general history of U.S. relations with Central America, other than with Panama, is *Inevitable Revolutions: The United States in Central America* by Walter

LaFeber; on the Panama Canal issue, see William Jorden's *Panama Odyssey;* and for the important original documents, see *The Central American Crisis Reader,* edited by Robert Leiken and Barry Rubin.

Subjects covered in my epilogue include recent U.S. relations with Western Europe, with the Soviet bloc, and with its economic competitors in the Far East. On Soviet-American relations, see *The Soviet Paradox* by Seweryn Bialer as well as *Gorbachev's Russia and American Foreign Policy,* edited by Bialer and Michael Mandelbaum; *The Rivals* and *Dangerous Relations* by Adam B. Ulam; and *U.S.-Soviet Relations in the Era of Détente* by Richard Pipes. Interesting studies of Europe include *A Continent Astray: Europe 1970–1978* by Walter Laqueur and *Beyond American Hegemony: The Future of the Western Alliance* by David Calleo—who also has written a major study of America in the global marketplace, *The Imperious Economy.* On the Japanese challenge, see *Trading Places: How We Allowed Japan to Take the Lead* by Clyde Prestowitz. Useful general primary sources on the recent past include the memoirs of Henry Kissinger, Richard Nixon, Cyrus Vance, Jimmy Carter, and Zbigniew Brzezinski.

My own book takes a strongly biographical approach to the history of U.S. foreign policy, so it might be appropriate to add some pertinent biographical works not mentioned above. For U.S. presidents in the pre-World War II period, these include *Theodore Roosevelt and the Rise of America to World Power* by Howard K. Beale and *Herbert Hoover and Economic Diplomacy: Department of Commerce Policy, 1921–1928* by Joseph Brandes. For secretaries of war and defense, see *Turmoil and Tradition* by Elting Morison (on Henry Stimson) and *James Forrestal: A Study of Personality, Politics, and Policy* by Arnold A. Rogow. A biography of Robert S. McNamara by Deborah Shapley is forthcoming. On secretaries of state, there exists a complete series of studies from Cooper Square Publishers in New York called *The American Secretaries of State and Their Diplomacy,* but one should also consult *Dean Acheson: The State Department Years* by David S. McLellan and *Waging Peace and War: Dean Rusk in the Truman, Kennedy and Johnson Years* by Thomas J. Schoenbaum. On the diplomats closely covered in this book, see also *William C. Bullitt and the Soviet Union* by Beatrice Farnsworth; *So Close to Greatness: A Biography of William C.*

Bullitt by Will Brownell and Richard Billings; *George Kennan and the Dilemma of U.S. Foreign Policy* by David Mayers; and *Henry Cabot Lodge: A Biography* by William Johnson Miller. (Some significantly unsuccessful attempts have been made at a biography of Averell Harriman; a biography of Kennan by John Lewis Gaddis is in progress.)

The central figures of my book have written a number of interesting books themselves that are not mentioned above. By William Bullitt: *It's Not Done, The Great Globe Itself,* and his co-authored work with Sigmund Freud, *Thomas Woodrow Wilson, Twenty-Eighth President of the United States: A Psychological Study.* By David Bruce: *Seven Pillars of the Republic* and *Revolution to Reconstruction.* Books by George Kennan include: *Russia, the Atom and the West; The Marquis de Custine and His "Russia in 1839"; From Prague After Munich; Democracy and the Student Left; The Cloud of Danger: Current Realities of American Foreign Policy;* and *The Nuclear Delusion: Soviet-American Relations in the Atomic Age.* Kennan's more scholarly works are *The Decline of Bismarck's European Order; The Fateful Alliance: France, Russia, and the Coming of the First World War;* and *Soviet-American Relations, 1917–1920,* vols. I and II. Before doing his war memoirs, Averell Harriman produced two books: *Peace with Russia?* and *America and Russia in a Changing World.* By Chester Bowles: *Tomorrow Without Fear; The New Dimensions of Peace; Africa's Challenge to America; American Politics in a Revolutionary World; Ideas, People and Peace; The Coming Political Breakthrough; The Making of a Just Society; A View from New Delhi;* and *Mission to India.* By Henry Cabot Lodge: *The Cult of Weakness; The Storm Has Many Eyes;* and *As It Was.*

Newspapers and periodicals were vital to my research, as they are to any book on American foreign policy. By far the most useful newspaper has been the *New York Times,* in part because of its comprehensive index, although the *Christian Science Monitor* and *Washington Post* also have special relevance. Foreign newspapers that should be consulted are the London *Times* and *Daily Telegraph; Le Monde* and *Le Monde Diplomatique;* and the *Neue Zürcher Zeitung.* The pertinent mass circulation magazines are *Time, Life, Saturday Evening Post, U.S. News and World Report,* and *Newsweek.* The less popular journals include *Foreign Affairs, Foreign Policy, The Economist, Encounter, Commentary, Atlantic,* and inevitably *The New Republic. The Department of State Bulletin* and the *American Foreign Service Journal* of course should be consulted by historians of the subject, along with the *Reader's Guide to Periodical Literature.*

On the unpublished sources consulted for this book, the most important personal papers and letters examined are those of Chester Bowles (Yale University), David Bruce (Virginia Historical Society), John Foster Dulles (Princeton University), Allen Dulles (Princeton University), James Forrestal (Princeton University), George Kennan (Princeton University), Walter Lippmann (Yale University), and Adlai Stevenson (Princeton University). Crucial as these collections may have been, many others were consulted in the course of my research.

As in filming a television series, logistics and expense had some influence on where I spent time reading documents. The other manuscript sources examined included the collections at Yale University of Arthur Clarence Walworth, Edward M. House, Yale in World War II, Anson Phelps Stokes, Clive Day, George Parmly Day, Ethel Fogg and William Brooke Clift, William Adams Delano, Chauncey M. Depew, Irving Fisher, David Brewer Karrick, Paul Palmer, Harry Weinberger, Philip H. Coombs, Arthur Bliss Lane, John F. Montgomery, Dwight Mac-Donald, Francis G. Newlands, Paul Palmer, Max Lerner, Henry L. Stimson, and Frank L. Polk. At Columbia University, the following collections were examined: Lincoln Steffens, Wellington Koo, Bernard Baruch, Lewis Galantiere, Harriman-Abel book manuscript, Lincoln Schuster, Columbia University Press, CRIA Collection, Frances Perkins, Wallace Sayre, David Kemp Owen, David Flaherty, W.W. Norton, Eustace Seligman, Frank Tannenbaum, Eleanor Belmont, Andrew Wellington Cordier, Curtis Brown, Justin O'Brien, Allan Nevins, Columbia Forum, Jacques Barzun, Carnegie Endowment, Harper & Row, Frederick Smedley, and Benjamin Nelson. At Princeton University, relevant material may be found in the collections of Lewis Fischer, Ferdinand Eberstadt, Hamilton Fish Armstrong, David Lilienthal, Arthur Krock, Livingston Merchant, John Van Antwerp MacMurray, Fred I. Kent, Karl Lott Rankin, and Emmet John Hughes. In the Library of Congress, the following manuscript collections also were consulted: James Martin Barnes,

George Biddle, Stuart Chase, Henry A. Wallace, Vannevar Bush, Emanuel Cellar, Ira C. Eaker, Joseph and Stewart Alsop, Jack Kroll, J. Robert Oppenheimer, American Foreign Service Association records, Alfred M. Kunz, Theodore Stark Wilkinson, and Leland Harrison. At Harvard University, the most relevant collections are those of Christian A. Herter, John P. Marquand, John Reed, Oswald Garrison Villard, Henry Cabot Lodge, Sr., Stuart Symington, Joseph C. Grew, and William Phillips. I found the Franklin D. Roosevelt Library at Hyde Park particularly helpful for information on Robert Murphy and Sumner Welles during World War II.

Numerous useful interviews are available at various libraries, especially in the Columbia University Oral History Project. The Columbia project includes two very pertinent interviews with Averell Harriman and interviews with Prescott Bush, Chester Bowles, Robert Murphy, James Shotwell, Adolf Berle, Charles D. Cook, Luther H. Evans, Raymond Baldwin, Arthur J. Goldberg, James P. Warburg, William Benton, Richard Bissell, Charles Bohlen, Harvey Bundy, William Clayton, Eleanor Dulles, Milton Eisenhower, Thomas K. Finletter, Felix Frankfurter, Loy Henderson, Herbert Hoover, William Knowland, Walter Lippmann, Clare Boothe Luce, John McCloy, Henry Morgenthau, Jr., Reinhold Niebuhr, Eleanor Roosevelt, Harrison Salisbury, Eric Sevareid, Henry Stimson, Dorothy Bowles, Henry Wallace, Thomas Emerson, Paul Nitze, and Dean Acheson. The Columbia Marshall Plan Project also includes interviews with Emilio G. Collado, Lewis Douglas, Norman Ness, Arthur Stevens, James Stillwell, and Ivan White. At Princeton, there is a collection of interviews on John Foster Dulles with George Kennan, Averell Harriman, David Bruce, Henry Cabot Lodge, Jr., and Robert Murphy. A number of pertinent interviews may be found at the John F. Kennedy Library: Dean Acheson, Chester Bowles, David Bruce, McGeorge Bundy, Chester Cooper, Averell Harriman, Howard Jones, George Kennan, Walter Lippmann, Henry Cabot Lodge, Jr., Robert Lovett, J. Graham Parsons, Sir Patrick Reilly, W. H. Sullivan, Llewellyn Thompson, Peter Thorneycroft (Lord Thorneycroft).

Interviews of the following people were filmed for the television series I originated: Arthur Schlesinger, Jr., Hamilton Fish,

Sr., Eric Segal, Jeane Kirkpatrick, Clark Clifford, Walter Judd, Michael Straight, Eleanor Dulles, Timothy Dickinson, Milton Friedman, Malcolm Forbes, John Kenneth Galbraith, McGeorge Bundy, George Ball, Carlos Fuentes, Frank Mankiewicz, Ralph Nader, Marcus Raskin, George McGovern, Eric Sevareid, Walter Karp, Karen Liffakers, Martin Mayer, Bruce Kovner, Noam Chomsky, Anne Bullitt, Paul Nitze, Michael Straight, Alger Hiss, Douglas MacArthur II, Charles Kindleberger, Corliss Lamont, Joseph Alsop, Victor Reuther, Richard Bissell, Roger Makins (Lord Sherfield), Edward Teller, Curtis LeMay, Milton Katz, Sir Frank Roberts, Caspar Weinberger, William Colby, Egon Barr, Lucius Battle, Edgar Jean Faure, André Fontaine, Clare Boothe Luce, Charles Burton Marshall, Leonard Miall, Eric Roll (Lord Roll of Ipsden), Alice Acheson, Edwin Martin, Maurice Couve de Murville, Robert Bowie, Anna Chennault, Wolfgang Schenk, Jack Foust Matlock, Slava Tynes, Melor Sturuva, Genkikh Trofimenko, Valentin Berezhkov, Ivan Krasnov, Nikolai Chervov, Valentina Terekhova, Alexander Gordeev, Galina Segeyevna Ulanova, Leonid Belkin, Alla Michaelenko, Nina Semizovova, Nguyen Xuan Oanh, Vo Nguyen Giap, Bui Tin, Li-An Chen, James Kline, and Naohiro Amaya. Filmed discussions also were conducted with Otto Hess, Ella Barowsky, and Peter Hertz on the subject of Berlin during the aftermath of World War II; with West German anti-nuclear demonstrators of a great range of ages and backgrounds; with U.S. soldiers on jeep patrol along the Berlin Wall; with Americans visiting Moscow during May 1988; and with elderly Americans in downstate Illinois on the subject of U.S. isolationism during the 1930s.

I conducted my own interviews with Arthur Schlesinger, Jr., Averell Harriman, Clark Clifford, George Kennan, Henry Cabot Lodge, Marshall Shulman, John Bullitt, Lincoln Gordon, George McGhee, Edwin Plowden (Lord Plowden), Walter J. Leavy, Oliver Shewell Franks (Lord Franks), Michael Forrestal, Hubert Miles Gladwyn Jebb (Lord Gladwyn), Miriam Camp, Henri Froment-Meurice, George K. Young, Pierre Uri, Etienne Hirsche, Hervé Alphand, and Walter Salant.

Notes

1. A lot of this information was made available to him by young American diplomats who were equally brilliant and well-informed, such as Allen Dulles in Switzerland and Christian Herter. These two later went with Bullitt to the postwar peace conference in Paris, where Allen Dulles functioned as Bullitt's assistant.

2. The idea of America's special mission in the world quite often has given shape to American reform movements; therefore, it is not surprising that Wilson's progressivism culminated in the Fourteen Points. But this was America's first direct entanglement in Europe's Great Power politics for more than a hundred years—not as imperial competitors or diplomatic mediators, but primarily on behalf of certain American ideals. Unlike President Theodore Roosevelt, Woodrow Wilson was opposed in principle to imperialism and protectionism. Nor did he object to a de facto alliance in order to implement his program and transform the imperial metropoles of Europe.

3. An enthusiastic backer of the *New Republic,* Justice Brandeis considered Bullitt "a good friend & co-worker of mine," who might help secure American support for the Jews in Palestine at the postwar peace conference. "B. has no sympathy for the missionaries & has a grandmother or so who was a Jewess."

4. Steffens wrote in a letter that "this gay boy did a man's work, soberly, sanely, shrewdly—even wisely, after we got to Moscow. There was no more swank then." Bullitt's young secretary and playmate, Robert Lynch, was more skeptical. He remembered later that Bullitt was obsessed with his own righteousness and convinced that President Wilson, by coming to terms with the Bolsheviks, could make himself "the greatest man in the world since Jesus Christ." Bullitt claimed afterward that the phrase, "we have seen the future, and it works," was his own idea, which he and Steffens discussed *before* their arrival in Russia. In Moscow, they found widespread poverty and starvation which Bullitt attributed to the Allied embargo.

5. A believer in selective government regulation, Hoover had supported Theodore Roosevelt in 1912 and later spent five years running various programs for food relief in Europe; when all of his programs ended in 1923, they had expended more than $5 billion in public monies and private donations. Hoover's lieutenants in the American Relief Administration became, in effect, the economic directors of Central Europe during the armistice period. This was the first international relief effort of its size in history; and it was to serve as a precedent for even more ambitious programs during the 1940s. In fact, the success of Hoover's programs, which were endorsed by President Wilson, helped to make foreign aid an important part of the internationalist liberal agenda.

Despite his conviction that "we cannot ever remotely recognize this murderous tyranny without stimulating actionist radicalism in every country in Europe," Hoover managed to come up with 833,875 tons of food for Soviet Russia in 1921–22. His efforts probably saved the lives of some 10 million people. There is an irony here, since the relief program helped the Bolshevik regime to survive—and 10 million is the approximate number of people that Joseph Stalin deliberately starved to death ten years later.

6. After returning to America in early 1919, Walter Lippmann had published a *New Republic* article saying that a peace treaty based on the Fourteen Points no longer was possible—the reactionary forces were too determined and Bolshevism was too virulent. But he warned the Europeans: "If you make it a peace that can be maintained only by the bayonet, we shall leave you to the consequences and find our own security in this hemisphere." Ten years later, Lippmann decided that he had been too critical of the Versailles Treaty; he should never have rejected it and allied himself with isolationist conservatives. As for Henry Cabot Lodge, Sr., he claimed with some justification that the League of Nations was too much an old-fashioned alliance and not the sort of world parliament that he and other "isolationists" had been hoping for.

7. Sigmund Freud long had been popular among young American intellectuals. Bullitt had concentrated in psychology at Yale, and his interest in the subject was sustained by Walter Lippmann, who lent him several books by Freud. When published thirty years later, the Freud-Bullitt book was denounced by almost everyone in the psychoanalytic community. Most reviewers asserted that Freud had very little to do with it. One of them suggested in the *New Republic* that Bullitt may have had a repressed hostility to Freud because the latter had not analyzed him properly—so he tricked Freud into co-authoring a terrible book in order to make Freud look like a silly fool.

8. Bullitt's emotionalism about the Russian Revolution was dramatized during a trip to Moscow two years before, when he went to visit John Reed's grave in the wall of the Kremlin. A witness reports that "two of us watched from the distance while Bullitt, carrying a large wreath, walked solemnly toward Reed's grave. We saw him place the flowers on the stone and stand there with bowed head for many minutes. When he returned to the car, tears were rolling down his cheeks and his features were drawn with sorrow." One of the first things he did as ambassador was to visit Reed's grave with his daughter and lay another wreath on it. Bullitt made plans to build a new American Embassy in Moscow that would resemble Thomas Jefferson's Monticello, but the Soviet government later reneged on its promise of land.

9. Adolf Berle's fear that de Gaulle might be Fascist reflected a suspicion that was quite widespread in the American government. Roosevelt wrote to Churchill in September 1942, "I consider it essential that de Gaulle be kept out of the picture and be permitted to have no information whatever, regardless of how irritated and irritating he may become."

10. The First Lady indicated an approval of this plan and a concomitant disapproval of Robert Murphy. Over tea at Morgenthau's farm in late 1944, Mrs. Roosevelt told her husband that Bob Murphy, a devout Roman Catholic, simply would not do as an occupation official—not given the attitude of the Pope, who was a notorious believer in private property. Whatever his views on private property, Murphy appeared quite naive about Soviet Russia during the war. During a good will trip to Moscow in 1943, he seemed almost as credulous as his companion, Ambassador Joseph E. Davies, about Stalin's good intentions.

11. Kennan wanted a Foreign Service academy that would inculcate "the basic qualities and traditions of early-American XVIII century diplomacy." The academy should be small, competitive, Spartan, and "it would have to be a cardinal principle that no man could graduate who had not shown himself to be thoroughly a gentleman." Really Kennan's apparent complexity amounted to a simple preference for his literary version of the past—a nostalgia for Harvard-Yale-Princeton during World War I, for Germany under Bismarck, for everything he associated with the eighteenth century. He hated almost every form of ideology-driven diplomacy—whether Communist or bourgeois—and believed firmly in the eighteenth century system of realpolitik.

12. Churchill had first met Harriman at Cannes years before and took great care to treat him well. The prime minister was anxious to show Americans like Harry Hopkins and Harriman that he was not another opportunistic Lloyd George, bent on tricking the United States into defending England's selfish interests. So Harriman was given almost all information, sometimes even admitted to cabinet meetings. On weekends Churchill received Harriman at Chequers as a family member, and they traveled together all over the world. Whenever the two disagreed, they did so forthrightly; indeed, the only thing Harriman had trouble explaining was American isolationism, which he did not understand himself.

13. Harriman functioned during the war very much like Robert Murphy—as a dealmaker for Franklin Roosevelt. In Russia, this required a great deal of cold-bloodedness. "We knew that Stalin had his security agents behind the lines ready to shoot down their own troops if they turned and retreated," Harriman recalls. "We were appalled by this, but we realized that it did make the Red Army fight. That was the thing that mattered." Even so, Harriman may have misunderstood what motivated the Red Army in 1942–45.

14. During a meeting with Harriman, the President said with respect to Poland that "he was helpless to do anything constructive till after the election." At another meeting, he "indicated that he wanted to have a lot to say about the settlement in the Pacific but that he considered the European questions were so impossible that he wanted to stay out of them as far as practicable except for the problems involving Germany."

15. Most of the approximately $10 billion in foreign aid contributed by the United States before 1948 was distributed by the United Nations Relief and Rehabilitation Administration, mainly for basic food and shelter. This program shows as well as anything the altruistic aspect of American policy right after the war. Most of the aid money went to East European areas occupied by the Red Army, since they needed it more and the United States assumed that they would be less able to pay for relief than the western countries. But there is considerable evidence that the United Nations Relief and Rehabilitation Administration was influenced by officials with a strong ideological sympathy for the Soviet Union.

16. The concern of some East Europeans was that the terms of the Marshall Plan would force a continuation of the old European trading patterns, under which primitive Eastern economies provided food and raw materials in exchange for high value-added goods from the West. This concern probably was exaggerated, and Communist autarchy and statist economics were in any case a dubious alternative. However, George Marshall later admitted that the Marshall Plan was framed so as to "make it quite impossible for the Soviet Union to accept." Moreover, the motives of certain U.S. officials from the start were partly commercial; one of the Marshall Plan's initiators, William Clayton, wrote in a memo: "Let us admit right off that our objective has as its background the needs and interests of the U.S. We need markets—big markets, in which to buy and sell."

17. That incident made a deep impression on James Forrestal, who took his own life in 1949 by jumping from a window twelve floors up. In contrast, Henry Wallace dismissed the incident as an irrelevant suicide, saying the Czechoslovak coup d'état was a legitimate response to U.S. actions in Europe—a harsh judgment that would do a lot to diminish Wallace's reputation in America. President Truman delivered a very effective speech to Congress in March 1948, warning politicians about the significance of the events in Czechoslovakia.

18. France received more Marshall aid per capita than any other country, and the aid was seen by many of its officials as very important. Failure to reform France's currency and the monetization of its deficits was a serious worry, but with U.S. aid the budget and trade deficits could be ignored. Some Americans—especially American politicians—wanted to impose fiscal discipline on France by threatening to withhold aid, but Harriman and Bruce resisted such tactics. In fact, the twin deficits in France may have been appropriate for a country in its position of capital formation.

19. "In French domestic political circles our advice will be misinterpreted and we will be accused of intervention and domination," they reported. Harriman had to act with particular discretion in France to avoid substantiating Soviet accusations of imperialism.

Elsewhere in Europe, this was less of a problem. The English did not care so much about appearances; and Germany was under occupation in any case. In Italy, it was possible for Harriman to attend a stag lunch for cabinet members and sit in afterward on an informal cabinet meeting.

20. Although Europe needed East-West trade far more than America did, U.S. diplomats knew that some restrictions were needed to prevent an outcry in Congress. Harriman overestimated Western Europe's need for food and raw materials from the East; and Acheson rightly doubted his belief that such trade would loosen Russia's hold on Eastern Europe. However, when Marshal Tito decided suddenly in 1948 to pull Yugoslavia farther away from the Soviet bloc, all agreed that he must be given economic support.

21. Averell Harriman understood that what America had to offer was not money or machines—the Europeans already were providing that themselves—so much as the new American methods of corporate administration. And as early as 1927, he had seen that labor and managerial reforms in Europe would first require a continental market like that of the United States.

22. Various forms of economic planning long had been a temptation for U.S. liberals—successful in two world wars, unsuccessful in the Great Depression. Most of the former New Liberals had come to accept that planning worked well in a crisis with a limited number of commodities for a small number of claimants, claimants such as the military services or European governments. They believed only in occasional and temporary intervention by the government. Long-term socialist planning for an entire civilian economy they left to foreign officials, without much optimism that it would make a difference to economic growth. Harriman's ECA functioned more as an advisory and watchdog agency than as a planning unit. Averell Harriman himself, however, had a definite weakness for economic controls and regulation and, along with many other liberals, gave in to the temptation more often in his later years.

23. A few months earlier, Acheson had made a speech in which he excluded Korea from America's "defensive perimeter" along the western Pacific—a speech that later prompted both left- and right-wingers to accuse him of "inviting" the Communist invasion. Acheson, they claimed, had made an egregious mistake or else had wanted the Communist invasion as an excuse for U.S. rearmament. These accusations, however justified or unfair, were quite typical of Acheson's obloquy in the United States. It is probable, in any case, that Stalin gave North Korea a green light for the invasion before Acheson's speech.

24. One rule of thumb for American diplomats was always to treat such new ideas as though they had originated in France. In this case it was easy, because Premier René Pleven was serious about rearmament and well disposed toward the United States. (William Bullitt once described him to Roosevelt as "an old and close friend of mine. I consider him one of the most subtly intelligent and reliable human beings that I have ever known.") In 1950, Pleven asked for a copy of the European Army blueprint and it soon became the "Pleven Plan." Immediately, Charles de Gaulle denounced the whole idea and also criticized the acceptance of U.S. money to pay for France's defense in Europe and Indochina. A man of premature hopes and outmoded fears, de Gaulle argued that in order to retain the respect of America and Germany, as well as their support over the long haul, France would have to pay for its own defense.

25. Even the experimental New Deal seems to have felt the pull of this liberal tradition. Up at his Hyde Park manor, Franklin Roosevelt wanted to reform modern business so that it would not corrupt both owner and worker. *The Modern Corporation and Private Property*—an important intellectual standby of the New Deal, co-authored by Adolf Berle—argued that private property was not at fault so much as the unnatural connection that had developed in corporations between their owners, managers, and employees. Labor unions should have more power—but so should the stockholders, who paid too little heed to their property, were corrupted by the system, and voted Republican. A general redistribution of income would discourage the corruption that ensued from excessive power or dependence.

26. Perhaps a round hundred would have seemed vulgar. In his first two seasons as American ambassador, Bruce helped to dispose of at least 1,268 pheasants, 121 partridge, 66 hare, 380 rabbits, 4 woodcocks, and about 200 ducks.

27. Like Harriman and Lovett, Bruce had considerable experience with European businessmen and he knew something about the dynamics of large-scale, heavy industry. But U.S. diplomats also had to understand Europe's political dynamics, which meant reconciling the existence of a European customs union with the economic requirements of the non-member countries and with the concerns of international economic agencies. Dean Acheson, along with members of the West German government, worried that the new High Authority might encourage cartels. "We recognize member govts must be in position to state before their respective parliaments that purposes and means of action incorporated in treaty are consistent with economic policies of either liberalism or socialism and with either private or public ownership," Acheson wrote. "Nevertheless, throughout treaty emphasis shld be placed on idea that new system is directed above all to bring change to present ossified structure."

28. Not that all of Acheson's attackers had a different social or educational background. Bill Bullitt, for example, suggested in 1948 that Acheson had been an appeaser of Russia during the war. And Bullitt's accusations were supported by Adolf Berle, who testified before Congress that Acheson had appointed a Communist sympathizer and been the leader of a pro-Soviet cabal at State, which Berle had tried unsuccessfully to oppose. Even Walter Lippmann, who once nominated Acheson for the Century Club, called for his resignation as Secretary in the autumn of 1950. Acheson's old friend, Archibald MacLeish, observed that the new barrage of criticism in 1950 did not outwardly bother the Secretary of State, who saw it as his duty to draw fire away from the President.

29. Allen Dulles proceeded to hire mostly liberals for the CIA. Earlier, both Lodge and Foster Dulles had opposed right-wing attempts to prevent the stationing of more U.S. troops in Europe. Even on China, the two of them were sympathetic to Democratic policies. Soon they would be swept up in the partisan battles of the Korean War, but in early 1950 Lodge doubted the wisdom of America's defending the island of Taiwan—a non-Communist stronghold off the shores of China where Chiang Kai-shek had fled with two million supporters. Meanwhile, Foster Dulles had negotiated the Japanese peace treaty and taken a generous line on aid to the Far East; he also favored guaranteeing the defense of Taiwan and did not want to recognize Communist China. But he did say, "If the Communist government of China proves its ability to govern China without serious domestic resistance, then it, too, should be admitted to the United Nations."

30. Another European whom Dulles met at the Paris Conference was Jean Monnet, forming an acquaintance that Monnet would describe in 1958 as "a growing friendship ever since." Their friendship grew closer on Wall Street during the 1920s, when both were involved in arranging American loans to Europe; and a decade later, Dulles helped to bankroll Monnet's international financial consulting firm.

31. One charge leveled by Harriman during the 1952 campaign was that Dulles's rhetoric about the "rollback" of communism sounded dangerous and irresponsible—although Harriman himself had called for rollback a few years before. In early 1953, George Kennan also made a speech criticizing rollback and so was pressured to retire from the Foreign Service, to his enormous chagrin. However, Kennan felt there was another reason why Dulles had, in effect, fired him. "We had the same kind of mind in certain respects," says Kennan. "He knew that he was going to have to follow in practice the line I had laid down, and I think he didn't want me around in Washington in any responsible capacity, because he didn't want it to be said that I was inspiring his ideas." An interesting similarity was that Kennan and Dulles—both of them Presbyterians—felt that world leadership would be good for Americans, forcing them to examine their faith and to act.

32. Mendès-France signed an armistice in July 1954 that divided Vietnam between north and south: the North would be Communist under Ho Chi Minh, and the fate of "South Vietnam" was to be settled by an election two years later. It was a good bargain

for the West, but neither South Vietnam nor the United States were signatories of it. Indeed, the Vietnam armistice and the apparent indifference of Mendès-France to the European Army made many U.S. diplomats highly suspicious of him—a man "without compunction or bowels," Bruce said.

33. By now, the most serious opposition to West Germany's NATO membership was to be found in West Germany itself. The joint Allied occupation of Austria had ended in 1955 with an East-West agreement to neutralize and demilitarize that country—a great diplomatic breakthrough. Constant Soviet offers of a similar treaty for German reunification—in exchange for German neutrality and demilitarization—went over especially well with the German Social Democratic Party. Having already voted against the European Army and the European Coal and Steel Community, the Social Democrats proceeded to oppose German rearmament and German membership of NATO. Many Germans also raised a clamor, which George Kennan encouraged in 1957, against the deployment of tactical nuclear weapons in West Germany.

Soviet pressure against these steps resembled later Soviet opposition, during the 1980s, to the deployment of intermediate nuclear missiles in West Germany. In both cases the Social Democrats and many other Germans caved in to Russia, seeing American policy as the greater danger to peace. One result naturally has been strong bipartisan sentiment in Washington to remove U.S. troops from West Germany.

34. In 1961, Bruce had described Macmillan's proposal as "the most thrilling and momentous made by a British Government in peacetime for generations. If ultimately successful, it will further the prospects of a grander Atlantic Union including the U.S. and Canada." Of course, one reason why de Gaulle rejected British membership was the prospects of it serving as a Trojan Horse for America—and that is one reason why American officials were so annoyed by his actions. Ambassador Bruce noted that "the French, although a most agreeable and attractive race, and in many respects an admirable one, are often, even to their friends, somewhat irritating." A few years later, Averell Harriman and Dean Acheson would come to agree. "What a tiresome creature that man is," said Acheson of de Gaulle. William Bullitt went further when de Gaulle recognized Red China in 1964, calling the President of France a "salaud" (slob) to his face.

35. De Gaulle had made what was, in that sense, a very practical point; while denouncing what was desirable, perhaps he advocated what was real. Woodrow Wilson also had called for not just freedom of trade, but the political independence of separate nation-states; his anti-imperialism was based not just on a desire for free trade, but on the inescapable reality of national feelings. Thus, national identity must be respected in any Wilsonian system of international cooperation.

A basic question still remained: Where did the Wilsonian desire for international cooperation end, and where did the Wilsonian desire for national self-determination begin? Although a line did have to be drawn somewhere, de Gaulle usually drew it according to the most narrow-minded and traditional view of what was best for France. He almost destroyed the Common Market in 1965, preserving it only after being guaranteed protected markets for French farmers; by 1967 he was suggesting that French nuclear weapons be aimed in all directions, including the United States. Telescoping history, he gave the U.S. and Russia too little blame or credit for ideological zeal and saw little to choose from between them. Communism could be contained, but the imperialism of the washing machine was something more insidious. Thus, the greater prosperity of Europe was a threat to French identity.

36. However much or little Citizen Bowles had to do with it, prices did remain quite stable for several years. On the other hand, price stability did not mean lower profits or lower wages during World War II. Although Bowles had wanted to keep business profits at their prewar, Depression levels—for moral reasons—profits soared during the war because of much higher volume. Meanwhile, wage rates did not rise much after 1942, but many more people had well-paying jobs. World War II was a time of special restrictions on available goods, and so much of the extra money earned went into such sectors as savings or the consumption of food, which was relatively plentiful.

37. Bowles found a kindred spirit in Vice President Wallace, who spoke out against colonialism during the war. He admired the Vice President for his "general 'earthiness' and feeling for the people," and these two self-made millionaires agreed on domestic politics as well. "I don't want to over-use the word 'fascist,' " Bowles wrote to Wallace, "but it does seem to me the only phrase that can be applied to the kind of thinking which I ran into among some groups in business." Bowles and Wallace were among those purist liberals who had reservations about the Darlan deal of 1942 and accepted it mainly out of loyalty to President Roosevelt.

38. A textbook case of all this was the Philippines, where Chester Bowles was asked to run the U.S. aid program in 1950. A great deal of U.S. aid already had gone astray in the Philippines, and a corrupt oligarchy there was fighting against left-wing guerrillas. In 1952, President Ramon Magsaysay enacted a variety of social and economic reforms urged upon him by the United States and the rebellion eventually was defeated. But Washington's memory can be very short—twenty years later a corrupt dictatorship, also backed by the United States, nearly destroyed everything that Ramon Magsaysay had accomplished, and the left-wing insurgency revived.

39. Truman, Acheson, and Harriman generally saw a lot of wisdom in what Bowles reported on India. However, they did not feel the same sense of immediate crisis, and they shared a certain cultural bias against the non-European countries. This bias was especially strong in Dean Acheson, who seldom took any personal interest in the under-developed areas. He felt quite scornful of Nehru and thought his sister ridiculous: "I have never been able to escape wholly from the childhood illusion that, if the world is round, the Indians must be standing on their heads—or, perhaps, vice versa." Truman's Point Four declaration had come almost entirely from political advisers like Clark Clifford and Chester Bowles; the State Department, including Acheson, Kennan, and Lovett, had been against it.

40. During the 1950s, the CIA in some areas rivaled State in creating policy, mainly because of the fraternal tie between Allen and Foster Dulles. Allen Dulles liked clandestine operations, which he felt could be used like jewels to dazzle the politicians into supporting his agency. President Eisenhower heard only oral reports on such operations from Allen and Foster Dulles and he tried to keep his distance—but Eisenhower kept a tight rein on the CIA itself, appointing David Bruce in 1955 to chair an intelligence oversight committee. As early as 1947, Bruce had warned his old friend Allen Dulles about the danger of secret operations; now, he and Lovett expressed dismay at what was going on. We need a strong intelligence service, Bruce said, but I find these "rogue elephant operations abhorrent." Furthermore, "where will we be tomorrow?" Actually, the CIA was well disciplined, and its clandestine operations never escaped the control of any president.

41. Although Dulles made these statements mainly to play well in Peoria, it is true that he had become almost obsessed by the Soviet-American confrontation—and he may have underestimated the amount of harm such rhetoric did to America's standing abroad. In the early 1950s he had engaged in some wild histrionics on this subject, talking in biblical terms about the anti-Communist mission of all decent people. President Eisenhower, on the other hand, felt relatively phlegmatic about neutral countries. Free trade and anti-colonialism were concepts as familiar to him as they were to Dulles, but Ike could better understand the reality of national pride and the temptations of non-alignment.

42. Stevenson also lent an ear to the Democratic Party "think tank," which held its first meeting at Bowles's house in 1953. Party think tanks make strange bedfellows. This one included, off and on, such diverse entities as Averell Harriman, George Ball, John Kenneth Galbraith, Paul Nitze, Arthur Schlesinger, Adolf Berle, and George Kennan, with Bowles generally in charge of foreign policy. Most intellectuals were Democrats in any case, but it is surprising that such a variety of them made a cult of Adlai Stevenson. At one meeting in 1955—which included Bowles, Schlesinger, and others—Adolf Berle notes that he "reported on Latin America. But by the time everyone had got through demolishing (a) NATO, (b) SEATO, (c) bases in Japan, (d) about everything else, I wondered whether this bunch had solidity enough to handle any situation. Their in-

stincts are of the best. But this is a rough, tough, world." The group expanded and became the Democratic Advisory Council during Eisenhower's second term—a more "hard line" group that included Dean Acheson.

43. Since 1957, Bowles had been working with Under Secretary of State Christian Herter and Allen Dulles of the CIA to push Eisenhower's foreign aid initiative. Always convinced that Americans basically agreed with him—that only the congressional pachyderms stood in the way—Bowles scolded President Eisenhower for saying foreign aid was unpopular. Eisenhower should present his program in a clear and positive light, not as a Cold War weapon. When Secretary Dulles died in 1959 and was replaced by Christian Herter, Bowles felt that State became more receptive to his advice.

John F. Kennedy was one of eight senators in 1959 to say that there should be less military aid to the underdeveloped countries and more civilian aid. Later on he would claim, not entirely accurately, that the "fundamental task of our foreign aid program in the 1960s is not negatively to fight communism." But it is true that the two-to-one ratio of military to civilian aid was reversed during his presidency.

44. The Kennedy campaign suggested that Eisenhower, besides being dull and senile, had been too partisan in his foreign policy appointments. Kennedy promised to restore a genuine bipartisanship in this area and did so by hiring a number of liberal, northeastern Republicans. Ike's Under Secretary of State, Douglas Dillon, became Kennedy's Treasury Secretary. John McCloy was made the President's special assistant on arms control and disarmament. Christian Herter and Henry Cabot Lodge took charge of Kennedy's new "Atlantic Institute," until Herter moved in 1963 to head the Trade Expansion Act Organization. And to the crucial position of National Security Adviser Kennedy appointed McGeorge Bundy, a Boston friend of Herter who had been dean of Harvard College.

45. Older Foreign Service officers complained that Bowles ignored the experienced diplomatists, filling embassies and the upper levels of State with his own creatures. That of course was similar to complaints made about Dulles in 1953. It is true that Bowles promoted a lot of young FSOs quickly—he wanted young ambassadors for the young countries. He sent a Puerto Rican as Ambassador to Venezuela; he hired a black press agent and sent two black ambassadors to Africa; he tried to put that diplomatic oddity, George Kennan, back into harness by making him Ambassador to Yugoslavia. An unusually high portion of his appointees were Foreign Service professionals or experts on their countries, including New Class types from the colleges and think tanks.

46. If anything, the opposite was true. Though a lot depends on the culture of a given country, generally it is the developed economies that can best afford a limited degree of socialism. One area where Western technical aid could be effective was that of agricultural productivity, where it helped to bring about the so-called Green Revolution in certain parts of the world. However, the Green Revolution occurred under private auspices as well; it flourished best in countries where agriculture was not socialized and the farmers could profit from it. It also led to disastrous side effects of a kind that one finds in most revolutions—while increasing productivity, the Green Revolution encouraged large-scale cash cropping, forcing subsistence farmers off the land so suddenly that they could find no alternative employment.

47. Typical of the former was David Bruce, then Ambassador to France. In 1949, Bruce complained that on the subject of Vietnam, "there appeared to be divided councils in Washington rather than the full agreement on and hearty implementation of policy such as the critical situation demanded. This division of councils seemed to stem in large part from concentration on the more abstract concepts of the problem such as colonialism, nationalism, independence, self-determination, etc. Of course we are against colonialism because it didn't work and couldn't work, and for nationalism because it was the strongest force in Southeast Asia. But could we afford to be purists and perfectionists?" He managed to convert General Eisenhower to this view, although in 1950 Eisenhower had considered the Indochina War to be an unwinnable colonial conflict. Later on, Bruce strongly urged more American intervention in Indochina, saying it would not necessarily identify the U.S. with colonialism: "That, I hear, is the thesis of Nehru. I question it."

48. Having once joined the attack on Truman for "losing" China, Kennedy saw Communist China as a tremendous threat and Red Chinese expansion as a real possibility. Chester Bowles and Averell Harriman also worried about Chinese expansion to the south; however, they wanted to soften Kennedy's China policy so as to encourage a Sino-Soviet split. Bowles had written to John Foster Dulles that "after a decent interval of chest pounding and name calling," the Chinese might calm down, and at that point America should be in a position to pull them away from Russia. Unfortunately, that point had not been reached by 1961. Harriman made some overtures to China in 1961–62, but his overtures were for the most part rudely rebuffed.

49. This cable had the strong support of Harriman and Michael Forrestal, the latter a White House aide and son of Harriman's old friend. Also in favor of dumping Diem was Robert F. Kennedy, the President's brother. But after being sent out with the approval of George Ball and the unreflecting consent of Rusk and President Kennedy, the cable aroused considerable opposition from other quarters. To Harriman's intense annoyance, Secretary of Defense Robert McNamara, the Joint Chiefs of Staff, Vice President Johnson, and the CIA all came out against it. Their dissent gave rise to furious debate, leading Kennedy to declare: "My God, my government is coming apart."

50. The mugwumps were a reformist group in the post-Civil War period—ineffectual in their own lifetime, but whose children were the chief proponents of the early Progressive movement. Older mugwumps wanted most of the standard Progressive reforms in domestic politics but, unlike many of their Progressive children, stood for the old American principles of anti-imperialism and free trade. They deplored American expansion in the Spanish-American War, which they feared would corrupt the United States at home.

An important first-generation mugwump was Henry Adams, who did see some benefit to Teddy Roosevelt's interest in international affairs: "The problem that Roosevelt took in hand seemed alive with historical interest, but it would need at least another half century to show its results." One way of restoring international unity, Adams thought, would be an "Atlantic combine" of bourgeois republics that could eventually draw in Germany and even czarist Russia. This Atlantic combine might save the world, he thought—which is what many New Liberals thought of the League of Nations. Not surprisingly, Adams was happy and proud about the de facto Atlantic Alliance of 1917. Like the New Liberals, Adams also was in favor of a strong and reformist central government. One of his favorite protégés, whom he encouraged to take an interest in political reform, was Henry Cabot Lodge, Sr. Lodge later helped get the United States into the Spanish-American War for a partisan reason—to win some political glory for the Republicans. Adams came to regard him as a friend lost, corrupted by politics, who should have known better.

51. In that sense, perhaps, Lodge deserves some credit for not taking the 1960 campaign very seriously, limiting his public appearances and spending his afternoons in aristocratic repose. "Being a politician is something like being an actor," he believed. "You don't stay on too long." In 1960 he fell back into the role of soldier-aristocrat—so much so that the American press corps, always sensitive on such a point, felt that he treated them too much like common people. Senator Kennedy had far more respect for their special status and shared their resentment of Lodge. "That's the last Nixon will see of Lodge," said Kennedy with bitterness, on seeing the two of them nominated together. "If Nixon ever tries to visit the Lodges at their house in Beverly, they won't let him in the door." Paradoxically, Kennedy later criticized Nixon for having "no class."

52. Lodge left the convention early, unwilling to witness Goldwater's nomination. During the autumn of 1964, he was on constant call from the White House and, in typical mugwump style, he would not do anything for the Republican ticket. In September, he was given the "Splendid American" award by William J. Lederer, co-author of *The Ugly American*. Lederer said that Lodge was what was needed in Vietnam, despite his good looks. On receiving the award, Lodge warned that appeasement of communism in Southeast Asia would resemble the appeasement of Nazi Germany and Imperial Japan.

53. Unlike the objections of ultraliberals like Chester Bowles, Ball's dissent was based on his fear that Vietnam was diverting America's money and attention away from what

ought to be its first priority: Europe. The CIA also took a gloomy view of America's involvement in Vietnam, saying that bombing in North Vietnam would help Communist morale and do little harm to their war effort; American troop buildups in the South always could be equaled by the North Vietnamese. Some American generals still resisted another land war in Asia, but almost all of them gave it strong support once the commitment was made. Eisenhower and Adlai Stevenson also supported Johnson's new policy in 1965. Because of his constant fear of leaks to the press, Johnson had far too small a group advising him on Vietnam.

54. The 1966 Vietnamese Assembly elections went well—although the Buddhists were excluded—and a large number voted in the face of Communist terror. Lodge wrote thus about the elections to President Johnson:

> This election should end once and for all the notion which
> seems to be held in a few places that the Viet Cong is a
> socially-conscious group of liberals on the model of western
> socialism. This is a western idea which the Viet Cong, during my
> time here, has done nothing significant to promote. At no time
> has any enthusiasm been asked or given for any Viet Cong
> program. The Viet Cong emerges clearly from this election as an
> organized group of terrorists who, under western law, should be
> called "criminals" since all of their methods are forbidden by
> the rules of land warfare and are crimes under western law. I
> refer to assassination, torture, kidnapping, etc. Without these
> crude methods there would be no Viet Cong. Without the Viet
> Cong there would be no recruits. And without the recruits there
> would be no war.

Lodge also helped to arrange the September 1967 presidential elections after ceasing to be Ambassador to South Vietnam.

55. Even such dissenters as Senators McGovern, Church, and Mansfield could not bring themselves to oppose funding for U.S. troops already in the field. The most important dissenter, perhaps, was Senator Robert Kennedy, who went public against the President after bombing was resumed in 1966; the bombing of North Vietnam, Kennedy asserted, might be putting us on "a road that leads to catastrophe for all mankind." Senate hearings on the war, arranged in 1966 by Senator Fulbright ("Senator Halfb-right," Johnson called him), gave Ambassador George Kennan an opportunity to worry on television that Vietnam was diverting America's attention from more important problems—such as Europe, the Soviet Union, and obligations at home. But the Senate hearings had little effect on congressional opinion or on the course of the war.

56. The Grand Old Man of American water projects, David Lilienthal, also lent a hand in Pacification—though he did not wish to be associated with the word, which had fallen into disfavor among his New York friends. Johnson liked to trot Lilienthal out as a man who would bring the New Deal to the world: "Dave, you give them some of that philosophy, that good TVA philosophy like your letter to me. As much as you want." Lilienthal proceeded to call for unity in the development projects and asserted that the Vietnamese were an extraordinary people. "I have found more fear and timidity at my club in New York than I found in some of the villages that had been exposed to the ravages of attack by the Viet Cong." Lodge, Harriman, and Ellsworth Bunker told Lilienthal afterward that they had found this a "moving statement." (Lilienthal's New York club—the Century—still was one of the social centers of U.S. foreign policy, along with the Council on Foreign Relations and the Metropolitan Club of Washington.)

57. Many European students were simply Americanized and restless—feeling confined by an older generation that came from another era—and their protest often took a Marxist form. Henry Cabot Lodge had defended America's Vietnam policy before fringe-group critics in Europe as early as 1965, when he spoke to a teacher-student sit-in at Oxford University. In England the venerable Bertrand Russell, who once had regarded America as the last bastion of Western civilization, participated in anti-war sit-ins

and tried to set up a "war crimes" tribunal to put President Lyndon Johnson on trial.

58. The overthrow of a reformist government in Guatemala was, in part, a misplaced reaction to the imminent Communist takeover of northern Vietnam—and perhaps Dulles's most foolish move in his generally competent Secretaryship. At a cabinet meeting during the Vietnam crisis that year, Dulles made reference to the Munich crisis of 1938 and the danger of appeasing aggression. To prevent another Munich, it might be necessary to begin "drawing a line" against Communist expansion, "particularly given the differentiation made by foreign nations between overt aggression and internal subversion." By this he meant that other Latin American countries would not help him to invade Guatemala because they could see no evidence of Soviet involvement. After Vice President Nixon was almost murdered by a Venezuelan mob in 1958, the Eisenhower administration started to take a more positive approach, initiating a modest increase in financial aid to Latin America.

59. In 1965 Bunker lamented, "When we are faced with the problems of Viet-Nam or Castro's attempts to subvert and overthrow the governments of his Latin American neighbors, adrenalin pumps in our bloodstream and we become emotionally involved." Simmering ever since Eisenhower's second term, the Panama issue did create a lot of emotion among Americans in the Zone and their supporters in Congress. President Johnson decided, on the urging of Bunker and others, to renegotiate the Panama Canal treaties but nothing actually was signed by the time he left office. The negotiations were revived in 1973 under Bunker's direction.

60. Nixon was sufficiently worried by the student protest to appoint a commission headed by a liberal Republican, Governor William Scranton, to study it. The commission concluded that America was "so polarized" by student revolt that it would threaten "the very survival of the nation." This was preposterous. Although the protests did continue on some campuses, the upsurge of 1970 was a last hurrah. The end of selective service that year, as well as the rapid American withdrawal from Vietnam, had a moderating effect on most students. Unfortunately, Nixon left it to Vice President Agnew to criticize the Scranton Commission.

61. In 1970 David Bruce was persuaded to replace Henry Cabot Lodge—once again as a token Democrat to appease media criticism—but Bruce could accomplish no more in the plenary meetings than Lodge. Henry Kissinger professed a keen admiration for David Bruce, who seemed to stand for everything that Kissinger was not: "Handsome, wealthy, emotionally secure, he was free of that insistence on seeing their views prevail through which lesser men turn public service into an exercise of their egos. His bearing made clear that he served a cause that transcended the lifespan of an individual; he exuded the conviction that his country represented values that needed tending and that were worth defending. His dignity forswore the second rate; his understated eloquence confirmed that in persons of quality substance and form cannot be separated." Bruce eventually quit in frustration over Kissinger's and Nixon's cavalier treatment of him.

62. One reason why the Panama treaty had been such a bitter issue in Washington is that Torrijos was giving help to the Nicaraguan guerrillas. The House of Representatives held hearings in 1979 on Panamanian aid to the Nicaraguan rebels which resulted in an extraordinary "secret" session of the entire House, the first in 130 years, to discuss Panama's shipments of Cuban weapons to the guerrillas. The dictator of Nicaragua, Anastasio Somoza, began manipulating the Panama treaty debates in Congress, exchanging pro-treaty votes for support for his regime. Torrijos later felt disillusioned by the events in Nicaragua, saying that his blind support for the guerrillas had been his greatest foreign policy mistake. Perhaps his disappointment was a case of injured vanity. After the "Sandinista" victory, Panamanians arrived in Nicaragua to find that Cubans had filled the most important military advisory roles. Soviet and East European advisers soon would follow.

63. The Catholic Church in Latin America also had grown more politicized, placing a new emphasis on changing secular society in favor of the poor. Church members started criticizing Latin America's economic dependence on the U.S. and, at their most extreme, advocating a quasi-Marxist "liberation theology." Although liberation theolo-

gians denounced Walt Rostow's theory of capitalist development in the Third World, generally they were critical of both capitalism and communism. While their reasoning was hard to follow, their conclusions were pretty clear: Poverty could be eliminated not by capitalist investment but by radical changes in the political structure. Even the Roman Catholic bishops of Latin America said in 1968, "Faced with the need for total change of Latin American structures, we believe that change has political reform as its prerequisite." Quick change was real, they believed, whereas slow change was illusory—surely the opposite of the truth, given the experience of our century.

64. A great admirer of Woodrow Wilson, Carter shared few of Wilson's strengths and many of his shortcomings. For example, Omar Torrijos and Muammar Qaddafi lauded two aspects of Jimmy Carter that also sat well with most North American voters. Qaddafi noted approvingly that Carter was a "God-fearing man." And Torrijos wrote in a letter to Carter that the two of them were going to establish "a great and profound friendship" because both of them were from rural areas: "Rural life is basically the same all over the world, and it creates a special way of thinking." Unfortunately, rural virtue and religious conviction never have been enough to inspire a successful foreign policy. Carter made himself the champion of a not very successful U.S. imperialism of sensitivity.

65. The fate of the Common Market provides an example of the entropy of American power. After the death of de Gaulle, England finally nitpicked its way into the Common Market; Spain, Portugal, and Greece were admitted later. But this did nothing to correct the EEC's worst faults, and its expansion positively discouraged unity. The EEC continued to protect European farmers, especially French farmers, from overseas competition in exchange for giving German industry a larger market. By the 1970s, the EEC economies had congealed again into cartelization and *dirigisme,* and the political direction of Western Europe was back in crisis. The planned elimination of intra-European tariffs threatens also to create higher tariffs against trade with countries outside the EEC.

66. The Gorbachev détente has far more in common with that of Khrushchev than that of Brezhnev, although this time a regression is less likely to be so extreme. Khrushchev had been ousted because he grew too anti-Stalin during the early 1960s—among Soviet leaders, he was perhaps the last true believer in Soviet ideology. Third World sympathy did a lot to encourage him—the Soviet dream of world revolution was revived—and he tried to revitalize it in Russia. There was genuine hope in Russia during the 1950s about a Soviet revolutionary brotherhood with the Third World, but Khrushchev's reforms were seen as dangerous and they raised questions about the legitimacy of the regime. After Khrushchev's humiliating withdrawal of Soviet missiles from Cuba, Brezhnev was careful to think more about military projection, and he started cracking down on internal dissent as early as 1973.

America's worry over the Nixon-Brezhnev détente, well advanced by the mid-1970s, was based on understandable concern over European hostility, Soviet advances, and American retreat. Under Brezhnev, the USSR had entered a military/political apogee. The 1965–75 period seemed a prosperous decade by Soviet standards, while the U.S. economy came under increasing strain after 1973. And the Soviets acquired a different sort of self-confidence as they grew militarily more powerful. But Brezhnev went so far in taking advantage of a post-Vietnam and post-Watergate disarray in the West that his détente was destroyed. Moreover, the Soviet rate of economic growth began to decline in the 1960s even as the rate of growth in defense spending rose, and the chickens came home to roost in the 1980s.

67. According to Jeffersonian reasoning, the frontier was essential to the republic's good health, because to maintain civic virtue there must be a continuous outward expansion so that corrupted city populations did not overwhelm rural individuality— hence the myth of rural virtue. When it was no longer possible for the United States to expand over contiguous territory, the rural, frontier virtues still had to be maintained in a country that seemed too crowded and urban. One method of doing so might be a form of non-imperial, overseas involvement. The new frontier might give coherence to the chaos of domestic U.S. politics, thought Henry Adams—no U.S. government could act rationally, nationally, and consistently at home, but with the right people in charge

it might do so abroad. Perhaps Adams can be forgiven for not anticipating that foreign policy, instead of chastening the Senate, eventually would become the same cause of political chaos and debate as domestic policy.

68. While some of them turned neo-isolationist, others took refuge in a movement called "neoconservativism"—essentially a liberalism that has re-examined itself and decided to step back for a while, perhaps for a long time, because things have changed too fast. Neoconservatism bore some superficial resemblances to genuine conservatism, such as a fear of Big Government. Neoconservative intellectuals feared that political corruption was flowing more from a newly powerful government than from newly powerful businesses. Of course, the notion that the New Deal was basically Tammany Hall writ large was an old one among Republicans, but many once and future liberals now were taking it quite seriously. It appeared to them that politicians, judges, and bureaucrats occupied a position that Big Business had occupied at the turn of the century—able, in effect, to bribe corrupted citizens into supporting them by means of targeted spending programs and judicial decisions.

69. Americans during the eighteenth century believed in two important modes of behavior: the mission of building shining cities on hills and the art of making money plenty. From the very first, anti-colonialism was based not merely on the sanctity of national independence and personal liberty, but on a desire to make bigger profits from unimpeded commerce. Considering the protectionist policies practiced by the United States throughout most of its history, it is quite bizarre the degree to which free trade and commerce permeated early American political thought. The Founding Fathers assumed that mankind was naturally peace-loving and therefore wanted free trade; they professed a hatred of tarriffs as harmful to prosperity, provocative of war, and violating natural law.

70. As president, George Washington was just as distressed as Ronald Reagan by the factionalism of American politics and by its deleterious effect on U.S. diplomacy, where he believed that the Congress had no right to interfere. The Constitution had been in part an effort to end the distortion of foreign policy by various utopian notions emanating from the Congress of the 1780s. President Washington felt that the Congress's delay in providing money to implement a treaty with Great Britain was an infringement of his powers that violated the spirit of the Constitution. His famous valediction was an attempt to define a true national interest that would find favor with all factions.

Index

316 INDEX

Lodge *(cont.)*
  career, 211–15; and Vietnam, 203–4,
  210–11, 216–25, 228, 231, 233; and
  Vietnam peace talks, 252, 254–55
Lodge, Henry Cabot, Sr., 23, 212–13,
  276
London Conference, 1950, 129
"Long Telegram" (Kennan), 86–88, 90
Lovett, Robert, *x,* 7, 43, 106, 107–8,
  144, 156; on Congress and Marshall
  Plan, 111; and military aid to Europe,
  128
Luciano, Lucky, 61

MacArthur, General Douglas, 135,
  138–40, 151, 222
McCarthy, Joseph, 150–51, 209
McCarthyism, 253
McCloy, John, *x,* 43, 62, 149
McCoy, General Frank, 211
McGovern, George, 253, 256
MacLeish, Archibald, *xv,* 27, 66
MacMillan, Harold, 60–61, 164–65, 167
McNamara, Robert, 221–22, 228–29,
  234
Madison, James, 281
Malay States, 136, 233
Mao Tse-tung, 136
Marines, U.S., 222, 247–48, 262–63
Marshall, George, 93, 100–101, 103,
  109, 121; and Kennan, 100, 102–3
Marshall Plan, 100–27, 214, 233, 246;
  assessment of, 130–32; Bruce and,
  148; for Central America, 266;
  economic and psychological aspects
  of, 130–32; opponents of, 111–12;
  and public support for, 189; run by
  UN, 191; and Third World, 177–78,
  196
Marx, Karl, 36, 274
Marxism, 36, 77, 87, 200, 236; Stalin
  on, 74
Marxism-Leninism, 89–90; and Central
  American insurgencies, 263–65; and
  Third World, 274
media. *See* press
Mediterranean area, 90, 96
Mellon, Ailsa, 144–45, 147
Mellon, Andrew, 144–45
Mendes-France, Pierre, 158–59, 160,
  206
middle class: conservatives and Red
  Scare, 20–21; upper, in America, *x–xi;*
  upper/under class coalition, 235–36
Middle East, 271, 272–73; *See also* Suez
  Canal crisis
Middle West (U.S.), 70
military intervention, 232–33, 238, 278.
  See also Central America; Latin
  America; South Vietnam

Military Security Agency, 130
military spending: and Acheson, 127–30,
  133, 139–40; and Bowles, 172;
  Eisenhower and, 152; Reagan and,
  274
mission, sense of, 25–26, 183–84, 196,
  201, 276
Monnet, Jean, 40, 64, 149, 158–61, 161;
  and de Gaulle, 59–60; and European
  Army, 141; and loans to France, 121;
  and Schuman Plan, 125
Monnet Plan, 121, 123
Morgenthau, Henry, 62–63, 66, 79, 84
Morgenthau Plan, 116
mugwumps, *vii,* 2, 9, 169, 212, 216,
  276; and internationalist liberalism,
  278–79
multilateral institutions, *viii–ix,* 25, 64,
  97, 216, 276
Munich crisis, 38–39
Murphy, Robert, *x,* 37, 41, 45, 69, 231;
  background and career, 48; and
  Darlan, 47–52; and de Gaulle, 58, 60;
  in French North Africa, 58–60; and
  German occupation, 61–62; to
  Moscow (1943), 75; at Paris Peace
  Conference, 16; and postwar
  Germany, 116; and provisional Italian
  government, 61; and Vichy
  government, 46
Mussolini, Benito, 61
Mutual Security Agency, 130

Nasser, Colonel Gamal Abdel, 187
national autonomy concept, 9, 25, 97,
  276
National Liberation Front, Vietnam, 207
National Security Advisers, 221, 224
National Security Council, 238
National War College, 89, 100
NATO, 127–31, 217, 245; and American
  payoff to France, 206; and American
  Suez policy, 187–88; and Eisenhower,
  152; and European Army idea, 156;
  French troop withdrawal, 164, 167;
  Germany in, 140–41; and Germany in,
  160; and Khrushchev Berlin
  ultimatum, 162; Korean War and,
  139–42; Reagan and, 270; resistance
  to U.S., 167; Soviet manipulation of,
  272–73
"natural aristocracy" concept, 145, 281
Nazi Germany: and American
  occupation plans, 61–62; attacks on
  Allied shipping, 108; Bullitt and, 35,
  38; and France, 38–39; Murphy in, 48;
  in North Africa, 50–52; and Poland,
  80; and Soviet-American relations, 68,
  73, 75–76; surrender of, 44, 57, 73,
  84; and Vichy government, 45–50